GLOBAL MARKET BRIEFINGS

doing business with
THE REPUBLIC OF
CYPRUS

CONSULTANT EDITOR:
PHILIP DEW

**KOGAN
PAGE**

London and Sterling, VA

First published in Great Britain and the United States in 2004 by Kogan Page Limited.

120 Pentonville Road
London N1 9JN
UK
www.kogan-page.co.uk

22883 Quicksilver Drive
Sterling VA 20166–2012
USA

© Kogan Page and individual contributors, 2004

ISBN 0 7494 4140 2

British Library Cataloguing-in-Publication Data

A CIP record for this book is available from the British Library.

Library of Congress Cataloging-in-Publication Data

Doing business with the Republic of Cyprus / consultant editor, Philip Dew
    p. cm.
Includes index.
    ISBN 0-7494-4140-2
    1. Cyprus--Commerce. 2. Cyprus--Commercial policy. 3. Cyprus--Economic conditions. 4. Investments, Foreign--Cyprus. 5. Business enterprises, Foreign--Government policy--Cyprus. 6. Commercial law--Cyprus. 7. Taxation--Cyprus. I. Dew, Philip.
HF3757.Z6D65 2004
330.95693--dc22

                        2003024781

Typeset by Saxon Graphics Ltd, Derby
Printed and bound in Great Britain by Thanet Press Ltd, Margate

In Cyprus, when we talk business the world listens.

For the international businessman having the facility to readily communicate with all other global markets is the difference between success and failure. That's why, in Cyprus, we have invested in one of the most advanced telephone and communications systems in the world which enables you to reach 98% of all the world's telephones 24 hours a day, seven days a week, 52 weeks a year.

The island is also served by 38 scheduled airlines and every conceivable service, facility and business support - from specialised legal advice to international banking and accountancy to language skills to land, sea and air transportation facilities - is readily available.

Furthermore, culturally and geographically, Cyprus is perfectly positioned to form a launch platform for trade with the Middle East, Africa, Asia and the Far East. Which means that whatever your business , we have the means to help you do more of it. So, when you are ready to talk business, talk to Cyprus. We guarantee you it will not fall on deaf ears. For further information please contact:

CYPRUS

THE MINISTRY OF COMMERCE, INDUSTRY AND TOURISM
1421 NICOSIA, CY-CYPRUS. FAX:00357 -2 375120   www.cyprus-prof-serve.com

Contents

Foreword   xi
Lynn Parker, H.E. The British High Commissioner to Cyprus

Foreword   xii
Yiorgos Lillikas, Minister of Commerce, Industry and Tourism

List of Contributors   xiv

Map 1: Cyprus and its Borders   xxv
Map 2: Nicosia and the Surrounding District   xxvi

Part One: The Background

1.1 Geography and History   3
     Philip Dew, The Philip Dew Consultancy Limited
1.2 The Economy   7
     Fiona Mullen, Assistant Editor, Financial Mirror, Nicosia
1.3 Government, Politics and Accession to the European Union   15
     Dr James Ker-Lindsay, Executive Director, Civilitas Research
1.4 Professional and Business Services   21
     Kostas Christophidis, Assistant Director General, Cyprus
     Employers and Industrialists Federation (OEB)
1.5 Tourism   26
     Cyprus Tourism Organization Information Centre
1.6 Banking, Finance and Insurance   34
     Sofronis Eteocleous, Manager, Economic Research and
     Planning, Laiki Bank
1.7 Telecommunications in Cyprus   37
     Andreas Theodorou, Regulatory Affairs, Business Management
     Support, Cyprus Telecommunications Authority
1.8 The External Sector   41
     Fiona Mullen, Assistant Editor, Financial Mirror, Nicosia
1.9 Manufacturing Industry   47
     Kostas Christophidis, Assistant Director General, Cyprus
     Employers and Industrialists Federation (OEB)

Part Two: Accounting and Fiscal Environments

2.1   Accounting Principles and Reporting Requirements   53
      Yiannakis Theoklitou, Partner, Ernst & Young
2.2   Taxation of Income in Cyprus   61
      Pieris Markou, Tax Partner, Deloitte & Touche, Nicosia,
      Cyprus and Antonis Taliotis, Tax Partner, Deloitte & Touche,
      Limassol, Cyprus
2.3   Other Taxation   73
      Pieris Markou, Tax Partner, Deloitte & Touche, Nicosia,
      Cyprus
2.4   Effective Use of Cyprus Double Tax Treaties   78
      Peter G Economides, Chairman, Totalserve Management Ltd
      and Senior Partner, PG Economides & Co.
2.5   Cyprus Double Tax Treaties: Summary of Withholding Taxes 85
      Peter G Economides, Chairman, Totalserve Management Ltd
      and Senior Partner, PG Economides & Co.

Part Three: Legal Environment

3.1   Legal Environment and Framework   91
      Demosthenes Mavrellis, Consultant, Chrysses Demetriades
      & Co. Law Office
3.2   Legal Dispute and Arbitration Proceedings   95
      Demosthenes Mavrellis, Consultant, Chrysses Demetriades
      & Co. Law Office
3.3   The Regulation and Supervision of Banking in Cyprus   98
      Central Bank of Cyprus
3.4   Cyprus International Trusts   105
      Demosthenes Mavrellis, Consultant, Chrysses Demetriades
      & Co. Law Office

Part Four: Establishing a Business in Cyprus

4.1   Using Cyprus for International Business   111
      Emily Yiolitis, Director / Legal Consultant, Totalserve
      Management Ltd
4.2   Foreign Participation in Cyprus Companies   117
      Demosthenes Mavrellis, Consultant, Chrysses Demetriades
      & Co. Law Office
4.3   Shipping & Ship Management   121
      Costas Georghadjis and Antonis Taliotis, Deloitte & Touche

Part Five: Property Ownership and Living in Cyprus

5.1   The Cyprus Real Estate Market and Foreign Investment   133
       Antonis Loizou, FRICS, Chartered Surveyor, Senior Partner,
       Antonis Loizou & Associates, Chartered Surveyors
5.2   The Acquisition of Immovable Property by Aliens in Cyprus   142
       Demosthenes Mavrellis, Consultant, Chrysses Demetriades
       & Co. Law Office
5.3   Living in Cyprus   145
       Lewis Scudder

Part Six: Financial Environment

6.1   Banking and Finance in Cyprus   153
       Sofronis Eteocleous, Manager, Economic Research &
       Planning, Laiki Bank
6.2   Anti-money-laundering Measures in the Banking and
       International Business Sectors   160
       Central Bank of Cyprus
6.3   Insurance in Cyprus   164
       Sofronis Eteocleous, Manager, Economic Research and
       Planning, Laiki Bank
6.4   The Cyprus Development Bank   169
       The Cyprus Development Bank
6.5   Cyprus Securities and Exchange Commission   176
       Dr Marios Clerides, Chairman, Cyprus Securities and
       Exchange Commission
6.6   The Cyprus Stock Exchange   179
       The Cyprus Stock Exchange

Part Seven: Marketing in Cyprus

7.1   Advertising and the Media in Cyprus   183
       Vasilis A P Metaxas, Managing Director, Pyramis DDB
7.2   Public Relations in Cyprus   191
       Christina Pissi Patsalides, Director, Christian Alexander Public
       Relations & Event Marketing
7.3   Marketing   196
       Soulla Kellas, Director, Customized Research and Annarita
       Hadjigavriel, Regional Director, ACNielsen AMER
7.4   Marketing Research   200
       Soulla Kellas, Director, Customized Research and Anna Rita
       Hadjigavriel, Regional Director, ACNielsen AMER

Part Eight: Human Resources Issues

8.1 Compensation, Benefits and Employee Regulations   207
     Michael Antoniou, Head, Industrial Relations & Labour
     Legislation Department, Cyprus Employers &
     Industrialists Federation (OEB)
8.2 Industrial Relations   219
     Michael Antoniou, Head, Industrial Relations & Labour
     Legislation Department, Cyprus Employers & Industrialists
     Federation (OEB)
8.3 Human Resources Management   224
     Jacovos Christofides, Human Resources Consultant

Part Nine: Appendices

Appendix 1 Useful Information   235
Appendix 2 Useful Addresses and Telephone Numbers   243
Appendix 3 Contributors' Contact Details   270

Index   279

Index of Advertisers and Sponsors   285

Other titles in this series by Kogan Page   287

Foreword

Cyprus is far more than a beautiful island. It is the most economically advanced of the new wave of EU member countries. Its location, sound economy, good communications and high quality of life makes it attractive both as a place to do business and as a regional base for operations in the Middle East, North Africa and further afield.

In addition to Cyprus' tourism, shipping, financial and corporate sectors, it is a lively and sophisticated market for consumer products of all kinds. English is widely spoken and used in the business community.

I hope that this guide will help those who are unfamiliar with Cyprus to get to know it better and to appreciate how much it has to offer.

Lyn Parker
H.E. The British High Commissioner to Cyprus

Foreword

It is with great pleasure that I welcome this book which I am sure will prove a useful aid to entrepreneurs around the world. The extensive information it contains relating to a wide range of economic and commercial activities about Cyprus make it a valuable source to all those engaged in international business.

Cyprus, especially now with its accession to the European Union, offers all the conditions that are conducive to business expansion. In recent years Cyprus has developed into an international centre for transit trade, tourism, international business and maritime activities as well as banking and business services. This successful transformation process was based on the exploitation of the comparative advantages of Cyprus. The most important are the strategic geographic location of the island, the prevalence of conditions of macroeconomic stability and social cohesion, the high quality of life, the high educational level of its manpower, the favourable fiscal environment, the low by international standards cost of living as well as the modern infrastructure and telecommunications. In fact an increasing number of businesses from all over the world are presently using Cyprus as their base and are establishing joint ventures with the locals. Furthermore, the strength and dynamism that characterizes our business community is another major factor that encourages foreign investors to cooperate with Cyprus and consider it as a potential business partner.

Cyprus, due to its small but dynamic domestic market and the open nature of its economy, considers access to international markets as of utmost importance. As a result trade has always been one of the main sectors of the Cyprus economy contributing considerably to the economic growth of the island. The European Union countries constitute the most important trading partners of Cyprus followed by the Arab and Central European countries.

The Government of Cyprus, through the Ministry of Commerce, Industry and Tourism, and within the framework of supporting and developing trade, follows a policy which aims at the expansion and diversification of trade. The Ministry attaches also particular attention to the promotion of professional services, a sector that is again a major contributor to the Gross National Product, while at the same time promoting Cyprus as an international business centre.

Publications of such quality as this one are instrumental in further achieving this goal and at the same time act as a comprehensive and indispensable guide on Cyprus for companies and professionals.

I would like to take the opportunity and congratulate the publishers for their initiative and wish them success in their endeavours.

Yiorgos Lillikas
The Minister of Commerce, Industry and Tourism

List of Contributors

ACNielsen AMER was established in 1982. With regional head quarters in Cyprus, the company quickly grew by setting up offices across the Middle East, North Africa and Eastern Europe. ACNielsen is the world's leading market research firm, offering measurement and analysis of marketplace dynamics, consumer attitudes and behaviour, and new and traditional media in more than 100 countries. Clients include leading consumer product manufacturers and retailers, service firms, media and entertainment companies and the Internet community.

Andreas Theodorou is the head of the Regulatory Affairs Unit of the **Cyprus Telecommunications Authority (CYTA)**, dealing mostly with European Union legislation and regulatory issues. The Regulatory Affairs Unit is also the unit responsible for the interface with the Commissioner's Office. He has a BSc and a Masters in Business Administration from George Mason University in the United States and a BT Diploma in Telecommunications Studies. He has a thorough working knowledge of European legislation on telecommunications and on the regulatory issues involved. He has participated as a member of the Cyprus EU accession negotiation team and in the preparation of Cyprus' positions for presentation at the ensuing negotiations. For the past four years he has worked on regulatory issues such as interconnection and universal service and has prepared informative papers for the general management of CYTA, as well as providing expert advice internally.

Anna Rita Hadjigavriel is Regional Director at **ACNielsen AMER**, managing the client and sales function across 13 MENA (Middle East and North Africa) countries. She has over 13 years' research experience with tremendous knowledge of the region. She is a member of the World Association of Research Professionals (ESOMAR).

Antonis Loizou is the senior partner of **Antonis Loizou & Associates – Chartered Surveyors**. The firm provides valuations for all types of property for whatever purpose, be it financing, asset evaluation, issue of shares, compulsory acquisition, sale and acquisition, litigation cases or taxation. It is also extensively involved in project management of property development projects and has managed the construction in the recent past of more than ten hotels, two bank headquarters buildings, numerous commercial and residential projects and two shopping centres, all on behalf of clients.

In addition, the firm has a very strong estate agency division, which deals with Cyprus real estate, both locally and abroad. It holds international exhibitions, publishes information booklets and over the years has established itself as the largest real estate agent in Cyprus. The firm also has an educational/information service, gives lectures and publishes articles on financial/property matters including, annually, an informative booklet on real estate.

The firm employs 56 people, including civil engineers, valuers/surveyors, architects, accountants and lawyers in addition to support staff and is by far the largest and most diversified firm of property consultants in Cyprus and the Eastern Mediterranean.

Antonis Taliotis is a tax partner of **Deloitte & Touche**, based at the Limassol office. He has been with Deloitte & Touche, Cyprus since 1996, joining them from the Cyprus Inland Revenue. He studied and trained in the United Kingdom and is a member of the Institute of Chartered Accountants in England and Wales and of the Institute of Certified Public Accountants of Cyprus. He has extensive experience in national and international tax, is the author of various articles and is a regular speaker at international tax conferences. He was a member of the University of Vienna team that advised the Cyprus Government on the tax reform that harmonized the Cyprus tax legislation with that of the EU and also satisfied the Government's commitments to the OECD. He services a large number of both international and local entities and is acting as the tax consultant of the Cyprus Shipping Council.

Central Bank of Cyprus is the country's central banking organization and is tasked with: the supervision of banks; the definition and implementation of monetary policy, including credit policy; the conduct of exchange rate policy; the holding and management of official international reserves; the promotion, regulation and oversight of the smooth operation of payments and settlement system; the performance of the tasks of banker and financial agent of the Government; and participation in international monetary and economic organizations.

Christian Alexander Public Relations & Event Planing was founded in 1998 and specializes in the planning, organizing, execution and supervising of PR functions that are either part of a larger campaign or form specific PR activities. The firm is a member of the

UK Institute of Public Relations, the Association of Communications and PR Consultants of Greece and the PR Association of Cyprus. Being totally committed to good business ethics, the company uses the whole gamut of PR techniques, staying in close contact with the above professional bodies, to ensure up-to-date information on all aspects of PR.

Christina Pissi Patsalides has a BA in Sociology and Industrial Relations, was the founder of **Christian Alexander Public Relations & Event Planning** in 1998 and has worked for the past ten years in the field of public relations. She started her career in a Management Consultancy in Toronto, Canada, where she was responsible for the PR and image making of company managers for two years. Coming back to Cyprus in 1994, she was hired on a one-year project setting up the Public Relations Department of a large insurance company. In 1995 she was hired as public relations manager of one of the largest advertising agencies in Cyprus.

She is a member of the UK Institute of Public Relations, the Association of Communications and PR Consultants of Greece and the PR Association of Cyprus. She has worked on many governmental, semi-governmental and private company projects.

Chrysses Demetriades & Co. Law Office was founded in 1948 by the late Chrysses Demetriades, Barrister of the Middle Temple, and has grown and developed into the largest law firm in Cyprus, with offices in Limassol (headquarters) and Nicosia. It is represented also in Piraeus, Greece. The practice is a full-service law firm, providing advice to and acting for an extensive list of domestic and international clients, as well as state, semi-state and local authorities. The firm has also undertaken the drafting of legislation for foreign governments.

Costas Georghadjis is Head of the Audit and Assurance function at **Deloitte & Touche**, based at the Limassol office. He has been with Deloitte & Touche since 1989, when he joined the Birmingham office in the United Kingdom, and became a partner of the Cyprus firm in 1996. He studied and trained in the United Kingdom and is a member of the Institute of Chartered Accountants in England and Wales and of the Institute of Certified Public Accountants of Cyprus.

He has participated in the audit of several national and multinational corporations and has been involved in various special engagements, including privatizations, listings, valuation and acquisitions. He specializes in the shipping and insurance industries and is an expert on International Accounting Standards.

The Cyprus Securities and Exchange Commission in its present form was created in April 2001, with the enactment of the Securities and Exchange Commission legislation that came into force in June 2001. The Law set up the commission as an independent government body and has entrusted it with the supervision and regulation of the Cyprus capital market.

Cyprus Stock Exchange commenced operations as a legal entity in the form of a public corporate body in 1996 by virtue of the Cyprus Stock Exchange Laws and Regulations of 1993 and 1995.

Cyprus Telecommunications Authority (CYTA) is a corporate body established by law and has been responsible for the provision, maintenance and development of telecommunications both nationally and internationally since 1961. A state-owned organization, currently enjoying monopoly rights in most telecommunications services, CYTA has proved highly instrumental in developing telecommunications in Cyprus and thus contributing to and supporting the Government's vision of turning the island into a renowned international services centre. CYTA has invested in building an extensive international network and turning the island into one of the most important telecommunications hubs in the Eastern Mediterranean.

Cyprus Tourism Organization, founded in 1971, is a semi-governmental organization overseen by the Ministry of Commerce, Industry and Tourism and charged with the responsibility for tourism planning, product development, marketing and general management of the national tourism industry. It fulfils its role through its main offices in Nicosia and its regional offices in Cyprus and abroad. The CTO maintains 18 tourist offices overseas to market and promote Cyprus tourism, to service the tourist trade and to provide information to prospective holidaymakers.

Deloitte & Touche in Cyprus has its origins back to 1958. It is the second largest professional services firm on the island in terms of revenues with 14 partners, over 300 personnel and with offices in all major towns of Cyprus. It is one of the biggest contributors to the success of Cyprus as an international financial and shipping centre. Recently, Deloitte & Touche worked closely with the University of Vienna on the reform of the tax legislation of Cyprus for the purpose of harmonization with the European Union. Deloitte & Touche won the First Services Award of the Employers & Industrialists Federation of Cyprus (OEB) in 1999 for Economic Achievement & Quality. The criteria that were considered in the decision-making process were the quality of the services provided and of the personnel, the increase in the firm's turnover in Cyprus, as well as the expansion of its international business both geographically and financially. The firm's services include auditing, tax, consulting and financial advisory services. Deloitte & Touche serves many local and international clients, and is the premier provider of services to the largest number of international ship owners and ship management companies. The firm's clients include the leading organizations across all sectors of the Cyprus economy ranging from banking, insurance and financial services to the tourist, industrial and trading sectors.

Demosthenes Mavrellis is a solicitor of the Supreme Court of England and Wales, an Attorney-at-Law, New York, a member of the Cyprus Bar Association and a consultant with the **Chrysses Demetriades & Co. Law Office** in Limassol.

Emily Yiolitis, MA (Oxon), LLM (EUI), graduated in Law from Trinity College, Oxford University in 1997 and continued her studies in European Law at the European University Institute in Florence, graduating in 1999. She is a member of the Cyprus Bar Association and a Director and Legal Consultant of **Totalserve Management Ltd**, a leading Cyprus trust and management company. Emily heads the International Registration and Trusts Departments of Totalserve. Emily is also secretary of the Cyprus branch of the Society of Trust & Estate Practitioners.

The areas of particular interest to her are international trust and tax structures, as well as corporate planning. She participates regularly in international conferences and writes articles on her topics of interest.

The **Employers and Industrialists Federation (OEB)**, an independent organization representing the business community of Cyprus, comprises 40 main professional associations and 400 major individual enterprises in the manufacturing, services, construction and agriculture sectors of the economy. Having been founded in 1960 by just 19 pioneering businessmen, the OEB today has 3,000 members who, between them, employ over 60 per cent of the private sector workforce. The OEB is acknowledged as a spokesman for the business community and is consulted as such by the Government.

Ernst & Young was formed in Cyprus in 1989 as a result of the merger of Arthur Young/Russell & Co. and Ernst & Whinney. The predecessor firm of Russell & Co. was established in 1937 and was the first accounting practice registered in Cyprus. The firm's expertise includes taxation, corporate recovery, investigations, business plans, financial proposals, investment appraisals, share valuations, information technology and business process re-engineering.

The Financial Mirror is Cyprus's leading English-language business weekly. Published for ten years, the independent newspaper's core readership consists of influential decision makers in local and international business, in government and in embassies at home and abroad. In July 2003, and in a first for the divided island, it launched the Cyprus Business Forum, a monthly publication for Greek and Turkish Cypriot businesspeople that is circulated on the whole island.

Fiona Mullen is Assistant Editor of the **Financial Mirror**. Formerly Director of Country Reports and a Senior Europe Analyst at the Economist Intelligence Unit in London, she has been analysing and writing about the Cyprus economy for several years.

Jacovos Christofides is an independent human resources consultant. He holds a BSc in Industrial Engineering and an MBA. His areas of specialization are the strategic implementation of human solutions in high technology environments, and the management of innovation. He was one of the founding partners of Apola Human Solutions Ltd in 1997, where he was responsible for the overall strategic management of the company and the successful execution of projects in key client accounts. Following Apola's acquisition by Hyperion in December 2000, he continued as the Managing Director of Apola until July 2003, when he again became an independent consultant. He has given lectures to various academic and business institutions and has implemented numerous projects and audits related to the efficient organization and management of human resources. Mr Christofides is accredited by the Institute of Technology of Cyprus and by the Human Resources Development Authority of Cyprus.

James Ker-Lindsay is Executive Director of **Civilitas Research**, a strategic consulting firm providing tailored political risk analysis and industry research services covering South-East Europe – the Balkans, Greece, Cyprus and Turkey. Working with an extensive network of over 150 leading academics, consultants and journalists, the company delivers independent assessments and forecasts to a diverse range of clients, including financial institutions, government departments and major corporations. It also provides regular insights and commentary on regional affairs for the international media. Founded in 2001, Civilitas Research is strategically located in Nicosia, Cyprus.

Konstantinos (Kostas) Christophidis is Assistant Director General at the **Cyprus Employers & Industrialists Federation (OEB)**. He is a member of a number of committees and boards, including: the Board of Directors of the Cyprus Certification Company; the National Council for the Environment; the Executive Committee of the

Technology Institute; the Consultative Committee for Technical & Professional Education; the Consultative Committee for Consumer Matters; and of various tripartite committees.

Laiki Group. The origins of the Cyprus Popular Bank Ltd go back to 1901, when the Popular Savings Bank of Limassol was founded. In 1924 the savings bank was converted into a fully fledged banking institution and was registered as the first public company in Cyprus, under the name The Popular Bank of Limassol Ltd. In 1967 the Bank expanded throughout the island and its name changed to the Cyprus Popular Bank Ltd, reflecting its truly pancyprian character.

A very important landmark in the history of the Group was the connection with Hongkong Bank in 1971, which acquired a stake of 22 per cent in the share capital of the Cyprus Popular Bank. This association enhanced the Bank's outlook for further development, since it secured a wide network of correspondents all over the world. The international character of HSBC and its huge financial capabilities inspired increased confidence in the Bank.

In 1974, the Bank began its international expansion with the opening of its first branch in London. In 1983, in an aggressive move, the Bank took over the Cyprus operations of Grindlays Bank, which was the largest and oldest foreign bank on the island. This led to a substantial increase in its market share and was considered as the most important event in the history of banking in Cyprus. A milestone in the international expansion of the Group was the establishment of a subsidiary bank in Greece in 1992, the European Popular Bank, which was renamed to Laiki Bank (Hellas) S.A. on 1 January 2000.

In 2000, the Bank established Laiki eBank, which was the first electronic banking service in Cyprus. During the same year the Bank adopted a new corporate identity, that of Laiki Group. In 2001, Laiki Group upgraded its representative offices in Australia to a full service bank, Laiki Bank (Australia).

Today the Group operates 120 branches in Cyprus, with 36 more in Greece, six in the United Kindom and five in Australia. The bank also operates six representative offices: two in Canada, one in New York, one in South Africa, one in Yugoslavia and one in Russia.

Laiki Group offers general banking services in retail, commercial and corporate banking, as well as trade financing and card services. It also offers specialized financial services through its subsidiary companies, including in the areas of general insurance, life insurance, finance, investment and factoring.

Lewis Scudder, a Kuwait-born expatriate American, is an ordained clergyman in the Reformed tradition. He is also a scholar, having done graduate work in Beirut and Montreal in Middle East and Islamic

Studies respectively. Author of the official history of the Arabian Mission in the Gulf (*The Arabian Mission's Story*, Eerdmans, 1998), he is an editorialist, journalist, translator and writer on a variety of topics, as well as editor-in-chief of the Middle East Council of Churches' English language magazine, *NewsReport*. He has worked with the MECC since the late 1960s and directly for it, off and on, since 1981. Since the late 1960s he and his family have been frequent visitors to Cyprus and finally took up residence there in 1994, now owning their own home.

Marios Clerides is Chairman of the **Cyprus Securities and Exchange Commission**. He has a BSc, an MSc and a PhD (labour economics) from the London School of Economics. Prior to his present appointment on a five-year contract he was employed by Hellenic Bank, initially as Head of Planning and Economic Research and thereafter with additional responsibility for marketing, Hellenic Bank Investments (the merchant bank subsidiary of Hellenic Bank), card services (credit cards), retail banking and the Bank's Treasury/ International Department. He also teaches a course on 'Cyprus Banking and Financial Markets' at MSc level at the University of Cyprus.

Michael Antoniou is Head of the Industrial Relations & Labour Legislation Department of the **Cyprus Employers & Industrialists Federation (OEB)**. He holds a Law Degree (LLB) from Athens University and a Master of Laws (LLM) from the University of Wales, Cardiff. He worked as a lawyer until 1991, when he was recruited by OEB as an Industrial Relations and Labour Legislation Officer. He was promoted to his current position in 2000.

He is a member of the European Social Dialogue Committee and various Cyprus bodies, including: Industrial Disputes Tribunal, Labour Advisory Body, Social Insurance Council, Redundancy Fund Council, Insolvency of Employers Fund Council, Council of Health and Safety at Work, Council for the Rehabilitation of the Disabled, Consultative Committee for the Elderly, Committee for Equal Treatment of Men and Women at Work and Consultative Committee on Radio and Television. He is also a former member of the Consultative Committee on Tertiary Education and The Prisons Council.

Publications include: *Unification and Codification of the Cyprus Labour and Social Legislation*, January 1998; *The Cyprus Termination of Employment Legislation as interpreted by the Case Law*, September 2000; and *Social Policy and Employment: Harmonization of the Cyprus Legislation with the EU Acquis*, October 2002.

Peter G Economides is a Fellow Chartered Certified Accountant (UK). He has extensive experience in international tax planning and trusts. He regularly publishes articles in the international professional press and lectures on international tax planning and asset protection trusts.

He is senior partner of **PG Economides & Co., Chartered Certified Accountants** and the Chairman of the leading Cyprus trust and management company, **Totalserve Management Ltd**, with offices in Cyprus, Greece, United Kingdom, Bucharest and Beirut. He is a member of the International Tax Planning Association and various other international accounting, tax and trust associations. He is the Honorary Consul in Cyprus of Cape Verde.

Philip Dew owns and manages his own Cyprus-registered business development consultancy, has worked and resided in the Middle East for over 30 years, is an Arabic speaker and has undertaken many assignments for clients from across the world. This is the sixth title in the *Global Market Briefing* series on which he has been Consultant Editor, the others being on the United Arab Emirates, Bahrain, Iran, Oman and Qatar. Over the past year he has also authored two business books: *Saudi Arabia: Restructuring for Growth* and *Bahrain: Financial Capital of the Middle East*.

The Philip Dew Consultancy Limited was founded in 1982 to support local and international principals in the comprehensive development of their businesses in the Middle East. The basic services provided include: identification, investigation and evaluation of market opportunities; market research and feasibility studies; identification of partners, principals and associates; development of marketing and business strategies; and on-the-ground support and assistance to market entrants, including the provision of background and cultural information.

Pieris Markou is a tax partner at **Deloitte & Touche** in Nicosia. He has more than 11 years of experience in Cyprus taxation and VAT. He studied and trained in the United Kingdom and is a member of the Institute of Chartered Accountants in England and Wales and of the Chartered Institute of Taxation. Pieris has also been an active member of the Institute of Certified Public Accountants of Cyprus since 1992, has served as Chairman of the VAT Committee and is currently Vice Chairman of the tax committee of the Institute of Certified Public Accountants of Cyprus, participating in a number of meetings with the Minister of Finance, the House of Representatives and the Tax and VAT Commissioners for the formulation of the Government's policies on taxation.

Pieris specializes in international tax planning for many multinational groups. He is one of the firm's major negotiators on corporate and personal tax for resolution of client tax matters. He has been involved in many restructuring projects of major international businesses operating through Cyprus and on a number of due diligences of industrial and service companies for the purpose of satisfying stock exchange requirements.

Pieris is an author of many articles in the local press and various publications with an international audience and is a speaker at many conferences, both in Cyprus and abroad, on international taxation, tax and VAT in Cyprus. Pieris was also the contributor to the tax section of the internally developed software program WinTax, the first ever personal tax software program developed in Cyprus.

Pyramis DDB (DDB Cyprus) was founded in 1968 as 'P.I.R.A.M.I.S.' to provide a host of marketing and communication-related services. Eventually the company focused exclusively on advertising and was, consequently, renamed Pyramis in 1976. Being at the forefront of the industry since its earliest days it co-founded the Cyprus AAA in 1981. Based on Pyramis' creative work and consistent financial performance DDB Worldwide chose the company in 1997 as its affiliate in Cyprus and, in 2000, bought a 70 per cent share in the agency, renaming it Pyramis DDB, a fitting tribute to its many achievements and standing in the market. The agency will undergo a final name change to 'DDB Cyprus' by the end of 2003. It is consistently a top-five full service agency handling a diverse portfolio of blue-chip multinational and local accounts. Contact: info@ddbcy.com.

Sofronis Eteocleous, Manager of Economic Research & Planning, **Laiki Group**, has an MA in Economics from the University of Bonn and an MA in Public Administration from Albany University, US. After a number of years in the Cyprus Ministry of Finance, where he attained the status of Director of Research and European Union Matters, he joined Laiki Group in 2000.

Soulla Kellas is Director for Customized Research at **ACNielsen AMER**. She is the ESOMAR (the World Association of Research Professionals) Representative for Cyprus. She has close to 20 years' market research experience, gained in the agency environment both in the United Kingdom and in Cyprus. Presently, she has overall responsibility for driving customized research across the Emerging Markets region.

The Totalserve Group has been providing professional business consulting services since 1972 and today has offices in Cyprus, Greece,

United Kingdom, Bucharest and Beirut. The services offered comprise international tax planning, corporate advice and consultancy, international trusts, management and administration, shipping and ship management, financial services and information technology. The client portfolio includes multinational corporations, high net worth individuals, banks, financial institutions and other professionals.

Vasilis A P Metaxas studied applied art, advertising and marketing in Athens and London and has worked in Greece, the United Kingdom and the Middle East, both on the agency side and as a client. He repatriated to Cyprus in 1990 and joined **Pyramis DDB** (DDB Cyprus), becoming its managing director and a partner in 1996. Versatile in all aspects of the communication process, he has written numerous articles on industry subjects. Contact: vmetaxas@ddbcy.com.

Yiannakis Theoklitou, is the partner in charge of Assurance and Advisory Business Services (AABS) in Cyprus and South-East Europe for **Ernst & Young**, Nicosia. He is a Fellow of the Institute of Chartered Accountants in England and Wales and has a degree with distinction in Accountancy, Economics and Business Law from the University of Stirling, Scotland.

He has substantial experience in managing projects both within Ernst & Young and with other clients. His service line leadership position requires good project management skills, including the coordination of activities in eight different countries, with over 800 professionals, as well as responsibility for quality of service delivery. In addition, he possesses substantial knowledge of International Accounting Standards (IAS) and their application, as well as substantial relevant experience in the petroleum industry.

Professionally he has been a member of Ernst & Young International's IAS Policy Committee in regard to adoption of IAS in Greece; Chairman of an Ad Hoc Committee to review financial statements of Cyprus listed companies for compliance with IAS; a member of the Audit and Accounting Standards Committee of the Institute of Certified Public Accountants of Cyprus (ICPAC); and a member of the ICPAC Working party for harmonization of Cyprus Companies Law with EC Directives.

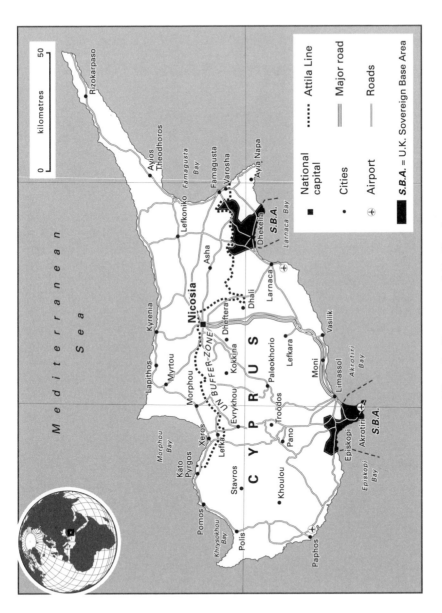

Map 1 Cyprus and its Borders

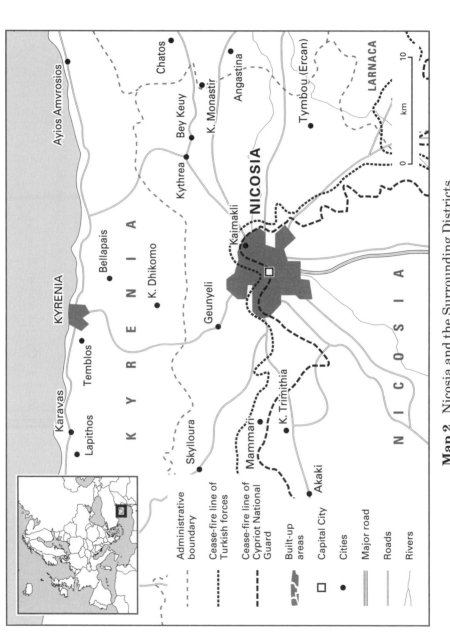

Map 2 Nicosia and the Surrounding Districts

Part One

The Background

1.1

Geography and History

Philip Dew, The Philip Dew Consultancy Limited

Geography

Location, area and population

Cyprus is located at the eastern end of the Mediterranean Sea, 75 km south of Turkey, 105 km west of Syria and 380 km north of Egypt. The island has an area of 9,251 sq. km, making it the third-largest island in the Mediterranean after Sicily and Sardinia.

The present population of Cyprus is estimated at 810,000, of whom some 78 per cent are Greek Cypriots, 18 per cent Turkish Cypriots and the balance mainly foreign residents and workers. The population growth rate approximates to 1 per cent per annum.

The capital of the island, Nicosia (Lefkosia), is the seat of government, has a population of about 210,000 and is located roughly in the centre of the country. The second-largest town, and the island's main commercial port, is Limassol (Lemesos), with 164,000 inhabitants. Located on the south central coast it is also an important tourist resort. Larnaca (Larnaka), to the south east, has a population of about 73,500 and has the country's second commercial port, its main international airport and also its oil refinery. Paphos (Pafos), in the south west, which is primarily a tourist resort, is home to Cyprus' second international airport and has a population estimated at about 50,000.

Until 1974 the towns of Famagusta, on the east coast; Kyrenia, along the north coast; and Morphou, in the agricultural area of the western Messaoria, were all important centres in the island's tourist industry. Today, they are all within the boundaries of the 'Turkish Republic of Northern Cyprus', as is the northern part of Nicosia. Until early 2003, they were accessible primarily through Turkey, although day visits were permitted to tourists and expatriate residents from the south, but only between clearly defined hours. However, as of the second quarter of 2003 the borders between the Republic of Cyprus and the north of the island were opened up to allow also the passage of locals, for the first time in 30 years, but again only on a day basis but with extended hours.

Geology

Geologically, Cyprus can be divided into three primary zones: the Troodos massif at the heart of the island, the Kyrenia range to the north (also known as the Pendadaktylos or five fingers range) and the Messaoria plain, which divides the two. Surrounding these is the coastal plain comprising many coastal valleys extending along virtually the whole coastline.

The Troodos range, situated in the central-west of the island and rising to 1,951 m on Mount Olympus, comprises mainly igneous rocks and forests. The Kyrenia range is mainly limestone, with some dolomite in older formations, and rises to a maximum height of 1,024 m. The Messaoria plain (the central plain) between the two mountain ranges, which rises to a height of just 180 m close to Nicosia, is sufficiently fertile to support agriculture, especially at its western extent. The coastal areas also tend to be fertile, having largely alluvial soil and, as a result, are also well suited to agriculture.

Most exploitable mineral resources are to be found in the ophiolitic complexes of the Troodos range (the ophiolite indicates the island was once deep below the sea). The most important minerals are the cupiferous pyrites (Cyprus' name being derived from the resulting copper) and the chromite deposits. Asbestos was also once exploited at the appropriately named Amiantos deposits, but these are now closed for environmental and health reasons. Umber, gypsum and bentonite are also to be found; the latter having many industrial uses.

Climate

Cyprus has a typical Mediterranean climate, with hot, dry summers between mid-May and mid-September; rainy but changeable winters between mid-November and mid-March; and, in between, short spring and autumn seasons.

Temperatures are highest in July and August, with average daily mean temperatures reaching 29°C on the central plain and 22°C on Troodos, with maxima up to 36°C and 22°C respectively. Winters tend to be mild, with an average mean in January of 10°C on the central plain and 3°C in the mountains and minima of 5°C and 0°C respectively.

Average annual total rainfall is 500 mm, with a maximum on Troodos of up to 1,100 mm. Snow falls most years above 1,000 m but rarely falls at lower levels.

History

The history of Cyprus can be traced back some 11,000 years to Neolithic times, although it is a relatively young republic, having gained its independence only in 1960. Over the many intervening centuries the island's location close to Europe, Asia and Africa has ensured considerable external influence, which has in so many ways made Cyprus and its people what they are today.

The first historical records of the country attaining importance relate to the period when it fell under the control of the Egyptians in the second millennium BCE. Subsequently the Phoenicians established a settlement on the island, to be followed later by the Mycenaeans. Over the ensuing 700 years Cyprus was to become successively an Assyrian protectorate, a province of the Persian Empire, under the influence of the Ptolemies of Egypt and then, in about 30 BCE, a dominion of the Roman Empire. Christianity is reported to have come to Cyprus under the Romans, with the Greek Orthodox Church – the main church of Cyprus today – becoming well-established in the late fourth century CE.

In 649 CE an attack by the Arabs heralded a new era in Cyprus' history; for more than 300 years the island was constantly an object of dispute between the Muslims and the Byzantines. The latter ultimately gained control towards the end of the tenth century CE, which they retained until 1191 when Richard the Lionheart took possession of the island before selling it to the Knights Templar, who in turn sold it to Guy de Lusignan, the deposed King of Jerusalem, thus initiating what became known as the Lusignan (Frankish) period in Cyprus' history, which also lasted for nearly 300 years.

In 1489 Cyprus was ceded to the Venetians, who viewed the island as a last bastion against the Ottomans. The Ottomans attacked and finally took the country in 1571. Cyprus then remained part of the Ottoman Empire until 1914, although the administration of the island had earlier passed to the British in 1878, under the terms of the Cyprus Convention. Following the end of the First World War, in which the Turks had supported the Germans, Turkey ceded all rights to Cyprus under the terms of the 1923 Treaty of Lausanne. Cyprus then became a British Crown colony in 1925.

British control was maintained for another 35 years, with the island attaining independence only after a national liberation struggle had been launched in 1955 against colonial rule and for the union of Cyprus with Greece (enosis). Cyprus became a fully independent republic on 16 August 1960, after the signing of the London-Zurich Agreement the previous year. Following independence Cyprus became a member of the United Nations, the Council of Europe, the British Commonwealth and the Non-Aligned Movement. More recently, the country has been accepted to accede to the EU.

The years following independence proved most uncertain for Cyprus as serious problems arose over the interpretation and working of the Constitution. In the event, the situation dissolved into violence in December 1963, leading to the establishment of a United Nations peace-keeping force on the island the following year. The commencement of inter-communal talks in 1968 resulted, for a time, in a marked reduction in the level of violence, only to take a turn for the worse in 1974 when the Cyprus National Guard, with apparent support from the military junta in Greece, staged a coup which so concerned Turkey as to cause them to make what proved to be a successful invasion of Cyprus. Following the invasion the Turkish forces pressed forward, taking the northern one-third of the island along a line joining Famagusta, Nicosia and Morphou. Subsequently, the 'Turkish Republic of Northern Cyprus' was proclaimed. Despite on-going discussions over many years, the island remains divided as at mid-2003, although hopes prevail of a resolution to the matter before Cyprus accedes to the EU in May 2004.

The Economy

Fiona Mullen, Assistant Editor, Financial Mirror, Nicosia

Economic structure

The past 50 years has seen Cyprus move from an economy based on agriculture to an economy dominated by services. In 2002, services accounted for 77.1 per cent of gross domestic product (GDP), or CYP 4.8 billion, in a total economy worth CYP 6.2 billion (USD 10.1 billion). Manufacturing accounted for just 9.6 per cent of GDP, construction for 6.9 per cent, agriculture 4 per cent, and electricity, gas and water, just 2.1 per cent.

A breakdown of GDP by sector shows that private consumption dominates: accounting for 68.2 per cent of GDP in 2002. A high proportion of private consumption is typical of a developed country. However, the share of gross fixed investment is somewhat low, at 18.7 per cent of GDP in 2002, while expenditure on research and development, according to a Statistical Service survey, was 0.27 per cent of GDP in 2001, compared with an EU average of 1.94 per cent. There are a number of explanations for low investment ratios: a risk premium in

Table 1.2.1 Key economic indicators 2002

GDP (CYP million)	6,192
GDP (USD million)	9,339
Population (thousand)	713
GDP per capita (USD)	13,841
Real GDP growth (%)	2.2
Exports of goods (CYP thousand)	511,277
Imports of goods (CYP thousand)	−231.5*
Tourism arrivals (million)	2.418
Tourism revenue (CYP million)	1,131
CYP:USD 1	0.663

Source: Cyprus Statistical Service, Central Bank of Cyprus

* January–September

the eyes of investors because of the division of the island, low natural resource endowment for heavy industry and, in the past, a range of foreign exchange restrictions that hindered borrowing in cheaper foreign currencies, which discourage foreign investors. Many restrictions have now been lifted and the capital account will be fully liberalized by the time Cyprus joins the EU on 1 May 2004.

Another significant factor, however, is the huge collapse of the once ill-regulated Cyprus Stock Exchange. After its peak of well over 800 in November 1999, the stock exchange index struggled to reach its base level of 100 for most of 2002 and the first half of 2003.

Living standards

Cyprus is the wealthiest of the ten countries that will join the EU on 1 May 2004, with GDP per capita of CYP 8,684 (USD 9,339) in 2002. According to EU estimates made in 2003, GDP per capita at purchasing power parity (ie adjusted for relative cost of living) was 85 per cent of the EU average in 2002. Relative wealth is also kept high by widespread ownership of land. Some 59 per cent of Cypriots do not have a mortgage, according to a survey conducted in 2003 by the Central Bank of Cyprus and the University of Cyprus. This compares with just one-third in the United States. Moreover, many people also own village houses or other property handed down from their parents (there is no inheritance tax in Cyprus).

Tourism: vulnerable to external shocks

Within the sector of services, tourism is the most dominant. Figures on GDP do not separate out tourism as an individual sector, but it is

Table 1.2.2 GDP by expenditure

	CYP million (2002)	real % change (2002)	real % change (1998– (2002)
Private consumption	4,224	2.4	5.4
Government consumption	1,097	3.1	2.7
Gross fixed investment	1,157	10.1	4.6
Increase in stocks	72	–	–
Exports of goods and services	2,668	–5.0	2.3
Imports of goods and services	–3,069	–0.4	3.6
Statistical discrepancy	41	–	–
GDP	6,192	2.2	4.2

Source: Cyprus Statistical Service

broadly accepted that tourism accounts for about 20 per cent of GDP, when the contributions of transport, hotels and restaurants, and retail and wholesale trade are taken together. In 2002 Cyprus attracted 2.4 million tourists, or 3.6 tourists per inhabitant. When investigating market opportunities, therefore, it is important to note that the potential pool of consumers is closer to 3 million. Tourism revenue accounted for CYP 1.1 billion, or 18.3 per cent of GDP in 2002. More than half of Cyprus' tourists come from the UK.

Dependence on tourism makes economic performance in Cyprus highly vulnerable to external shocks, however. After a record 2.7 million tourists in 2000 and 2001, the sector suffered badly in 2002–03, owing to a range of external factors: the attacks on the United States in September 2001, continued fighting between Israel and the Palestinians, which affected cruise tourism, uncertainties in the long run-up to the Iraq war in 2003, combined with a strong euro-pegged Cyprus pound relative to sterling, which made Cyprus an expensive destination for Britons. Tourist arrivals in January–May 2003 fell by 12.9 per cent year on year. For 2003 as a whole, it is possible that tourism arrivals will fall by more than 10 per cent for the second year in a row. Efforts to raise the quality and spending of tourists are mainly long term in nature (see below), and will therefore take time to bear fruit.

Financial and business services grow

In an effort to move away from dependence on tourism, the Government has encouraged growth in the financial and business services sector. 'Financial intermediation' has therefore risen from 4.9 per cent of GDP in 1995 to 6.2 per cent of GDP in 2002. Business services, meanwhile, rose from 2.8 per cent of GDP in 1995 to an estimated 3.4 per cent of GDP in 2002. In the past, growth in the financial and business services sector was helped by generous tax incentives for the international business (offshore) sector and a much more flexible work permit regime for offshore businesses. Money also flowed to Cyprus during the Lebanese civil war and the break-up of the former Soviet Union. This attracted international banks, financial services, accounting and insurance firms as well as numerous 'brass plate' companies, sometimes with dubious activities.

However, under pressure from the OECD to tackle money-laundering, and as part of its preparations for EU accession on 1 May 2004, the Government was obliged to harmonize onshore and offshore tax rates in a major tax reform passed in July 2002. Despite some reports to the contrary, a clean-up of the sector means that Cyprus would now be a very difficult place to launder money. Cyprus is no longer on the OECD Financial Action Task Force blacklist and the Russian Central

Bank also took Cyprus off its own blacklist in 2003. The Government also announced in 2003 that it will fully implement the new EU savings directive. This includes the automatic transfer of information to the home tax authorities within the EU about interest paid to non-residents of Cyprus who are resident in another EU country. This does not apply to residents of non-EU countries, however.

The tax reform entailed an increase for international businesses and a decrease for local ones. However, the new corporate tax rate is only 10 per cent and income tax rates are still considerably lower than in much of Western Europe. This, combined with some 40 double taxation treaties, still makes Cyprus an attractive location for financial and business services, according to the Cyprus International Business Association.

Government services are significant

Government services also play a significant role in the economy, accounting for around 20 per cent of GDP, mainly because utilities, such as ports, airports, Cyprus Airways, postal and telecommunications services, electricity and water are either fully or majority state-owned or are run as semi-government organizations. Privatization is not obligatory under EU rules, and is not favoured by the current government, but these sectors are gradually being opened up to competition.

Manufacturing and agriculture

Manufacturing has been the poor relation in recent years, falling from 11.7 per cent of GDP in 1995 to 9.6 per cent of GDP in 2002. The limited availability of raw materials on the island, combined with rising labour costs, has reduced the competitiveness of once traditional industries such as textiles, clothing and food-processing. Two significant exceptions are pharmaceuticals, where the production of generics has led to something of a boom in this sector, and the export of the traditional halloumi cheese.

Mining, which is negligible, has also been growing in recent years, thanks to strong growth in the aluminium product sector, while the contribution of agriculture, dominated by potatoes and citrus fruits, has fallen slightly.

Recent economic policies

Since Cyprus started EU accession negotiations in March 1998, policy has focused on implementing the many thousand pages of EU legislation and norms. Compared with the East European applicants,

Table 1.2.3 GDP by sector

	CYP (million) 2002	Real % change 2002	Real % change 1998–2002
Agriculture and hunting	236	5.8	4.5
Fishing	12	1.9	9.5
Mining and quarrying	19	7.0	9.3
Manufacturing	594	−0.3	0.4
Electricity, gas and water	128	7.7	8.0
Construction	430	4.2	0.7
Wholesale and retail trade	753	2.0	3.6
Restaurants and hotels	507	−7.0	4.3
Transport, storage and communication	570	4.3	9.4
Financial intermediation	387	0.9	6.7
Real estate, rental and business activity	842	5.0	4.8
Public administration and defence	544	2.4	3.4
Education	312	3.4	3.4
Health and social work	212	2.9	3.1
Other community social and personal services	243	3.9	4.9
Private households with employed persons	34	9.8	11.3
Total gross valued added	*5,821*	*2.2*	*4.2*
Imputed bank service charges	−245	−9.3	7.7
Import duties	205	−2.5	5.5
VAT	410	2.2	4.2
Total gross domestic product	*6,192*	*2.2*	*4.2*

Source: Cyprus Statistical Service

Cyprus had the advantage that administrative capacity was already high, thanks, not least to a public sector that attracts well-qualified graduates because of its generous pay and conditions. Cyprus was therefore the first of the candidate countries to close all of the negotiating chapters. Energy and telecoms liberalization have gone more slowly, but it is highly unlikely that these will not be implemented before EU accession.

Both the current and the previous government have stated that they want to adopt the euro as soon as possible after membership. For technical reasons relating to the five Maastricht criteria and the rules of the Exchange Rate Mechanism, this would probably not be possible for any candidate country before 2007 at the earliest. As of mid-2003, Cyprus did not fulfil the Maastricht criterion on the general government budget deficit, which must be no more than 3 per cent of GDP, nor the criterion on inflation. However, assuming that tourism picks up from 2004, Cyprus has a good chance of meeting all of the criteria by mid-2006, the earliest point at which the European

Commission could make an assessment on all five criteria. Moreover, exchange rate stability has already been proven. The Cyprus pound is pegged to the euro and has traded within a narrow band against it, and its predecessor, the ecu, for more than ten years.

Recent economic performance

Cyprus does not face any significant structural problems and is therefore not at risk of any major economic crisis. Although it does need to fund a reasonably large current-account deficit, it has good access to international debt markets and foreign public debt is low, at around 15 per cent of GDP, while net private foreign debt (ie, taking account of foreign assets) is estimated to be around 20 per cent of GDP. Unlike less developed countries, moreover, Cyprus has no debt with the IMF.

However, the economy is facing some short-term problems. Cyprus' trend real GDP growth rate – the rate at which it can grow without sparking inflation – is officially estimated at 4 per cent per year, based on population and productivity growth. However, two bad years for tourism have led to below-trend growth. Real GDP growth was just 2.2 per cent in 2002 and is officially forecast to be only slightly higher in 2003. Real GDP growth in the first quarter of 2003 was just 2.4 per cent year on year, although it should be noted that this is well above EU growth rates. At the same time, inflation has been rising, to 4.9 per cent year on year in January–May 2003, owing to EU-related increases in VAT and other indirect taxes.

This, combined with a tax reform that shifted the emphasis of revenue onto consumption taxes in a year in which retail sales growth has been weak, led to a sharp rise in the government budget deficit in 2003. As of the beginning of July 2003, the Government was expecting a consolidated general government deficit of 5.3 per cent of GDP. This is well above the 3 per cent ceiling that would be required for Cyprus to adopt the euro, and led the Government to introduce a supplementary budget in mid-2003. If tourism fails to pick up in 2004, the budget deficit and current account deficit, which reached an estimated 6.2 per cent of GDP in 2002, could reach even more uncomfortable levels.

Challenges for the future

Cyprus has spent the past five years making significant improvements to the business environment by adopting thousands of pages of legislation to bring it in line with EU norms. Although this had led to higher costs for businesses in areas such as health and safety and the environment, an EU-compatible business environment should be attractive for companies wanting an EU base to trade with the eastern

Table 1.2.4 Latest economic indicators as of July 2003

	Period	Year on year % change
Real GDP growth	2003 Q1	2.4
Retail sales volume	2003 Q1	1.2
Consumer prices	2003 Jan–May	4.9
Tourist arrivals	2003 Jan–May	−12.9
Total exports of goods (CYP thousand)	2003 Jan	−18.5
Total imports of goods (CYP thousand)	2003 Jan	−10.4

Source: Cyprus Statistical Service

Mediterranean. This could be particularly important in view of the EU–Mediterranean free trade area gradually being implemented, which includes several neighbouring countries such as Lebanon and Egypt. It could also be important if the more recent US plans for a free trade area for the wider Middle East get under way.

The main challenge for Cyprus' economy in the future is to shift the economy away from dependence on tourism, at the same time as attracting higher-spending tourists. As a comparatively expensive destination that is much further away from mainland Europe than, say, Spain, Cyprus is losing its attraction as a 'bucket shop' holiday destination. Reducing the cost of labour does not seem to be an option, given the strength of unions in the hotel and airline sectors, which frequently call strikes and routine restrictions on foreign labour whenever there is a downturn in the sector.

Successive governments and the private sector have therefore concentrated on the longer-term aim of upgrading the Cyprus tourist product in order to attract higher-spend tourism. In the private sector, this has included following the Spanish model, with developers building holiday- or retirement-home resorts that include attractions such as golf. The Government is also planning new marinas, which would attract yachts, and has plans to increase the number of other sports facilities now that the British Olympic team has chosen Cyprus as a permanent base for warm-weather training. New marinas could also lead to a revival of the cruise industry, if there is a long-term settlement of the Israeli–Palestinian problem. However, 2003 has not been a good year to attract bids for such projects; therefore it will probably be 2004 before the marina projects get under way. The airport at Larnaca is also going through an upgrade.

In other sectors, the Government has made a start at encouraging 'incubators': small firms in the high technology field, which can be given grants to develop and commercialize research. Cyprus will benefit from having young, fairly skilled workers, most of whom speak

English with ease, as well as a population that is known for its entrepreneurial spirit. The University of Cyprus and some private firms are also taking an active role in this area, although business-people in the sector note that it took a good decade, plus a technology boom, before similar initiatives in Israel had a significant impact on the economy.

Another challenge, which no government has had the will to face, is to improve the flexibility of the labour market. Many companies in the private sector are under pressure from the unions to follow the government practice of automatically raising salaries twice a year under the inflation-indexation mechanism known as COLA, regardless of profitability or productivity improvements. This has led to criticism from both the EU and the IMF. In addition, many of the large employers, such as banks and hotels, also engage in sector-wide collective bargaining. While unemployment remains low by EU standards (at 4.3 per cent in May 2003 on an EU-compatible basis, compared with 8.8 per cent for the EU), there is little incentive to change these practices. However, the economy will no doubt face disruptions in the event that there is a reunification of the island. Public expenditure will probably rise and the Government will be under fiscal pressure to revise these practices, although they will be politically difficult to implement.

1.3

Government, Politics and Accession to the European Union

Dr James Ker-Lindsay, Executive Director, Civilitas Research

Overview

Following 80 years of British rule, Cyprus achieved independence in 1960. However, within three years conflict broke out between the island's Greek and Turkish communities and in 1974 Cyprus was divided following a military invasion by Turkey, which was staged in response to a Greek inspired coup. Today, the southern two-thirds of the island, which is mainly inhabited by Greek Cypriots, is controlled by the Government of Cyprus, which is still internationally recognized as the legal government of the whole of the island. In the North, the Turkish Cypriots have unilaterally declared independence and created the 'Turkish Republic of Northern Cyprus' (TRNC). However, despite numerous efforts to secure international acceptance, the TRNC is still only recognized by Turkey.

Thus far all attempts to try to reach a solution to the conflict and thereby bring about a reunification of the island have failed. Even the impending accession of Cyprus to the EU, on 1 May 2004, was not enough to bring the parties together, and the most recent effort to secure a settlement collapsed in March 2003. Nevertheless, although new negotiations are not currently scheduled, it is expected that discussions will start again at the end of 2003 or early in 2004.

The contemporary political scene

The political scene in the Republic of Cyprus is dominated by four main parties. The two largest parties are AKEL, the Cyprus communist party, and Democratic Rally (DISY), a right-wing party, each of which commands approximately 35 per cent of the national vote. Given the rough equality of support for the two main parties, and the fact that neither could command an executive or legislative majority on its own, the balance of power therefore has tended to fall into the hands of two smaller parties, the Democratic Party (DIKO) and the Socialist Party (EDEK), which between them currently have around 20 per cent of the vote. While DIKO was traditionally a centre-right party, in June 2003 it declared that it would henceforth adopt a social democratic stance; a decision that has led to calls for a merger with EDEK. The remaining 10 per cent of the votes are distributed among a number of smaller parties.

Supreme executive authority rests with the President of the Republic, who is both the head of state and the head of government. Elections for the presidency are held every five years, and in order to win a candidate must receive a clear majority of votes cast. If no candidate wins over 50 per cent in the first round, the two leading contenders go head to head in a second round run-off. The most recent presidential elections were held in February 2003 and were won by Tassos Papadopoulos, the leader of DIKO, who beat the DISY-sponsored incumbent, Glafkos Clerides. Mr Papadopoulos, a well-known lawyer, now heads a left-wing coalition government made up of ministers drawn from AKEL, EDEK and his own party. There are also three independent ministers; including George Iacovou, the foreign minister, and Kypros Chrysostomides, the government spokesman.

Cyprus has a strict separation of powers and so ministers cannot simultaneously serve as members of the House of Representatives (Vouli ton Antiprosopon), the island's single chamber legislative body that is elected every five years. Originally composed of 50 members – 35 Greek Cypriot and 15 Turkish Cypriot – the number of seats was increased to 80 in 1985. In order to main the 70:30 balance between Greek and Turkish Cypriots, as laid down by the constitution, only the 56 seats allocated to the Greek Cypriot community are filled at present. Following the last elections, held in May 2001, the composition of the House is as follows:

AKEL	34.7%	20 seats
DISY	34.0%	19 seats
DIKO	14.8%	9 seats
EDEK (KISOS)	6.5%	4 seats
New Horizons	3.0%	1 seat
United Democrats	2.6%	1 seat
ADIK	2.2%	1 seat
Ecologists	2.0%	1 seat

The three religious minorities – the Latins, Maronites and Armenians – each have a single representative who may only speak on matters that directly affect their community and does not have a vote. However, for the purposes of parliamentary and presidential elections, these three minorities are considered to be a part of the Greek Cypriot community and vote accordingly. Due to the continuing political situation, the Turkish Cypriots who choose to live in the southern, Greek Cypriot part of the island do not currently have voting rights.

The Turkish Cypriot political system

Since declaring independence in 1983, the Turkish Cypriots have developed a political structure that is more akin to a European presidential system in which the head of state has very little real power. However, Rauf R Denktash, the holder of the office since the creation of the TRNC, has been given sole authority to negotiate on the Cyprus issue. Apart from this, most other aspects of executive authority are exercised by a prime minister, a post currently held by Dervish Eroglu, who leads a centre-right coalition government formed by his National Unity Party (UBP) and the Democratic Party (DP). The next parliamentary elections are due to be held in December 2003, when it is expected that the predominantly left-wing opposition parties will make big gains. If they win, it is anticipated that they will force a parliamentary vote, relieving Mr Denktash of his current responsibility for negotiating on the Cyprus issue.

The Cyprus Issue

The single most important political issue in Cyprus is the continued division of the island. Although history in Cyprus is naturally open to debate, the contemporary situation can be traced back to 1878. It was then that Cyprus was passed over to British administration by the Ottoman Empire, which had ruled the island for 300 years. Almost immediately after the handover, representatives of the island's numerically larger Greek community requested that the island be united with the Kingdom of Greece. This call was resisted by the British Government, as were all subsequent attempts to revive the matter, and Cyprus remained a part of the British Empire until 1960, when it was granted independence.

In order to balance power between the island's two communities, and thus maintain peace between Greece and Turkey, the new republic was given an extremely complex constitutional structure. The president was required to be a member of the larger Greek Cypriot community (78 per cent of the population), while the vice-president would be drawn from the significantly smaller Turkish Cypriot community (18 per cent of the population). (The remaining 4 per cent is made up of Armenians, Latins, Maronites and others.) These two figures presided over a ten-member Council of Ministers that was made up of seven Greek Cypriots and three Turkish Cypriots and which was responsible for overall executive administration. The House of Representatives, the island's main legislature, was composed of fifty seats. Thirty five seats were held by the Greek Cypriots and 15 by Turkish Cypriots. In the civil service, judiciary and police the two communities were represented according to a ratio of 70:30 in favour of the Greek Cypriots, while the army saw a more equal representation at 60:40.

The complexity of the structure soon started to create tensions between the Greek and Turkish Cypriots. The Greek Cypriots considered the Turkish Cypriots to be over-represented in the machinery of state and unwilling to compromise. The Turkish Cypriots felt that the Greek Cypriots wanted to force them out of the political system and relegate them to second-class citizens. By December 1963 tensions had reached boiling point and fighting broke out. This led to the creation of a United Nations peace-keeping force, in March 1964, which still operates on the island. Although a number of efforts were made to try to resolve the differences between the two communities, no progress was made. In 1967 the democratic government in Greece was overthrown by a military coup, which ushered in a new period of instability on the island that culminated, in July 1974, with a coup aimed at overthrowing the government of Archbishop Makarios and uniting the island with Greece. Turkey responded by launching a military invasion of the island and, over the course of the following month, occupied the northern 36 per cent of Cyprus, including the eastern port city of Famagusta, the northern town of Kyrenia, and the western town of Morphou, the main citrus-producing area on the island.

Attempts to reunite the island soon got underway and in 1977 the leaders of the two communities agreed that any reunification would be based on the creation of a bi-zonal, bi-communal federal structure. This agreement was subsequently reconfirmed in 1979. However, no solution was reached in the following years and in 1983, using the opportunity of political uncertainty in Turkey, the Turkish Cypriots unilaterally declared independence for what they called the 'Turkish Republic of Northern Cyprus' – an entity that is recognized only by Turkey. Despite the setback, talks continued intermittently throughout the 1980s and 1990s with no success, largely as a result of the continued demands by Mr Denktash that the TRNC be recognized.

The prospect of Cyprus's accession to the EU opened the way for a resumption of talks in January 2002. These continued throughout the year and resulted in the preparation of a comprehensive peace plan by the UN Secretary General, Kofi Annan, which was presented to the parties in November of that year. While Mr Clerides, the Greek Cypriot leader, showed a willingness to accept the agreement, yet again Mr Denktash refused to sign up – despite the fact that he was facing massive demonstrations in favour of a solution by Turkish Cypriots and was coming under considerable pressure from the Turkish Government, the United States and the EU. The talks eventually came to an end on 10 March 2003, when a last-ditch proposal to put the plan to an island-wide referendum was rejected by the Turkish Cypriot leader.

European Union Accession

As a result of this decision to reject a referendum, Cyprus appears likely to enter the EU divided. The process of EU accession began in 1972 when the Republic of Cyprus signed an association agreement with the EEC that was designed to result in a full customs union within ten years. However, the events of 1974 delayed the implementation of the agreement, so in May 1987 a new association agreement was signed. This was followed, in 1990, with a formal application by the Government of Cyprus for full membership of the EU. The application was accepted in 1993, but because of a decision to delay the start of talks until after the Inter-Governmental Conference (IGC) that resulted in the 1997 Treaty of Amsterdam, the process of harmonization with the *acquis communautaire*, the Union's body of laws, did not start until March 1998.

At the time of the start of talks an offer was made to the Turkish Cypriot community to take part in the negotiation process. However, the offer was rejected on the grounds that the Turkish Cypriots would not be recognized as a separate negotiating party. Over the next three and a half years Cyprus made quick progress in closing the 31 chapters of the *acquis*. Indeed, at many points in the process Cyprus led the other nine candidate countries and by December 2002 the process had been completed. A decision was therefore taken at the Copenhagen European Council to admit the ten countries, including Cyprus, as full members of the EU in May 2004. The formal treaty of accession was subsequently signed in April 2003, in Athens. Unlike the other nine new entrants, Cyprus did not put EU membership to a referendum – a procedure that is not recognized under the Cyprus constitution. Instead the issue was voted on by the House of Representatives.

A solution is still possible

Unlike the other accession states, Cyprus never saw EU accession as desirable in terms of the economic benefits the island would reap. Apart from the fact that Cyprus will be a net contributor to the EU, it is widely felt that EU accession will actually damage several sectors of the economy. In particular it is expected that light industry will be affected, as will agriculture. However, EU accession was never based on economic factors. Instead, EU membership has always been regarded by the Greek Cypriots as a means by which to guarantee their security against what they perceive to be an ongoing threat from Turkey. Given Turkey's stated desire to join the EU, Cypriot accession has also come to be seen as a means of spurring Ankara to take action to solve the issue. While the first reason represents wishful thinking given the lack of a military capability on the part of the EU, it does appear that the prospect of Cypriot membership of the EU may well lead to a solution.

In December 1999, after many years of lobbying, Turkey was finally accepted as a candidate for membership of the EU. Although, strictly speaking, a solution to the Cyprus issue is not a formal prerequisite for Turkish membership, it has long been known that it will be very difficult, if not impossible, to envisage Turkish accession without a solution in Cyprus. This was made especially clear after the breakdown of the latest talks when senior figures within the European Commission highlighted the fact that as of 1 May 2004 Turkey would be in occupation of the territory of an EU member state. At the same time, Cyprus, as a full member of the EU, would from that point onwards be in a position to block moves to start talks with Turkey; a prospect that the Turkish Government is growing increasingly concerned about. It is therefore increasingly likely that another attempt will be made to revive peace talks and try to reach a solution prior to full Cypriot membership. After 30 years, 2004 may well be the year the Cyprus issue is finally solved.

1.4

Professional and Business Services

Kostas Christophidis, Assistant Director General, Cyprus Employers and Industrialists Federation (OEB)[1]

Background

Cyprus has fast become a major regional services centre attracting clients and businesses from many geographical locations with the net result that at the end of 2002 the services industry was the island's biggest economic sector contributing some 76 per cent to GDP (GDP – including retail trade).

A combination of unique features has made Cyprus a key regional services centre. These can be summarized as follows:

- *High quality – value for money.* Many enterprises in numerous sectors provide quality business support facilities. These match the highest international standards at a fraction of the cost.

- *Qualified professionals – no language barriers.* Highly qualified professionals with wide international experience, fluent in English and other languages, guarantee smooth and efficient services.

- *Expertise in servicing overseas clients.* Apart from the Cyprus market, many Cyprus services enterprises now successfully cater to foreign clients, either through branches abroad or directly from their Cyprus base. Cyprus has earned a reputation as a major centre of excellence in providing services and support among professionals.

- *Ideal geographical location.* Cyprus, at the crossroads of Europe, Asia and Africa, is easily accessible and ideally located for providing

---

1. Information in this article has also been provided by The Ministry of Commerce, Industry and Tourism.

business services in all these regions. Having very good business relations with all its neighbouring countries and as a full member of the EU from May 2004 Cyprus will enhance its role as a bridge between the EU and third countries.

- *Excellent telecommunications*. The state-of-the-art national and international infrastructure and the wide range of services offered, rank Cyprus among the most advanced countries in this field.

- *Pleasant environment*. With 340 days of sunshine per year, Cyprus has an excellent climate. Its archaeological wealth, scenic beauty, lovely beaches and mountain resorts offer many opportunities to mix business with pleasure. The island is also enviably crime free and secure, making it ideal for families.

Sector by sector overview

Accounting

This sector is highly developed and professional, with most major international accountancy companies being represented. In addition there are a number of local practices, all operating to the highest international standards.

Banking

Cyprus is well served by banks, of which there are nine commercial banks and three specialized institutions. The country is also a centre for international banking, with 30 well-known banks from a number of countries maintaining a presence.

International business

Well in excess of 30,000 international business enterprises have been granted permits to register in Cyprus, covering a wide area of business interests.

Business consulting

A comprehensive range of business consultancy services is offered by numerous professional practitioners in many fields, including, but not confined to, management consultancy, patent design, trademark registration, human resources, quality management, project management and coordination, environmental activities and the preparation of economic and feasibility studies.

Computing and information technology (IT)

Today, in excess of 70 computer hardware and software suppliers, IT consultants and Internet and e-commerce consultants offer a breadth of expertise in every aspect of computing and IT.

Design

Over 100 design companies offering a breadth of experience and expertise maintain a presence in Cyprus, offering their services to the fields of advertising, marketing, packaging and product design.

Education and research

The development of educational services has been a success story for Cyprus and is an area where much concentration is currently being placed to ensure future growth. Facilities are being provided by both government and the private sectors and many of the colleges offer places to international students as well as those from within the country.

State organizations include The University of Cyprus, The Higher Technical Institute, The Forestry College, The School of Nursing, The Higher Hotel Institute and The Mediterranean Institute of Management.

These facilities are well-supplemented by a host of private sector educational and training centres, offering a wide spectrum of subjects presented by well-qualified and professional tutors and professors.

A major initiative in mid-2003 is The Cyprus Institute[2], which is in the process of establishing a new research and educational institution with a strong scientific and technological orientation in partnership with other world-class institutions and with a truly international student body and faculty. Integral to the Institute will be a series of cross-disciplinary research centres which from the outset are expected to comprise those for energy, environment and water; technology and archaeology; information, communication and computation; economic development and conflict resolution; management and finance; human health and development; and computer-based science and technology.

Engineering

Cypriot engineers are well known worldwide but especially in the Middle East and North Africa, where their skills in civil, electrical and mechanical engineering have been employed in major projects over many years.

---

2. Information provided by the Cyprus Development Bank, the promoter of the Institute.

Cyprus-based engineering contractors and consultants are also to be found across the same two regions, often working in association with local companies to which they provide the necessary expertise.

Integral to this sector is The Technical Chamber of Cyprus (ETEK), which represents the interests of the whole gamut of engineering-related activities.

Legal services

The legal profession has been long established in Cyprus, with many practising lawyers having been trained in Greece, the United Kingdom and the United States.

Close associations with major international practices are maintained by the larger companies operating in the international environment.

Marine and shipping

As an island and therefore a seafaring nation, Cyprus has accumulated comprehensive experience and expertise in shipping, ship management and marine freight. Today, the island has become home to many ship-owning companies and an entrepôt for international shipping companies, so encouraging a host of land-based freight activities of the highest international standards and which are so important to the smooth running and cost effectiveness of the shipping business.

Private healthcare

Cyprus enjoys high quality healthcare to European standards and is able to offer its services price competitively when compared with other parts of the world. As a result the private sector seeks assiduously to develop medical and healthcare tourism to the country, especially from the Middle and Far East but also from Europe, in which it has proved most successful.

Risk management

Risk management in Cyprus is largely the field of the insurance companies and brokers operating there, many of whom maintain close associations with international brokers in the major centres of the world.

Sales and marketing

Cyprus boasts a well-developed infrastructure of sales and marketing professionals, many of whom have international experience, especially in the Middle East, Africa and Eastern Europe. The island has developed as a centre for market research and the provision of marketing-related consultancy services.

Tourism, travel and conferences

The hospitality industry is the major single contributor to the nation's GDP and constantly seeks to build on the country's year-round sunshine and relaxing lifestyle. In addition to tourists seeking sun and leisure, many international businesses now use Cyprus as a destination for conferences and other meetings. In addition to the provision of facilities for people to stay and meet, the island also boasts a number of companies offering a range of consultancy services interrelated with the hospitality industry.

The export of services

At this time, Cyprus' services are exported to Eastern Europe, the Middle East, the EU and North America.

Sectors of greatest potential

Presently, the most dynamic services sectors are tourism, accounting and finance, business consultancy services, and shipping and international marine, whilst the newly emerging sectors are private healthcare, tertiary education and information technology.

1.5

Tourism

Cyprus Tourism Organization Information Centre

Introduction

From modest beginnings in the early 1960s tourism has grown to become a vital element in the economy of Cyprus. Such growth has not always been smooth as visitor numbers have been adversely impacted on several occasions by events either within the country, as in 1974, in the nearby Middle East, as in 1991, or in the aftermath of 11 September 2001, when worldwide tourism saw a major decline. Despite this, implementation of the facilities necessary for encouraging yet greater numbers of visitors to Cyprus, including several categories of accommodation and a host of infrastructural works such as airport terminals, port facilities, roads, parks, sporting facilities, nature trails and marinas, has continued apace.

As Cyprus entered the twenty-first century a new strategic plan for tourism was announced for implementation through to the year 2010. This plan seeks a qualitative increase in visitor numbers whilst ensuring enhanced quality of the products, services and facilities offered, all within the context of sustainable development. Implementation of this plan has continued apace whilst, looking ahead, membership of the EU in May 2004 is perceived likely to provide a major fillip to further progress in terms of visitor numbers, revenues generated and foreign investment.

Cyprus tourism

Tourism in Cyprus is a year-round activity, albeit a vast proportion of visitors arrive in the country in the six months from May to October, when they can usually be categorized as 'sea, sun and sand' tourists arriving to relax and to escape from the rains and colder weather of more temperate climes. Tourism does, however, continue throughout the winter months, which are generally mild with many hours of sunshine, with conference attendees, third age visitors and special interest tourists, including those arriving for the short skiing season in the Troodos Mountains.

In recent years increased attention has been given to niche tourism and the number of visitors arriving to take in the extensive historical and cultural sites, the former dating back to Neolithic times; to participate in recently developed agrotourism in the picturesque hinterland villages; to walk the many delightful nature trails through Cyprus' 1,500 sq. km of forests; or to become involved in sports and sports training on both land and sea, has grown considerably in recent years.

As more facilities have been developed, for example golf courses, marinas, football pitches and parks in addition to every aspect of the basic infrastructure, so have the numbers of niche tourists grown commensurately.

The Cyprus Tourism Organization

The Cyprus Tourism Organization (CTO), founded in 1971, is a semi-governmental organization overseen by the Ministry of Commerce, Industry and Tourism and charged with the responsibility for tourism planning, product development, marketing and general management of the national tourism industry. It fulfils its role through its main offices in Nicosia and its regional offices in Cyprus and abroad. The CTO maintains 18 tourist offices overseas, in London, Dublin, Frankfurt, Paris, Stockholm, Athens, Zurich, Moscow, Milan, Amsterdam, Brussels, Vienna, New York, Tokyo, Tel Aviv, Budapest, Warsaw and Prague, to market and promote Cyprus tourism, to service the tourist trade and to provide information to prospective holidaymakers to Cyprus (full contact details appear in Appendix 2 Useful Addresses). It also has information and inspector offices in all the tourist regions.

Through the CTO, Cyprus is an active participant in many international tourism-related organizations including the World Tourism Organization (WTO), the European Travel Commission (ETC), the International Congress and Conventions Association (ICCA) and the European Federation of Conference Towns (EFCT). Cyprus is also represented at the annual meetings of international trade associations such as ABTA (UK), ASTA (US) and DRV (Germany).

The Strategic Plan for Tourism 2010

By the early 1990s the rapid development of tourism in Cyprus was seen to have impacted adversely on the country's natural resources, on the overall natural and built environments and on the people themselves. At the same time marked changes had begun to occur in the international tourism market, including intensified price competition and a greater demand for niche tourism such as cultural and nature-based tourism. Taking account of these factors Cyprus has sought to upgrade, enrich and diversify the 'product' being offered to ensure wider diversity of tourist experience for a broader cross section of visitors.

To this end the Strategic Plan for Tourism 2010 was drawn up by the CTO, with the active participation of tourism partners in both public and private sectors for subsequent approval by the Council of Ministers in January 2001. The basic target of the Plan is to increase total revenue from tourism in real terms (based on 1998 prices) to CYP 1.8 billion (GBP 2.36 billion, EUR 3.1 billion) by 2010 through pursuit of sustainable development policies and the repositioning of Cyprus as a destination offering great diversity of the tourist experiences within a limited geographical space. The new positioning strategy aims to expose the island's unique character to the visitor, which can be described as follows: 'A mosaic of nature and culture, a whole magical world concentrated in a small, warm and hospitable island in the Mediterranean, at the cross-roads of three continents, between east and west that offers a multidimensional, qualitative tourist experience.'

The two most important areas for bringing about the distinctiveness of Cyprus as a tourist destination are its rich cultural heritage (history, archaeology, tradition, local cuisine, religion) and its diverse environment (varied landscape, flora, fauna, geology) that are identified as the two main axes of the strategy around which the marketing, product development and quality/value strategies evolve.

The strategy assesses the priority segments to be targeted and the special interest products that need to be developed in order to meet their needs. The priority segments targeted are sun and sea as well as the segments of culture, conference and incentives, nature, hiking, cycling, cruise tourism, sports tourism, wedding ceremonies/ honeymooners, mega events, sea sports and yachting. The strategy suggests how the marketing tools will be used to target these segments in the selected markets and bring about the island's repositioning in the markets and provides for partnerships between the public and private sectors for destination marketing.

The 'special interest products', which will act as attractors to the targeted segments offering them opportunities for activities and entertainment in their area of interest (things to do and see), are prioritized in the strategy. Top priority products are the themed routes across the island, museums, agrotourism establishments/activities, national parks, nature trails and events, workshops and information centres on targeted segment topics of interest, health/fitness/pampering facilities, cycling and hiking facilities. Other high-priority products, catering for the needs of specific market segments, are marinas and football grounds, while golf courses, theme parks, marine parks, sea sports facilities constitute special interest products of medium priority.

The development of a complete tourist product of high quality is a strategic priority for Cyprus. This will be accomplished by building on every aspect of the tourist product: special interest products, accommodation, catering, inland transport, basic infrastructure (airports, ports, marinas, road network), shopping and merchandising. Public and private investments and partnerships are expected in all of these areas to facilitate the repositioning of the destination and the attraction of the targeted segments.

Regarding accommodation the strategy aims at encouraging new types of accommodation facilities (eg mixed use destination resorts), upgrading the existing tourist accommodation establishments and developing small-scale accommodation units of particular character and ambience.

Apart from the areas of marketing and product development, investment opportunities lie also in the sphere of quality/value enhancement: human resource development, establishment of quality mechanisms (quality and environmental management systems, certification, awards, etc) and programmes for the enhancement of competitiveness (pricing, cost, improvement of technological and management practices in SMEs and the like).

Tourist arrivals and receipts

In just over 20 years Cyprus has seen phenomenal growth in terms of both visitor numbers and tourist receipts, with both reaching a peak in 2001 when 2.7 million tourists visited the country and receipts totalled

Table 1.5.1 Tourist arrivals and receipts

Year	Arrivals	Receipts (CYP million)
1980	348,530	71
1985	769,727	257
1990	1,561,479	573
1995	2,100,000	813
1997	2,088,000	843
1998	2,222,706	878
1999	2,434,285	1,022
2000	2,686,205	1,094
2001	2,696,732	1,272
2002	2,418,233	1,132

Source: Government of Cyprus Official Statistics

Table 1.5.2 Tourist arrivals by country of origin, 2002 and 2001

	2002	2001	% change
United Kingdom	1,337,640	1,486,700	−10.03
Germany	173,711	214,149	−18.88
Greece	93,217	89,758	3.85
Sweden	99,750	127,415	−21.71
Norway	57,699	61,614	−6.35
Finland	45,438	48,751	−6.80
Denmark	31,800	33,009	−3.66
France	29,541	32,825	−10.00
Switzerland	64,582	76,608	−15.70
Netherlands	39,784	50,743	−21.60
Belgium/Luxembourg	24,191	31,001	−21.97
Austria	29,049	31,031	−6.39
Italy	12,178	21,907	−44.41
Ireland	56,649	51,875	9.20
Russia and other ex-USSR	122,961	128,504	−4.31
Poland	19,514	25,142	−22.38
Hungary	8,075	8,523	−5.26
Czech Republic	13,820	9,891	39.72
Other Eastern Europe	9,711	7,676	26.51
Other Europe	14,126	17,612	−19.79
Arab countries	28,515	28,641	−0.44
Gulf countries	17,616	22,154	−20.48
Israel	39,936	36,676	8.89
United States	20,560	23,295	−11.74
Canada	5,256	5,761	−8.77
Japan	372	598	−37.79
Other countries	22,542	24,873	−9.37
All countries	*2,418,233*	*2,696,732*	*−10.33*

Source: Cyprus Tourisam Organization

CYP 1.27 billion (GBP 1.66 billion, EUR 2.2 billion). A year later there was a marked decline in numbers in line with a downturn in world tourism arising from heightened concern about international terrorism.

Over the years the United Kingdom has been the major country of origin of visitors to Cyprus and in both 2001 and 2002 British nationals accounted for some 55 per cent of all tourist arrivals. In the same two years a further 20 per cent of all visitors emanated from just four countries: Germany, Russia, Sweden and Greece.

As to the future, the Strategic Plan foresees not only enhanced numbers of tourist arrivals but also increased expenditure per visit. In numerical terms a rise in the number of arrivals is envisaged to be around 3.5 million in 2010 (a year-on-year growth figure between 1999 and 2010 of 3.4 per cent). In attaining such a figure, and by targeting higher-income tourists with niche interests, Cyprus seeks also to attain growth in average expenditure per tourist in real terms (adjusted for inflation) from CYP 388 (GBP 485, EUR 665) in 1999 to CYP 512 (GBP 640, EUR 878) in 2010. Actual expenditure per tourist in current terms reached CYP 441.50 (GBP 588, EUR 806) in 2001 and CYP 468.24 in 2002.

Accommodation

Cyprus offers a comprehensive range of holiday accommodation, from luxurious, modern establishments to small, family-run operations. Such accommodation comprises hotels, hotel apartments, tourist villages, villas and apartments, camping sites, traditional houses, guest houses and youth hostels, many providing a wide array of sports and leisure facilities.

As at the end of 2002 Cyprus boasted 946 tourist accommodation units offering a total of 94,466 beds, as follows:

Table 1.5.3 Tourist accommodation, December 2002

Accommodation type	Number of units	Number of beds
Hotels	241	52,410
Hotel apartments	273	23,537
Tourist villages	17	4,958
Sub total	*531*	*80,905*
Villas	101	850
Traditional buildings	66	625
Tourist apartments	197	8,128
Furnished apartments	27	384
Hotels (without stars)	11	275
Guest houses	8	179
Camping sites	5	3,120
Sub total	*415*	*13,561*
Total	**946**	**94,466**

Source: Cyprus Tourism Organization

At the same date yet further accommodation was under construction, as follows:

Looking to the future, to accommodate the visitor numbers projected for 2010, 131,000 beds are necessary. The Strategic Plan encourages the construction of the additional beds in five categories: mixed-use resorts, 3 to 5 star hotels, tourist villas, tourist villages and smaller units of traditional character.

Table 1.5.4 Tourist accommodation under construction, December 2002

Accommodation type	Number of units	Number of beds
Hotels	7	1,342
Hotel apartments	3	488
Tourist villages	3	832
Traditional buildings	2	10
Total	*15*	*2,672*

Source: Cyprus Tourism Organization

The opportunities

In seeking to attract higher tourist numbers and greater visitor expenditure the CTO recognizes, as expressed in the Strategic Plan, the need to enhance not only the quality and availability of accommodation but also the standard and variety of the facilities to be made available for their use and entertainment. Thus, as has been mentioned, substantial attention is being given to enhancement of the overall infrastructure on the island.

Of highest priority in this regard is expansion and upgrading of the Republic's two airports at Larnaca and Pafos, to enable the greater passenger throughput anticipated and to provide passengers with high-quality lounges, shops and refreshment facilities. Attention is being given also to the country's seaports at Larnaca and Limassol, to enhance their status as major points of entry to Cyprus and as locations offering high-quality facilities and services to arriving and departing cruise passengers.

Ease of access by visitors to the many and varied attractions of the island necessitates good roads, cycle paths and pedestrian footpaths, as well as improved transportation links. To improve and beautify the streets of towns and villages, upgraded pavements and suitable street furniture are being provided.

Attention is being given also to the raising of the profile of Cypriot culture and the country's authentic products, thereby enhancing their attraction for visitors and creating increased opportunities for generating income for the indigenous population.

Indications are that substantial investment opportunities in Cyprus are, therefore, available for both local investors and foreign businessmen seeking to participate in the island's anticipated future prosperity, be they in the provision of visitor accommodation, the array of facilities the Government and CTO seeks to have made available, human resource development, enhancement of quality and competitiveness or destination marketing. Entry to the EU in 2004 seems likely to provide an added stimulus for foreign investors to become involved in the tourism sector of the Republic and, when agreement is reached concerning Northern Cyprus, yet further tourism-related opportunities are deemed likely to arise as Cyprus will try to capitalize on the provision of a more complete and diverse experience on the whole island, in line with its new strategic positioning of the island.

1.6

Banking, Finance and Insurance

Sofronis Eteocleous, Manager, Economic Research and Planning, Laiki Bank

The financial sector in Cyprus has exhibited rapid growth in recent years, driven by the good performance of the economy, stable macroeconomic conditions and the development of the island as an international business centre. Average annual GDP growth over the period 1995–2002 reached 3.9 per cent, while the average rate of unemployment and inflation over the same period stood at 3.2 per cent and 2.7 per cent, respectively.

The financial sector is one of the most dynamic sectors of the economy. The contribution of the sector to GDP in 2002 is estimated at 6.2 per cent, compared with 4.9 per cent in 1995. In 2002 the sector provided employment to 147,000 people, or 4.7 per cent of the gainfully employed population, compared with 123,000, or 4.3 per cent, in 1995.

Banking has the leading role in financial intermediation services. The value added generated by the banking sub-sector represented in 2002 a share of 83.9 per cent of the total value of the financial sector, compared with 79.9 per cent in 1995. Banks are the overwhelming providers of finance to the economy, even though this role was temporarily challenged during 1999 and 2000 with the boom on the Cyprus Stock Exchange. Total assets of domestic banks between 1996 and 2002 grew at an average annual rate of around 14 per cent, reaching CYP 15.5 billion at the end of 2002, which is equivalent to 251 per cent of GDP. Employment in the sector at the end of 2001 stood at 78,000 or 2.5 per cent of the gainfully employed population.

Non-bank financial firms, such as insurance companies and other financial institutions, play a secondary role in mobilizing savings and allocating resources for investment purposes. Insurance, however, plays a significant role in economic activity. Total insurance premiums in relation to GDP reached 4.4 per cent in 2001, while the same ratio for EU countries stood at 9 per cent. From these figures it is evident that there is room for further growth in the market. Supervision and regulation of the financial sector is divided between four different bodies:

- The Central Bank of Cyprus has responsibility for the supervision of banks. The rules, policies and practices of the Central Bank are in line with the EU directives and the recommendations of the Basle Committee on banking supervision.

- The Commissioner of Cooperative Development, under the Minister of Commerce, Industry and Tourism supervises Cooperative Credit Societies.

- The Office of the Superintendent of Insurance, under the Minister of Finance, oversees the functioning of insurance companies.

- The Cyprus Securities and Exchange Commission is responsible for supervising the operation of the Stock Exchange and ensuring compliance with the Stock Exchange Law and Regulations.

The financial sector in Cyprus is currently in a transitional stage due to the process of harmonization with the EU *acquis communautaire*. This process has propelled reforms and changes in the legal and operating environment, which will have an impact on the structure and functioning of the financial system. The most important changes relate to the following areas:

- introduction of a regime of floating interest rates as from 1 January 2001;

- gradual abolition of restrictions on inward and outward capital movements, which will be completed upon accession of Cyprus to the EU on 1 May 2004;

- adoption of the freedom of establishment and the freedom to provide services;

- strengthening of the regulatory framework;

- approval of legislation governing the establishment and supervision of investment service providers, which is in line with EU directives;

- adoption of the state aid rules of the European Commission, which will result in less government intervention.

Harmonization will gradually open up the country's financial system and integrate it with the single financial market of the EU and indirectly with the global financial markets. As a result, it will become more sensitive to international developments. The process of harmonization is leading to the creation of new opportunities and challenges, the improvement in the functioning of the market and the intensification of competition to the benefit of the consumers.

CYTA...
THE LOWEST TELEPHONE RATES
IN THE EUROPEAN UNION!

Teligen indicator

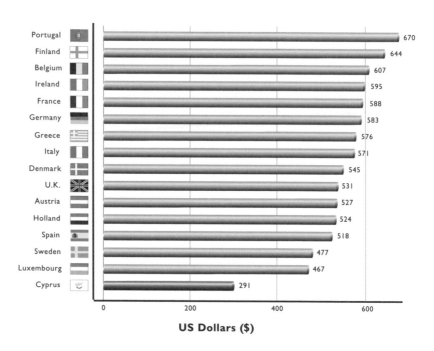

Country	US Dollars ($)
Portugal	670
Finland	644
Belgium	607
Ireland	595
France	588
Germany	583
Greece	576
Italy	571
Denmark	545
U.K.	531
Austria	527
Holland	524
Spain	518
Sweden	477
Luxembourg	467
Cyprus	291

US Dollars ($)

TABLE: OECD cost indicator (Organisation for Economic Co-operation and Development). The indicator refers to a basket of telecommunication services and includes subscription, local, trunk and international calls as well as calls to mobile phones.

SOURCE: TELIGEN

Focusing on the changing needs
of today's consumer

CYPRUS
OLYMPIC
COMMITTEE

OFFICIAL SPONSOR
CYPRUS OLYMPIC COMMITTEE

Telecommunications in Cyprus

Andreas Theodorou, Regulatory Affairs, Business Management Support, Cyprus Telecommunications Authority

Introduction

Cyprus today has one of the most technologically advanced telecommunications networks in Europe, with a fully digitalized national network, an extensive fibre optic submarine cable network connecting the island with all its neighbouring countries and with the rest of the world and a rich portfolio of services. Furthermore, with the cheapest basket of telecommunications services, according to a Teligen benchmark study, the claim that Cyprus is one of the most advanced telecommunication centres in the world is far from exaggerated.

The telecommunications market in Cyprus is currently in the process of being liberalized. The first licences in the form of general authorizations were granted in mid-2003 and there are plans to auction a second GSM licence later in the year.

The Cyprus Telecommunications Authority (CYTA), a corporate body established by Law, has been responsible for the provision, maintenance and development of telecommunications both nationally and internationally since 1961. A state-owned organization currently enjoying monopoly rights in most telecommunications services, CYTA is a financially sound organization that has proved highly instrumental in developing telecommunications in Cyprus and thus contributing and supporting the Government's vision of turning the island into a renowned international services centre. CYTA has invested in building an extensive international network and turning the island into one of the most important telecommunications hubs in the Eastern Mediterranean.

Overall, telecommunications in Cyprus are in the growth stage, especially in the mobile and data markets, while further development of the sector is expected after full liberalization. Strong competition is expected in all sectors of the market, presenting the incumbent provider with yet another challenge.

International network

In cooperation with neighbouring countries, CYTA has developed an extensive submarine fibre optic cable network in the eastern Mediterranean basin, employing state-of-the-art technology and full restoration to connect Cyprus with all neighbouring countries, including Greece, Israel, Lebanon, Syria and Egypt. In addition, participation in the submarine cable systems, SEA-ME-WE-2, SEA-ME-WE-3, LEV, BSFOCS and TAT-14, connect the island with the rest of the world. There are also satellite connections to the outside world through six major and a number of smaller satellite earth stations.

National network

The national network is fully digitalized and it is continuously being upgraded to enhance the number and quality of the services and facilities offered to customers. The introduction of the Integrated Services Digital Network (ISDN), an ATM/FR network, an Intelligent network and the introduction of the Asymmetric Digital Subscriber Line (ADSL) system to all urban telephone exchanges enable CYTA to offer high quality telecommunication services

Fixed telephony penetration is at 61.2 per cent, which compares favourably with the average penetration of the EU. In the last couple of years there has been a migration to mobile telephony and ISDN subscriptions, with the latter steadily rising to bring the penetration in channels to 9.5 per cent.

Mobile telephony

Mobile telephony has been experiencing huge growth lately, surpassing the penetration of fixed telephony. CYTA has followed a strategy of continuously expanding the mobile telephony network to improve quality and at the same time to offer new services. Network infrastructure has been extended to the point that geographically it covers approximately 95 per cent of the government-controlled area while population coverage exceeds 99 per cent.

Towards the end of 2001 GPRS technology was introduced and was offered commercially in 2002, thus enabling the provision of advanced content and multimedia services. In 2001 the first mobile portal in Cyprus was also introduced.

Furthermore, there are now 248 International Roaming Agreements with other mobile operators in 102 countries. There is also the possibility for those travelling outside of GSM coverage to connect to the satellite system of mobile telephony, THURAYA, which covers 40 per cent of the globe. In 2001 and 2002 there were drastic reductions in the tariffs of international and mobile telephony, making Cyprus a country with the cheapest telecommunications basket in Europe.

Value added services

In addition to the fixed and mobile networks and services, a host of other value added services are available to the Cypriot consumer, such as audiotex, data services and videoconferencing.

Internet services are being offered by various Internet Service Providers. ADSL services enabling customers to have access to fast Internet are available through CYTA and video on demand and other interactive services are being tested and soon will be offered commercially.

Regulatory situation

Cyprus had pledged, during the EU accession negotiations, to fully liberalize its telecommunications market by 1 January 2003. Unfortunately, delays in implementing the relevant harmonizing legislation and in setting up the regulatory body have resulted in delays in the liberalization process.

The new telecommunications Law was approved in March 2002 and, towards the end of the same year, the Office of the Commissioner of Telecommunications and Posts was set up. In late 2002 and early 2003 the new regulatory homework was prepared, which will enable the full liberalization of the market.

As of mid-2003 the general authorization for value added services has been awarded, while a second GSM licence will be awarded by October 2003.

A Reference Interconnection Offer was published by the incumbent operator towards the end of July 2003, and it is expected that before the end of the year regulations will be in force on the unbundling of the local loop.

Conclusion

By the end of 2003 the telecommunications market will be fully liber-alized, and competition is expected in all the main product areas but particularly in mobile telephony, international fixed telephony and data services. Shortly thereafter it is expected that the process of implementing the new EU regulatory framework will begin.

As of mid-2003 there were more than 20 companies that had expressed interest in providing telecommunications services and had applied to the regulator and were consequently granted general autho-rizations. It is expected that special licences will also be granted in the near future.

The External Sector

Fiona Mullen, Assistant Editor, Financial Mirror, Nicosia

Foreign trade in goods

As a small island with few natural resources, Cyprus regularly imports four times more, in Cyprus pound terms, than it exports. In 2002, that ratio rose to 5:1. Total imports amounted to CYP 2,487 million, while total exports were only CYP 511.3 million. Cyprus therefore runs a large merchandise trade deficit. In 2002, this amounted to CYP1,975.3 million (fob-cif), or 31.9 per cent of GDP.

The large port in Limassol has developed as an entrepôt, which means, in the event, that around half of total exports fall under the category of 're-exports': goods which are not consumed within Cyprus but are temporarily imported before being shipped on elsewhere in the region. On the import side, however, almost 90 per cent of imports are for home consumption.

The Eastern Mediterranean is important for re-exports

The EU is the largest market for exports. For example, more than three-quarters of agricultural exports go to EU countries. In 2002, the

Table 1.8.1 Exports and imports 2002

	CYP thousand
Total exports incl. others	511,277
Domestic exports	221,918
Re-exports	247,052
Total imports incl. others	2,486,612
Imports for home consumption	2,256,442
Trade balance (fob-cif)	1,975,335

Source: Cyprus Statistical Service

EU took 53 per cent of Cyprus' domestic exports, while Arab countries took a further 21 per cent. The United Kingdom is the largest single export market, both for domestic exports and re-exports. The United Kingdom took CYP 38.3 million of domestic exports and CYP 103.1 million of re-exports in 2002. The next largest market is Greece, which took CYP 22.4 million in domestic exports and CYP 22.1 million in re-exports in 2002. Germany, the Netherlands and Lebanon are the next most important markets for domestic exports. For re-exports, however, neighbouring countries are much more dominant, with Syria and Egypt taking third and fifth places respectively.

The re-export market suffered badly in 2002, owing to the downturn in Middle East trade after the attacks on the United States in September 2001 and as a result of uncertainty in the run-up to the Iraq war. Re-exports thus fell, in Cyprus pound terms, by 26.7 per cent, compared with the previous year. Domestic exports fared better, but still fell, by 5.1 per cent compared with 2001. Data for January 2003,

Table 1.8.2 Top domestic and re-export markets, 2002

Top domestic export markets	CYP thousand	% of total
United Kingdom	38,284	16.5
Greece	22,374	9.7
Germany	13,539	5.8
Netherlands	10,434	4.5
Lebanon	7,161	3.1
Russia	6,447	2.8
Jordan	6,259	2.7
United States	6,125	2.6
Italy	6,086	2.6
Spain	5,713	2.5
Top re-export markets	**CYP thousand**	**% of total**
United Kingdom	103,127	36.9
Greece	20,110	7.2
Syria	14,624	5.2
United Arab Emirates	12,684	4.5
Egypt	12,094	4.3
Lebanon	11,508	4.1
Russia	6,379	2.3
Italy	6,231	2.2
United States	5,417	1.9
Bulgaria	5,167	1.8

Source: Cyprus Statistical Service

the latest data available as of July 2003, show that the collapse of both domestic exports and re-exports continued into the new year. Domestic exports fell in January by 10.7 per cent year on year in Cyprus pound terms, while re-exports fell by 25.2 per cent in the same period.

Pharmaceuticals now the largest export

A breakdown of exports by category is available only for domestic exports. This breakdown shows that pharmaceuticals are the largest single export, accounting for CYP 43.1 million in 2002, or 19.4 per cent of the total. This was not always the case, but in recent years the pharmaceutical industry has benefited from growing demand for generic products. Citrus fruit exports were the next largest category in 2002, with domestic exports of CYP 18.3 million (8.3 per cent of the total), while potatoes followed with CYP 16.0 million (7.2 per cent). Finally, the next category of any significant size is exports of halloumi cheese, which reached CYP 10.9 million in 2002, or 4.9 per cent of the total. As Greece has done with feta, Cyprus has managed to secure EU recognition of halloumi as a traditional cheese of Cyprus; therefore no other country may export cheese of the same name. Apart from pharmaceuticals and halloumi, exports of other manufactured products, such as clothing and processed food, have been losing market share to countries with lower labour costs.

Greece rises in importance for imports

A breakdown of figures by country for imports for home consumption is not available, but as far as total imports are concerned, in 2002, Greece

Table 1.8.3 Top domestic exports by category, 2002

	CYP thousand	% of total
Pharmaceutical products	43,107	19.4
Citrus fruit	18,304	8.2
Clothing	15,994	7.2
Potatoes	11,104	5.0
Halloumi cheese	10,946	4.9
Cement	8,796	4.0
Furniture	5,922	2.7
Articles of paper or paperboard	5,532	2.5
Wines	5,126	2.3
Fruit and vegetable juices	4,667	2.1

Source: Cyprus Statistical Service

secured the top place as Cyprus' principal supplier of total imports for the first time, overtaking the United States, which was the top supplier in 2001. Economic integration between Greece and Cyprus has probably been influenced by Greece's adoption of the euro, to which the Cyprus pound is pegged, as well as the expansion of the large Cypriot banks, which are also now listed on the Athens Stock Exchange, into Greece. The United Kingdom, meanwhile, which used to be the largest supplier, particularly of food, has suffered in recent years from the BSE (mad cow disease) crisis, followed by foot and mouth disease. Italy, which was the second-largest supplier in 2002, remains an important supplier in areas such as floor tiles and clothes, while Germany, Japan and France number in the top ten thanks to imports of cars. Russia, which was the tenth top supplier in 2002, is an important supplier of oil.

Manufacturing inputs dominate

By category, figures for 2002 show that the largest import by category was intermediate inputs for the manufacturing sector, which accounted for CYP 431 million, or 17.3 per cent of the total. This was closely followed by non-durable consumer goods, accounting for CYP 414 million, or 16.6 per cent of the total. Imports of passenger motor vehicles were the next largest category, accounting for CYP 182 million, or 7.3 per cent of the total. Comparatively low levels of investment were reflected in the fact that imports of all capital goods for all sectors accounted for only CYP 247 million, or 9.9 per cent of the total.

Table 1.8.4 Top domestic export markets, 2002

	CYP thousand	% of total
Greece	237,260	9.5
Italy	229,725	9.2
Germany	218,825	8.8
United Kingdom	207,815	8.4
Japan	167,912	6.8
France	126,901	5.1
United States	123,643	5.0
China	99,630	4.0
Israel	92,582	3.7
Russia	88,373	3.6

Source: Cyprus Statistical Service

Table 1.8.5 Top imports by economic destination, 2002

	CYP thousand	% of total
INTERMEDIATE INPUTS	725,019	29.2
Manufacturing inputs	430,772	17.3
CONSUMER GOODS	713,567	28.7
Non-durable	413,559	16.6
TRANSPORT EQUIPMENT AND PARTS	397,201	16.0
Passenger motor vehicles	181,852	7.3
FUELS AND LUBRICANTS	269,697	10.8
CAPITAL GOODS	246,830	9.9
Manufacturing capital goods	61,059	2.5
UNCLASSIFIED	134,303	5.4
TOTAL	*2,486,616*	*100.0*

Source: Cyprus Statistical Service

Balance of payments

Cyprus' large trade deficit is normally partly offset by a considerable surplus on services. Exports of, or income from, services is dominated by revenue from tourism, with net travel receipts amounting to CYP 1,132 million in 2002. A year earlier was an overall deficit on income, which comprises interest, profits and dividends, while net transfer payments were positive. However, the positive balances tend to be insufficient to offset the trade deficit in full, and therefore Cyprus tends to run a current account deficit. Although full figures for 2002 were not available as of July 2003, the current account deficit in 2002 was an estimated 6.2 per cent of GDP.

A country with a large current account deficit needs to balance this by inflows into the financial account, in the form of foreign investment, loans, or in extreme cases, drawing on foreign currency reserves. Foreign direct investment into Cyprus – investment in plant or machinery, or equity participation of more than 10 per cent – has been historically low in Cyprus, although there was a rise in 2002. Inflows of portfolio investment into the small Cyprus Stock Exchange also tend to be minimal. In order to fund the current account deficit, therefore, Cyprus tends to rely on a large net surplus on 'other investment', which is dominated by the offshore sector, now known as the international business sector. Other investment is made up mainly of loans, credits, currency and bank deposits. The large figure for liabilities reflects money coming into Cyprus – new deposits by foreigners into the Cyprus financial system, and Cypriot entities taking out loans overseas (net of any repayment of loans already outstanding). The

Table 1.86 Balance of payments, CYP million

	2001 (year)	2002 (Jan–Sep)
CURRENT ACCOUNT		
Exports of goods (fob)	955.9	402.6
Imports of goods (fob)	–3,404.5	–1,671.3
Trade balance	–2,448.4	–1,268.7
Exports of services	3,059.8	1,863.4
Travel	*1,786.6*	*938.4*
Imports of services	–1,128.0	–883.4
Services balance	1,931.8	980.0
Income: credit	554.6	170.5
Income: debit	–604.1	–147.5
Net transfer payments	18.9	31.2
Current-account balance	–547.3	–234.5
FINANCIAL ACCOUNT		
Direct investment abroad	–209.0	8.2
Direct investment in Cyprus	154.8	136.0
Portfolio investment assets	–468.8	–413.7
Portfolio investment liabilities	555.8	188.3
Derivatives	0.0	-6.6
Other investment assets	–271.9	949.1
Other investment liabilities	1,591.4	–491.8
Financial account exc. reserves	1,352.3	369.5
OTHER ITEMS		
Capital account balance	0.0	0.9
Net errors & omissions	109.1	47.1
OVERALL BALANCE	914.1	183.0
Movement of reserves (– indicates increase)	–914.1	–183.0

Source: Central Bank of Cyprus

large figure for assets reflects money flowing out of Cyprus – Cypriot entities depositing money offshore, or foreign entities taking out loans from the Cyprus financial system.

Net external debt is low

Since liabilities are normally backed up by assets, this also explains why Cyprus' net external debt is considerably lower than total external debt, and is thus not a threat to macroeconomic stability. Data on foreign debt are not published regularly by the Central Bank of Cyprus, but according to an estimate by Fitch Ratings agency, total external debt in 2001 was USD 20 billion, almost twice the size of GDP, whereas net external debt was only USD 2 billion, around 20 per cent of GDP.

1.9

Manufacturing Industry

Kostas Christophidis, Assistant Director General, Cyprus Employers and Industrialists Federation (OEB)

Introduction

The manufacturing sector in Cyprus has undergone major changes over the past 20 years, owing largely to the Customs Union Agreement with and the accession process of the EU. During that time the highly protected manufacturing industry has had to adjust to a very competitive and demanding environment whilst passing through difficulties that have resulted in a decline in the growth of production, exports and employment. Integral to this has been erosion in competitiveness due to rising costs and insufficient productivity. The end result has been that a considerable number of labour-intensive industries have exited the market, whilst concurrently other manufacturing sectors became stronger and new industries have emerged.

Today, the manufacturing sector in Cyprus is fully harmonized with the *acquis communautaire* of the EU, contributes 10.2 per cent to GDP and employs about 12 per cent of the economically active labour force.

The most promising sectors, among those in operation, in terms of value added and exports, are pharmaceuticals, food, chemicals, beverages, building materials and plastic products. Perlite and copper, either raw or processed, are also showing good prospects for increased export. Other industrial sectors with growth potential include metal and wood-processing industries and machinery and electronics manufacturers.

Cyprus is attractive for foreign investment in the manufacturing sector because it combines many unique features that provide undoubted advantages. The island will be an EU member country in May 2004 with an excellent telecommunications infrastructure and modern and efficient legal, accounting and banking services. Also, its strategic location at the crossroads of three continents and its traditional, excellent political and trade relations with neighbouring countries make Cyprus an ideal place for business investment. In addition there is a favourable tax regime, including corporation tax at 10 per cent, double tax treaties with 40 countries and bilateral investment agreements with 16 countries. Furthermore, set-up and operating costs are low and managerial, clerical and technical staff are all highly qualified and readily found.

New Industrial Policy

In 1999 the Cyprus Government considered ways and means in which to assist in the reconstruction and development of the manufacturing sector, seriously taking into account proposals put forward by, among others, the Cyprus Employers and Industrialists Federation (OEB). The result was the introduction of the 'New Industrial Policy'. Subsequently, during 2003, this policy has had to be amended so as to comply with the state aid restrictions of the EU. The main aims of the New Industrial Policy are:

- attraction and development of new high-technology industries;
- assistance and reconstruction of Cyprus' traditional industry;
- productivity improvement;
- attraction of capital-intensive foreign investments.

The New Industrial Policy document consists of 12 chapters, each one referring to a specific government policy and including special schemes or measures promoting the targeted policy. The 12 chapters are:

- High-technology and Business Incubators;
- High-technology and Research & Development;
- Investors Service Centre (one-stop-shop);
- Promoting Mergers, Joint Ventures and Subcontracting;
- Testing and Laboratories for Quality Upgrading;
- Guarantees for Lending to Small and Medium Enterprises (SMEs);
- Consultancy Studies Subsidisation,
- Energy Saving;
- Tax Incentives;
- Encouraging Export Promotion;
- Developing the Free Zone in Larnaca;
- Government Support and Subsidies.

High-technology industry

One of the most important goals of the Cyprus Government is the attraction and development of high-technology industries through the creation of business incubators.

Such incubators are intended to provide the necessary support to inventors to enable them to develop innovative ideas while at the same time promoting the creation of new companies for the commercialization of their products. Business incubators are connected to research and they may have close links with universities or research institutes in Cyprus or abroad. They aim also at the development of new high-tech products that do not exist in the market at present and the creation of companies in high-tech areas.

Under the terms of the scheme the Cyprus Government may subsidize an incubating company up to CYP 120,000 for a period of two years to cover actual costs.

Government support and subsidies

In order to assist with the technological upgrading of the manufacturing industry, the Cyprus Government has introduced several state-aid schemes and grants. One scheme worthy of mention here is the Technology Upgrading Scheme, which provides government grants to cover the costs of buying new high-tech machinery or equipment as follows:

- 7.5 per cent for medium-size enterprises;

- 15 per cent for small enterprises;

- 20 per cent for large- and medium-size enterprises involved in the primary processing of agricultural produce, cattle breeding and fisheries, with a 30 per cent grant being made available for the small enterprises in the same sectors.

The maximum government grant for all the above is CYP 100,000 for a maximum period of two years.

Exports

The main manufactured export products are clothing, furniture, pharmaceuticals, copper, building materials and, to a lesser extent, agricultural origin products, especially foodstuffs such as dairy products, frozen processed food and marmalades.

Also, on the international front, Cyprus has signed bilateral trade agreements with a number of third countries and maintains close relations with international organizations involved in trade matters.

Cyprus is also increasingly used as a trans-shipment centre for the onward shipment of goods destined for the Middle East, the Gulf and Central and Eastern Europe.

Part Two

Accounting and Fiscal Environments

2.1

Accounting Principles and Reporting Requirements

Yiannakis Theoklitou, Partner, Ernst & Young

Introduction

The following is intended to be a brief summary of current record-keeping, reporting and auditing requirements and does not cover all aspects of financial reporting and, in particular, does not address financial statement requirements related to income taxes, or of regulated industries such as banking, insurance or public utilities. Record-keeping and reporting requirements are governed by the Cyprus Companies Law Chapter 113 and in the cases of public companies with securities listed on the Cyprus Stock Exchange, by the Stock Exchange Laws and Regulations. Filing requirements in respect of the latter are included at the end of this chapter. Although not covered in detail, filing requirements with the Income Tax authorities have also been summarized and are included at the end along with a tax calendar.

In the context of joining the EU on May 1 2004, Cyprus has had to harmonize its legislation with the EU Directives. Regarding financial reporting, the EU has indicated that it will allow Cyprus to go the full International Financial Reporting Standards (IFRS) way, provided it will also introduce those requirements included in the 4th and 7th Directives, which are not covered by IFRS.

Record-keeping requirements

The Companies Law requires every company to keep 'proper books of account,' which give a true and fair view of the state of the company's affairs and explain its transactions. Although the individual books that must be kept are not prescribed by the Law, they must show:

- all amounts received and expended and the matters in respect of which the receipt and expenditure takes place;
- all sales and purchases of goods;
- the assets and liabilities of the company.

In addition to the accounting records, companies are required to keep in Cyprus the following statutory registers and other records:

- register of shareholders;
- register of debenture holders;
- register of directors and secretary;
- register of directors' shareholdings;
- register of charges;
- minutes of directors' meetings;
- minutes of shareholders' meetings.

The books of account may be kept at such place as the directors of the company think fit, in Cyprus or abroad, provided that, if the books of account are kept in another country, accounts and returns showing the financial position of the business must be sent to Cyprus at intervals not exceeding six months.

Reporting requirements

All limited liability companies with the exception of 'exempt private companies' must file a copy of the financial statements, auditor's report and directors' report with the Registrar of Companies and the files containing such reports are open to the public for inspection.

A copy of the annual report and financial statements must be laid before the company in general meeting within nine months from the end of the financial year or twelve months in the case of a company having interests abroad.

Financial statements comprise a balance sheet and statement of results of operations. Although not required by Law, all companies prepare financial statements that also include a cash-flow statement and notes including disclosure of the accounting policies used.

Where a company has subsidiaries it must prepare and present before the company in general meeting, group accounts, which are usually in the form of consolidated financial statements. These should also include the balance sheet of the parent company.

Every balance sheet placed before the company in general meeting must be audited and must give a true and fair view of the state of affairs of the company as at the end of its financial year, and every profit and loss account of the company must give a true and fair view of the profit or loss of the company for the financial year.

Every balance sheet and profit and loss account must include the particulars prescribed in Schedule 8 of the Law with some exceptions for Banks and Insurance companies. The main requirements are summarized on page 60.

At present there are no different reporting requirements depending on the size of the entity and the matter is being debated in the context of the full adoption of IFRS as well as those aspects of the 4th and 7th EU Directives not covered by IFRS.

Exemptions

The 'exempt private company'[1] is a company which by its Articles restricts the right to transfer its shares, prohibits an invitation to the public to subscribe in its shares or debentures and limits the number of its members to 50. In addition, the company must certify annually that: no body corporate (except exempt private companies) is the holder of any shares or debentures and that no persons other than the holders have any interest in any of the shares or debentures; the number of debenture holders does not exceed 50; no body corporate is a director; no arrangement exists whereby the company's policy can be determined by persons other than directors, members or debenture holders or trustees for debenture holders.

Accounting principles

The Law does not prescribe accounting principles to be applied in the preparation of financial statements[2]. In fact, the Law permits a company to prepare its financial statements in accordance with accounting principles generally accepted in any country provided the financial statements show a 'true and fair view' of the company's affairs and disclosure is made of the items specifically mentioned in the Law.

However, the local professional body has adopted International Financial Reporting Standards (formerly International Accounting

---

1. Under a new draft bill this type of company will be abolished and all companies will have to file their annual report with the Registrar of Companies.

2. Under the new draft bill, preparation of financial statements in accordance with International Financial Reporting Standards will be mandatory for all companies.

Standards) and these are applied in the preparation of financial statements. In the case of the preparation of financial statements of companies listed on the Cyprus Stock Exchange application of IFRS is mandatory by Law.

Auditing requirements

The financial statements of all companies, including exempt private companies, must be audited by an auditor appointed by the shareholders.

The local profession is self regulated by Law and it has adopted International Standards on Auditing (issued by IFAC) as the generally accepted auditing standards, which must be applied in an audit of the financial statements.

In addition, the Stock Exchange Law requires the use of these standards when auditing the financial statements of companies listed on the Stock Exchange.

The auditor's report is required to expressly state whether proper books of account have been kept, whether the financial statements are in agreement therewith and to express the auditor's opinion as to the true and fair view of the financial position and profit or loss. Expression of compliance with the Companies Law is also required.

Auditors must be members of the Institute of Certified Public Accountants of Cyprus and they must be independent of the company. No officer or employee of the company can act as auditor.

In this respect the code of ethics of IFAC has been adopted by the local profession.

Listed companies

Companies with listed securities on the Cyprus Stock Exchange, have more onerous reporting requirements pursuant to the Cyprus Stock Exchange Laws and Regulations.

A brief summary of these requirements is as follows:

Annual audited financial statements

- A copy must be sent to the Council of the Stock Exchange and the Cyprus SEC by end April every year.

- A copy must be sent to all registered shareholders by the same deadline.

- The company must announce the date by which financial statements will be sent to shareholders.

Interim financial statements (six-monthly)

- At present do need to be audited and must be sent to the Stock Exchange within two months from the period end.

- Financial statements must comply with IAS 34 – Interim Financial Reporting or IAS 1.

- The company may either publish profit and loss accounts and state that interim accounts are available for inspection or it may choose to send accounts to shareholders, in which case it must notify the Stock Exchange and the SEC of the date by which accounts will be sent.

Indication of result for full financial year

- Every company must indicate its result for the full financial year within two months from the year end.

- It must include an explanatory statement that enables investors to establish trends, prospects and facilitate comparison with the previous year.

Company filing requirements for taxation, payroll deductions, withholding taxes and VAT

The fiscal year in Cyprus is the calendar year. For financial statements covering accounting periods other than the calendar year, taxable income is apportioned to the relevant fiscal years pro-rata.

Every company must file a provisional tax return before 1 August during the year of assessment and, on the basis of this return, pay the tax due in three equal instalments on 1 August, 30 September and 31 December respectively. This provisional return may be revised before 31 December during the year of assessment. Any balance due after the actual tax liability is calculated by the company is payable by 1 August following the year of assessment through a self-assessment process.

The final income tax return must be filed with the Tax authorities by 31 December following the year of assessment together with the audited financial statements and some additional information.

Payment of contributions to the national defence fund is made by the end of the six-month period to which it relates.

Income tax deductions under the PAYE system as well as other deductions such as social insurance are paid by the end of the month following the month for which the deduction was made. The same deadline exists for amounts withheld on the payment of dividends and interest.

Table 2.1.1 Tax calendar for a company that is resident in Cyprus for taxation purposes

Date	Obligation	Form	Penalties
By 30 April	Submission of Employer's return	I.R.7	
By 30 June	Payment of Defence for first six months	I.R.601	Interest at 9 per cent per annum 1st day after end of six months calculated on a daily basis
By 1 August	Submission of Provisional tax return for the current year	I.R.6	If any instalment is not paid by the due date, interest of 9 per cent per annum calculated for complete months is charged. If no temporary return is
By 1 August	Payment of first instalment of tax based on provisional tax return	I.R.6	submitted and a provisional assessment is raised by the tax authorities, interest as above is paid plus a flat amount of 5 per cent on the whole amount of temporary tax assessed. In addition, a 10 per cent penalty is imposed on the difference between the final tax due and the tax per the temporary assessment if the temporary taxable income is less than 75 per cent of the taxable income per the final assessment.
By 1 August	Payment of the balance of tax for the previous year by self-assessment	I.R.158	If tax is not paid by the due date, interest at 9 per cent per annum is imposed based on complete months. Also, if the tax return, audited accounts and the additional information are submitted late, an additional 5 per cent flat is imposed on the whole tax.
By 30 September	Payment of second instalment of tax based on provisional tax return	I.R.6	See above
By 31 December	Submission of company return of income, audited accounts and additional information	I.R.4 I.R.166	See above
By 31 December	Submission of revised provisional tax return if required	I.R.6	See above
By 31 December	Payment of third instalment of tax based on provisional tax return	I.R.6	See above

Table 2.1.1 continued

Date	Obligation	Form	Penalties
By 31 December	Payment of Defence for second six months	I.R.601	See above
By the end of the next month	Tax deducted from employees' emoluments under the PAYE system	I.R.61	Late payments result in the imposition of interest at 9 per cent per annum based on complete months from due date plus 1 per cent per month penalty for as long as the delay continues. This penalty cannot exceed 11 per cent of tax due.
By the end of the next month	Contribution to the defence fund withheld from interest and dividends	I.R.601	As for PAYE deductions
By the end of the next month	Social insurance deducted from employees' emoluments		3 per cent for each month payment is delayed with a maximum of 15 per cent of amount due
By the 10th of second month after period end	Submission of VAT return and payment of VAT due	VAT 4	10 per cent penalty and 9 per cent interest for amounts due plus CYP 30 per VAT return

Every employer must also file an employer's return detailing salaries, deductions and other particulars by 30 April following the fiscal year.

VAT returns must be submitted and the VAT due paid within 40 days from the end of the quarterly period they relate to.

Companies Law Chapter 113 – main schedule 8 requirements

Schedule 8 covers the basic disclosure content of a set of financial statements with respect to the balance sheet and profit and loss account both for an individual company as well as a company with subsidiaries presenting group accounts. The schedule is quite detailed in its disclosure requirements but it does not deal with recognition or measurement issues.

The following table summarizes the topics covered by Schedule 8:

Table 2.1.2   Reporting requirements

Balance sheet

2   Share capital, assets and liabilities must be summarized in such a way as is necessary so as to disclose the general nature of assets and liabilities. Includes specific requirements to disclose redeemable preference shares, interest on share capital, the share premium account and particulars of redeemed debentures that may be re-issued.

3   Includes disclosure requirements relating to preliminary expenses, discounts, commissions paid and expenses incurred in connection with the issue of shares or debentures.

4   Includes requirements regarding classification of assets, liabilities, provisions and reserves as well as disclosure of the methods used to arrive at the carrying amount of fixed assets under each heading.

5   Prescribes methods of arriving at carrying amounts of fixed assets.

6   Includes requirements regarding classification of reserves that must be disclosed under separate headings.

7   Includes requirements to disclose and explain movements in reserves for the year.

8   Includes detailed disclosure requirements relating to assets, liabilities and provisions.

9   Requires disclosure of the basis of foreign currency conversion.

10   Requires disclosure of the amount provided for taxation.

11   Imposes the need to present corresponding amounts for all items shown in the balance sheet.

Profit and loss account

12   Imposes disclosure requirements with respect to specific expenses such as depreciation, interest charged, taxation, amounts provided for redemption of shares or debentures, transfers to and from reserves, provisions, analysis of investment income and dividends paid and proposed.

13   Requires the disclosure of auditors' remuneration unless this is fixed by the company in general meeting.

14   Includes additional disclosure requirements for the notes as well as corresponding amounts.

Group accounts

15   Requires disclosure of intra-group indebtedness, shares held in the company by its subsidiaries, the reasons why a subsidiary has not been consolidated and disclosure of certain particulars including qualifications in audit reports.

16   Requires disclosures of group indebtedness where company is a subsidiary of another.

17   Prescribes the consolidation method.

Taxation of Income in Cyprus

Pieris Markou, Tax Partner, Deloitte & Touche, Nicosia, Cyprus and Antonis Taliotis, Tax Partner, Deloitte & Touche, Limassol, Cyprus

Introduction

The taxation system in Cyprus has recently undergone an overall reform, which was brought about primarily by the need to harmonize the whole taxation system with that of the EU in the light of Cyprus' accession in 2004 and the need to comply with the Code of Conduct of the OECD on Business Taxation.

The Cyprus Government, in implementing the new tax system, has committed itself in making such changes so as to maintain and enhance Cyprus' attractiveness as an international business centre.

New tax basis

In accordance with the new tax legislation, which came into effect on 1 January 2003, all discriminatory tax incentives, allowances and exemptions that previously applied to certain groups of taxpayers, are abolished. All residents of Cyprus are subject to a uniform method of taxation.

Under the new tax regime, the basis of taxation is changed from one of a source basis to that of a residence basis.

Income tax law

Legal entities

Scope of taxation

Legal entities are considered resident in Cyprus for tax purposes if they are managed and controlled from Cyprus. A company resident in Cyprus is liable to tax in Cyprus on its worldwide income and more specifically on all income accruing or arising both from sources within and outside the Republic. On the other hand, companies that are not resident in Cyprus, (ie which are managed and controlled outside Cyprus) are liable to tax in Cyprus on income accruing or arising from sources within Cyprus only.

Tax rates

A uniform corporate tax rate of 10 per cent is introduced for all companies whether operating locally or internationally. Public Corporate Bodies are taxable at the rate of 25 per cent. An additional 5 per cent corporate tax rate is imposed for the years 2003 and 2004 only, on profits that exceed CYP 1 million.

Exempt income

Under the new tax law, certain exemptions and provisions provide for certain types of income to escape taxation altogether. The main exemptions are as follows:

- Dividends received are exempt from income tax (see below for Special Contributions for Defence Law provisions).

- Profits of a permanent establishment situated outside Cyprus of a Cypriot resident are exempt from tax. This exemption does not apply if the permanent establishment engages directly or indirectly more than 50 per cent in activities that lead to investment income, and the foreign tax burden on the income of the permanent establishment is substantially lower than the tax burden of the Cypriot resident in the Republic. Substantially lower has been interpreted to mean less than half of the Cyprus tax rate (ie 5 per cent).

- The profit from the disposal of securities is exempt from tax, irrespective of whether the gain is of a capital or trading nature. Securities include shares, government stocks, debentures, bonds, founder's shares and rights thereof.

- 50 per cent of interest income is exempt from income tax, unless it is received in the ordinary course of business, or is closely connected to the ordinary course of business, in which case it is taxed as normal trade income (see also below for Special Contribution for Defence Law provisions).

Deductible expenses

In arriving at the chargeable income all expenses incurred wholly and exclusively for the purpose of earning the income are deductible.

In addition specific provisions provide for the deductibility of the following:

- interest for the acquisition of fixed assets used in the business;

- interest for the acquisition of a building for rental purposes;

- donations to approved charitable organizations.

Non-deductible expenses

In addition to expenses not incurred wholly and exclusively for the purpose of earning income the following expenses are also specifically not tax deductible:

- Business entertaining expenses, including hospitality expenses of any kind which are incurred for the purpose of the business and which exceed 1 per cent of the gross income or CYP 10,000, whichever is the lower.

- Private motor vehicle expenses.

- Interest in relation to the acquisition of a private motor vehicle, irrespective of whether it is used in the business or not, or other asset not used in the business. This restriction is lifted after seven years from the purchase of the private motor vehicle or the other asset not used in the business.

Wear and tear allowances

Depreciation expenses included in the financial statements are not deductible expenses for tax purposes but predetermined rates are used to calculate the wear and tear allowance that is deductible for tax purposes.

Losses and group relief

CARRY FORWARD OF LOSSES

Losses are carried forward indefinitely. Losses for the years 1997 onwards, which have not been offset against profits arising up to the year 2002, will be carried forward to 2003 and subsequent years without time restriction.

GROUP RELIEF

Losses for the current year only can be surrendered by a group company to another group company. Group relief will be given provided that both companies are members of the same group for the whole of a tax year.

Two companies are considered to be part of a group for group relief purposes if: one is a 75 per cent subsidiary of the other, or both are 75 per cent subsidiaries of a third company.

Loss of a permanent establishment outside the Republic

Losses arising from a permanent establishment outside the Republic can be offset against profits arising in the Republic. However, when a profit arises from such a permanent establishment, an amount equal to the losses that have been utilized in the past against profits arising in the Republic will be included in the taxable income.

Insurance companies

- Losses of the life business can be offset against profits of the general business.

- Losses of the life business can be offset against profits from other sources.

- Losses of the life business can be carried forward indefinitely.

Company reorganizations

In the event of a company reorganization, unused losses brought forward will be transferred to the new company and the provisions dealing with the set off or transfer of losses, will apply accordingly.

Special provisions are introduced for company reorganizations under the new tax law, so as to avoid any adverse tax implications arising from reorganizations. These provisions are in line with the EU directive on mergers, acquisitions and reorganizations.

Unilateral tax relief

Relief for taxes paid abroad is in the form of a tax credit for tax paid abroad on income subject to tax in Cyprus. The relief is given unilaterally, irrespective of the existence of a double tax treaty. Where a treaty is in force the treaty provisions (if more beneficial) apply.

International Business Companies – transitional provisions

International Business Companies (IBCs), or permanent establishments of overseas companies which during the tax year 2001 derived and continue to derive income or which are expected to have income that has not arisen until 31 December 2001 due to the nature of their operations from sources exclusively outside Cyprus, may elect to be taxed, for the tax years 2003, 2004 and 2005, at a rate of 4.25 per cent.

They will, however, not be entitled to the following benefits:

- exemption of 50 per cent of interest income;
- exemption of dividends income (except dividends received from other IBCs);
- exemption of profits from the disposal of securities;
- group relief for losses;
- the tax benefits of company reorganizations;
- unilateral credit relief for tax paid abroad (in the case where a double taxation treaty does not exist);
- exemption for profits of a permanent establishment abroad.

Losses up to the year 2000 will be offset against profits up to the year 2005 only, whereas losses for the years 2001 onwards will be carried forward indefinitely.

Once the election is made to be taxed under the transitional provisions, it is irrevocable for the three-year period.

Tax year

The tax year is the calendar year. Entities may choose an accounting year ending on a date other than 31 December. In such a case, the taxable income will be apportioned into the relevant tax years.

Payment of taxes and returns

Provisional declarations and payments on account of the current year corporation tax liability are required to be made on 1 August in the current year, payable in three equal instalments, 1 August, 30 September and 31 December. The calculation is based on the best estimate by the directors. Where the estimate is less than 75 per cent of the final taxable profit, a penalty tax of 10 per cent is imposed on the difference of the tax due and the provisional declaration.

A tax return must be submitted by 31 December of the following tax year and any remaining tax must be paid by 1 August following the tax year to which it relates.

A 5 per cent flat penalty is imposed on late submission of financial statements and tax computations on the balance of the tax due.

A delay in paying any of the instalments of the provisional tax declared or the final tax balance is subject to interest at the rate of 9 per cent per annum.

Individuals

RESIDENT IN CYPRUS

An individual is resident in Cyprus if such person is physically present in Cyprus for an aggregate period exceeding 183 days in the tax year. Resident individuals are liable to tax in Cyprus on their worldwide income whereas non-residents are liable to tax only on income accruing or arising from sources within Cyprus.

TAX RATES

The tax rates applying to individuals for the year 2003 and 2004 are summarized in Table 2.2.1.

EXEMPT INCOME

The following income is exempt from taxation:

- Dividends received are exempt from income tax (see also Special Contributions for Defence Law provisions).

- Profits of a permanent establishment situated outside Cyprus of a Cypriot resident are exempt from tax. This exemption does not apply if the permanent establishment engages directly or indirectly more than 50 per cent in activities which lead to investment income, and the foreign tax burden on the income of the permanent establishment is substantially lower than the tax burden of the Cypriot resident in the Republic. Substantially lower has been interpreted to mean less than half of the Cyprus tax rate (ie 5 per cent).

- The profit from the disposal of securities is exempt from tax, whether of a capital or trading nature. Securities include shares, government stocks, debentures, bonds, founder's shares and rights thereof.

Table 2.2.1 Individual tax rates, 2003–2004

YEAR 2003				
Taxable Income		Tax rate	Amount of tax	Cumulative tax
CYP	CYP	%	CYP	CYP
0	–	9,000	0	0	0
9,001	–	12,000	20	600	600
12,001	–	15,000	25	750	1,350
15.001 and above		30		

YEAR 2004 AND THEREAFTER				
Taxable Income		Tax rate	Amount of tax	Cumulative tax
CYP	CYP	%	CYP	CYP
0	–	10,000	0	0	0
10,001	–	15,000	20	1,000	1,000
15,001	–	20,000	25	1,250	2,250
20,001 and above		30		

- The whole of interest income. Interest income, which is received in the ordinary course of a business, including interest closely connected to the ordinary course of business, is not exempt but is included in the taxable income of the business (see also, special contribution for defence law provisions).

- The lower of 20 per cent of the remuneration from an employment, which is exercised in the Republic by a person who was a non-resident before the commencement of his or her employment, and CYP 5,000. This exemption applies for a period of three years from 1 January of the year following the year in which the employment commenced.

- The emoluments from salaried services performed abroad for an aggregate period in the tax year exceeding 90 days, for a non resident employer or a permanent establishment of a Cypriot employer.

- Widow's pension granted under approved schemes.

- Gratuity or lump sum paid on retirement or on death.

- Lump sum repayment from life insurance schemes or from approved provident funds.

DEDUCTIONS

In arriving at the taxable income all expenses incurred wholly and exclusively for the purpose of earning the income are deductible.

In addition specific provisions provide for the deductibility of the following:

- interest paid for main residence, up to CYP 500 (for year 2003 only);

- interest for the acquisition of fixed assets used in the business;

- 20 per cent of rental income;

- interest for the acquisition of a building for rental purposes;

- subscriptions to trade unions or professional bodies;

- expenditure for the maintenance of buildings under preservation order, depending on square metres;

- donations to approved charitable organizations.

NON-DEDUCTIBLE EXPENSES

In addition to expenses not incurred wholly and exclusively for the purpose of earning income, the following expenses are also specifically not tax deductible:

- Business entertaining expenses including hospitality expenses of any kind, which are incurred for the purpose of the business and which exceed 1 per cent of the gross income or CYP 10,000, whichever is the lower.

- Private motor vehicle expenses.

- Interest in relation to the acquisition of a private motor vehicle, irrespective of whether it is used in the business or not, or other asset not used in the business. This restriction is lifted after seven years from the purchase of the private motor vehicle or the other asset not used in the business.

PERSONAL ALLOWANCES

In calculating the taxable income, contributions to the Social Insurance Fund, approved provident funds, medical funds, General Medical Plan, or other approved plans, as well as insurance premiums to insurance companies for the life assurance of the taxpayer are tax deductible up to a maximum of one-sixth of the chargeable income before this deduction.

TAX FILINGS

Individuals are taxed on a calendar year basis. For employees, tax is deducted from their salary by the employer on a monthly basis under the PAYE system. All taxable persons are obliged to submit a tax return by 30 April following the tax year of assessment.

Special modes of taxation

Ship management companies

Income arising from ship management activities is subject to tax at 4.25 per cent. A company can elect to pay special tonnage tax if more beneficial (see also article 4.3).

Pension income from services rendered abroad

The pension income of any individual resident in the Republic, which arises from services rendered abroad, is taxed at a rate of 5 per cent for amounts exceeding CYP 2,000 per annum.

Intellectual property rights and similar income

The gross income arising from intellectual property rights, other exploitation rights, compensations or other similar income arising from sources within the Republic, of an individual who is not resident in Cyprus, is subject to withholding tax at a rate of 10 per cent. Rights granted for use outside the Republic are not subject to any withholding tax.

Film royalties

The gross income derived by a non-resident individual in respect of royalties arising from film projection in the Republic is subject to withholding tax at a rate of 5 per cent.

Profits of professionals, entertainers and the like

The gross income derived by a non-resident individual from the exercise in the Republic of any profession, vocation or public entertainment services, including football teams and other athletic missions, is subject to a 10 per cent withholding tax.

Special Contribution for Defence Law

The Special Contribution for Defence Law was introduced in 1984 for the purpose of funding the island's defence budget. Over the years this contribution resulted in just another extra tax. With the recent tax reforms the Special Contribution for Defence Law has been used as another means of funding the government budget by taxing certain types of income, as described below.

Dividends

Every resident person receiving dividends from a company, whether incorporated in the Republic or not, is subject to a special defence contribution of 15 per cent on the amount of the dividend, which is withheld at source.

Exemptions

- Dividends paid by a company resident in the Republic to another company resident in the Republic.

- Dividends received by a company resident in the Republic or a company not resident in the Republic which maintains a permanent establishment in the Republic from a company which is non-resident in the Republic and of which at least 1 per cent of the share capital is held. This exemption will not apply if the overseas company paying the dividend engages directly or indirectly more than 50 per cent in activities, which give rise to investment income AND the foreign tax burden on the income of the company paying the dividend is substantially lower than the Cyprus tax burden.

Substantially lower has been interpreted to mean less than half of the Cyprus tax rate (ie 5 per cent).

- Dividends paid out of dividend income that has suffered income tax at source of 20 per cent (under the previous regime) and are paid within a period of six years from the date of receiving such dividend income.

Interest

Every resident taxpayer who receives or is credited with interest is subject to special defence contribution at 10 per cent, which is withheld at source.

Interest that is received as a result of the carrying on of a business activity, including interest closely connected to the ordinary activities of the business, is not considered interest for the purposes of special defence contribution.

Interest from Government Savings Certificates, Government Bonds and deposits with the Housing Finance Corporation, as well as interest earned by approved provident funds, is subject to defence contribution at 3 per cent.

A person whose total annual income, including interest, does not exceed CYP 7,000 and who receives interest that has been subject to defence contribution at 10 per cent, has the right to a refund of the amount of defence contribution suffered in excess of 3 per cent.

Deemed distribution

A company resident in the Republic is deemed to have made a distribution of 70 per cent of its profits after tax, in the form of dividends at the end of the two-year period from the end of the tax year in which the profits relate, to the extent that the profit relates to Cypriot resident shareholders only and must account for 15 per cent defence contribution thereon.

The deemed distribution provisions do not apply to profits, to the extent to which they relate to non-resident shareholders.

In arriving at the amount of the deemed distribution, any actual dividend that is distributed during the two-year period from the end of the tax year in which the profits relate is deducted.

In cases where an actual dividend is paid after the two-year period, any deemed distribution reduces the actual dividend on which the defence contribution is withheld.

For the purpose of calculating the amount of the deemed distribution, 'profits' mean the accounting profits arrived at using generally acceptable accounting principles, but after the deduction of any transfers to reserves as specified by any law.

Any offset of group losses, as well as any amounts, including any additional depreciation, which emanate or are the result of revaluation of movable and immovable property, do not affect accounting profits.

In the case of a person not being resident in the Republic receiving dividends from a company that is resident in the Republic, emanating from profits which at any stage were subject to deemed distribution, the special contribution paid as a result of the deemed distribution which is attributable to such person is refundable.

Company dissolution
The aggregate amount of profits in the five years prior to the company dissolution, which have not been distributed or been deemed to be distributed, will be considered as distributed on dissolution and will be subject to defence contribution at 15 per cent.

These provisions do not apply in the case of liquidation under reorganization, in accordance with regulations to be issued.

Reduction of capital
In the case of a reduction of capital of a company, any amounts due or paid to the shareholders up to the amount of the undistributed taxable income of any tax year calculated before the deduction of losses from prior years, will be considered as distributed dividends subject to special defence contribution at 15 per cent (after deducting any amounts which have been deemed as distributable profits).

Rental income

Rental income is subject to special contribution for defence at the rate of 3 per cent after allowing as a deduction 25 per cent of the gross rental income.

Unilateral tax relief

Relief for taxes paid abroad is in the form of a tax credit for tax paid abroad on income subject to tax in Cyprus. The relief is given unilaterally, irrespective of the existence of a double tax treaty. Where a treaty is in force the treaty provisions (if more beneficial) apply.

Payment of special contribution

In the case of dividends and interest, special contribution for defence is due for payment at the end of the month following the month the dividend or interest is paid and in the case of rental income, in two instalments, on 30 June and 31 December of the year it is received.

Other Taxation

Pieris Markou, Tax Partner, Deloitte & Touche, Nicosia, Cyprus

Capital gains tax

Capital gains tax is imposed on gains from disposal of immovable property situated in the Republic, including shares of companies not listed on a recognized Stock Exchange that own immovable property situated in the Republic, at the rate of 20 per cent.

In computing the capital gain the value of the immovable property as at 1 January 1980 (or cost if the date of acquisition is later), the cost of any additions after 1 January 1980 or the date of the expense if later, any expenditure incurred for the production of the gain and the indexation allowance, are deducted from the sale proceeds.

Exemptions

The following disposals of immovable property are exempt from capital gains tax:

- Transfer on death.

- Gifts between spouses, parents and children and relatives up to third degree.

- Gift to a company whose shareholders are members of the donor's family and continue to be members of the family for a period of five years from the date of the gift.

- Gift by a family company to its shareholders, if the company had also acquired the property in question via donation and provided the property remains in the possession of the shareholder for at least three years.

- Gifts to charitable organizations or to the Republic.

- Exchange or disposal under the Agricultural Land (Consolidation) Laws.

- Exchange provided the gain is used for the acquisition of new property. The gain derived from the exchange reduces the cost of the new property and the tax is paid when the latter is disposed.

- Expropriations.

- Transfer of ownership or share transfers in the event of company reorganizations.

Table 2.3.1

	CYP
Disposal of principal private residence (subject to conditions)	50,000
Disposal of agricultural land by a farmer	15,000
Other disposals	10,000

Deductions

Individuals are entitled to deduct from the gains the following:
The above are lifetime deductions.

Immovable property tax

Immovable property tax is collected annually on all property situated within the Republic. The value is taken to be that of 1 January 1980. The due date is 30 September within the tax year on property held at 1 January in the same tax year.

There are various exemptions and these include cemeteries, places

Table 2.3.2

Value (CYP)	Rate (‰)
0 – 100,000	0
100,001 – 250,000	2.5
250,001 – 500,000	3.5
500,001 and over	4.0

of worship, public hospitals, schools, charitable institutions, agricultural land, land which belongs to the Government, etc.

The rates of immovable property tax are as follows:

Social Insurance contribution and other employment taxes

Employees are liable to contribute to the Social Insurance Fund 6.3 per cent of their gross salary.

The employer also has an obligation to contribute 6.3 per cent on the gross salaries of employees, as well as 1.2 per cent towards the redundancy fund and 0.5 per cent for industrial training.

Both the employee and employer contributions are subject to a salary ceiling, which for the year 2003 was CYP 22,104.

Self-employed persons have an obligation to contribute at the rate of 11.6 per cent. Various lower limits apply, depending on category of profession or vocation and the number of years in the business.

Social Coherence Fund

The tax reform of 2003 introduced this new law which requires employers to contribute on behalf of each employee 2 per cent on the amount of emoluments for the purpose of funding the Social Coherence Fund. There is no ceiling as regards the amount of emoluments.

'Emoluments' do not include the emoluments of a non-Cypriot national who is employed by an overseas government or an international organization or a company that owns a Cyprus ship or a ship management company, as well as the emoluments of a non-Cypriot for the years 2003, 2004 and 2005, who is employed by a company that has elected to be taxed (for income tax purposes) under the transitional provisions.

Value Added Tax (VAT)

Value Added Tax is imposed on the provision of goods and services in Cyprus, as well as on the importation of goods into Cyprus.

Rates

Standard rate (15 per cent)
The standard rate applies to any provision of goods and services in Cyprus not subject to the zero rate, the special rate or is exempt.

Reduced rate (5 per cent)
The reduced rate applies to hotel services, the provision of food in the course of catering, some fertilizers, animal food and pesticides.

Zero rate
Zero-rated supplies include the provision of food supplies, medicines, newspapers, magazines and books, children's clothing and footwear, some fertilizers, agrochemicals and agricultural machinery, public bus transport and exports.

Exemptions

Exempt supplies include rental of immovable property, financial services, hospital and medical services, postal services, insurance services and disposal of immovable property.

Who is obliged to register?

Every individual or company is obliged to register: a) at the end of any month, if the value of taxable supplies recorded in the last 12 months exceeds CYP 9,000; or b) at any point in time the value of taxable supplies are expected to exceed CYP 9,000 in the next 30 days.

Right of registration

Persons who trade outside the Republic in goods or services that would have been taxable if they were provided within the Republic, groups of companies and company divisions have the right to register.

VAT returns and payment of VAT

Any registered person must submit to the VAT Commissioner a VAT return within 40 days from the end of any tax period and pay the VAT due.

Penalties and interest

Late registration	CYP 50 for every month of delay
Late submission of return	CYP 30 once only
Late payment of VAT	10 per cent of amount due plus 9 per cent interest

Stamp duty

Stamp duty is payable on the execution of documents that relate to any property situated in the Republic or to any matter or thing to be performed or done therein, irrespective of the place where the document is executed.

Table 2.3.3

Type of document	Duty
Cheques	3 cents
Letters of guarantee	CYP 2
Letter of credit	CYP 1
Receipts for amounts from CYP 2 to CYP 20	2 cents
Receipts for amounts over CYP 20	4 cents
Customs documents	CYP 10–20
Bills of lading	CYP 2
Bills of exchange (payable at sight on first demand or within three days from demand or sight)	50 cents
Contracts	
– up to CYP 100,000	CYP 1.50 for every CYP 1,000
over CYP 100,000	CYP 2 for every CYP 1,000
– without fixed amount	CYP 20
Registration of a limited company	
– authorized capital up to CYP 5,000	CYP 75
– authorized capital from CYP 5,001 to CYP 10,000	CYP 125
– authorized capital from CYP 10,001 to CYP 8,000,000	CYP 125 for the first CYP 10,000 plus CYP 3 for every additional CYP 1,000
– authorized capital over CYP 8,000,000	CYP 24,098

Any documents relating to transactions the result of reorganization as defined in the Income Taxes Law are exempt from stamp duty.

The table below shows the types of documents and rates of stamp duty thereon.

Effective Use of Cyprus Double Tax Treaties

Peter G Economides, Chairman, Totalserve Management Ltd and Senior Partner, PG Economides & Co.

Double Tax Treaties – an overview

The main purpose of Double Tax Treaties is to avoid international double taxation, whereby the same profits are taxed in two or more states in respect of the same person or entity. Double tax treaties also clarify the scope of the taxing rights of each contracting state, allowing international business to be transacted with a degree of certainty and stability. This is why Double Tax Treaties are important tools for international tax planning, and constitute a substantive advantage for any jurisdiction that has entered into such arrangements. Moreover, Double Tax Treaties are significant for international business because they encourage investment from one country to another.

Double Tax Treaties are relevant for both income tax and corporation tax, providing relief in two principal ways. First, Double Tax Treaties allow the tax payable in one country as a credit against tax payable in the contracting state with respect to the same income. Second, the Treaties exempt certain classes of income from tax in one or the other contracting state. As a rule, treaties contain exemptions which provide that the enterprise of one territory will not be liable to tax on commercial or industrial profits made in the other territory unless it has a permanent establishment in that other territory. The majority of treaties determine the territory where the taxpayer resides as the appropriate territory where his or her total income should be assessed, with relief given for certain types of income, which are more appropriately taxed in the territory where they arise.

Double Tax Treaties – the unique position of Cyprus

The problem with accessing Double Tax Treaties via tax-efficient jurisdictions is that countries which are primarily 'onshore' in classification have little interest in concluding Double Tax Treaties with 'offshore' jurisdictions, since the latter often levy no tax whatsoever (eg the British Virgin Islands or the Bahamas). High tax countries on the other hand, may contract with each other but here again, most entrepreneurs are hesitant in paying the high tax involved, albeit once. This is where Cyprus enjoys a competitive advantage. Cyprus is a low tax jurisdiction (the tax rate till 31 December 2002 being 4.25 per cent) and has negotiated 32 Double Tax Treaties to date. Moreover, the rise in taxation brought about by the recently introduced legislation, effective from 1 January 2003, still retains the tax rate at an attractive European low of 10 per cent, and introduces various other fiscal benefits such as the exemption from taxation of any profits made from the sale of securities, thus in certain instances increasing the competitive advantages offered by Cyprus as an International Business Centre.

Anti-avoidance provisions

Limitation of benefits articles feature in a number of treaties concluded by Cyprus, and under the previous taxing regime, effectively excluded fiscally privileged companies from a number of benefits accruing thereto. The treaties concluded between Cyprus and Belgium, Canada, France, Germany, the United Kingdom and the United States all contain anti-avoidance provisions, the significance of which has been diminished or eliminated after the recent introduction of the unitary tax rate for international and local companies.

To give an example, the provisions in the Double Taxation Agreement between Cyprus and the United Kingdom in relation to dividends, interest and royalties do not apply if the recipient is a company liable to tax at a rate which is substantially lower than the rate usually imposed. This limitation of benefits article clearly targeted the Cyprus IBC, which, until recently, and more specifically until 31 December 2002, enjoyed the preferential taxation of 4.25 per cent instead of the 25 per cent widely applicable for local companies. Therefore if a Cyprus International Business Company was in receipt of royalties from the United Kingdom, the reduced withholding tax would not kick in because of this article. As of 1 January 2003, this limitation no longer applies because all companies in Cyprus are taxed at a uniform rate of 10 per cent.

Benefits of Double Tax Treaties

The conclusion or not by a territory of a network of Double Tax Treaties is a significant consideration in deciding a jurisdiction from which an entrepreneur or investor will carry out his or her business. Another significant consideration is the form of the Double Tax Treaties concluded. The majority of the treaties concluded by Cyprus follow the OECD Model Treaty, which provides clear and consensual rules for the taxation of income and capital.

Among other benefits, most double tax treaties concluded by Cyprus entail:

- elimination of double taxation in the Contracting State by way of a tax credit;
- reduced withholding taxes or dividends, interests and royalties;
- tax sparing provisions in the Contracting State for tax not imposed in Cyprus because of Cyprus tax incentives.

Tax credits

As noted above the primary purpose of these treaties is the avoidance of double taxation of income earned in any of the treaty countries. This is usually achieved either through the allowance of a credit against the tax levied by the country in which the taxpayer resides for taxes levied in the other treaty country or through tax exemption in one treaty country on the income taxed in the other treaty country. The effect of these arrangements is normally that the taxpayer pays no more than the higher of the two rates.

Withholding taxes

A detailed summary of the withholding taxes provided by the double tax treaties entered into by Cyprus with other countries appears in Chapter 2.5.

Tax Sparing Credits

A number of Cyprus Double Tax Treaties contain provisions for tax sparing credits. Tax sparing credit means the tax credit not only in respect of tax actually paid in Cyprus but also the tax that would have been otherwise payable had it not been for the incentives granted in Cyprus which result in exemption or reduction in tax.

The tax sparing credit provisions of Cyprus double tax treaties are outlined below, country by country.

Canada

There are tax sparing credit provisions in Canada in respect of Cyprus tax that would have been payable or deductible in Cyprus on profits or interest but for certain tax incentive exemptions or relief in Cyprus.

Czech Republic

In the Czech Republic, there are tax sparing credit provisions in respect of Cyprus tax that would have been payable on profits and interest in Cyprus but for tax incentive exemption or relief in Cyprus, and in respect of Cyprus tax that would have been deductible from any dividend paid out of profits, granted such incentive exemption or relief.

Denmark

In Denmark, there are available tax sparing credits of 15 per cent for dividends and 10 per cent for interest from Cyprus, if for purposes of promoting the economic development of Cyprus there is an exemption from or reduction of tax below the above percentages.

Egypt

There are tax-sparing provisions in respect of tax that would have been payable but reduced or waived under the legal provisions of either contracting State for tax incentives.

Germany

In Germany, tax sparing credits of 15 per cent for dividends and 10 per cent for interest are available, if there is an exemption from or reduction of tax below these percentages, as a result of incentives for promoting economic development in Cyprus.

Greece

In both countries, tax sparing credits are available for the whole of any tax that would be payable in respect of any profits or interest for which relief or exemption from tax is allowed as a tax incentive, and in respect of any tax that would be withheld from any dividends paid out of profits, for which relief or exemption from tax is allowed as a tax incentive.

India

In both countries, tax sparing credits are available for the whole of any tax that would be payable but for incentive relief designed to promote economic development. Withholding tax shall be deemed to have been paid on the gross amount of: dividends at 10 per cent or 15 per cent, as the case may be; interest at 10 per cent; royalties and fees for included services at 15 per cent; and technical fees at 10 per cent.

Ireland

In both countries, tax sparing credits are available for profits, interest and dividends that are exempt from tax or taxed at reduced rates due to tax incentive provisions of each State. In addition, in Ireland there are tax sparing provisions in respect of profits from the operation of ships under the Cyprus flag.

Italy

The Contracting State shall be deemed to have been paid, for tax credit purposes in the other State. In the case of Italy, these would include the full tax exemption in the case of operations of ships under the Cyprus flag.

Malta

In both countries tax sparing credits are available for the whole of any tax that would be payable but for incentive relief. Withholding tax shall be deemed to have been paid on the gross amount of: dividend at 15 per cent and interest and royalties at 10 per cent.

Poland

In both countries tax sparing credits are available for the whole of any tax that would be payable but for incentive relief. Withholding tax shall be deemed to have been paid on the gross amount of: dividends and interest at 10 per cent and royalties at 5 per cent.

Romania

In Romania, there are tax sparing credit provisions in respect of Cyprus tax that would have been payable in Cyprus on profits or interest but for tax incentive exemption or relief in Cyprus, and in respect of Cyprus tax that would have been deductible from any dividend paid out of profits granted tax incentive exemption or relief in Cyprus but for such tax incentive exemption or relief.

Syria

In both countries tax sparing credits are available for the whole of any tax that would be payable but for incentive relief. Withholding tax shall be deemed to have been paid on the gross amount of: dividends and royalties at 15 per cent and interest at 10 per cent.

United Kingdom

In the United Kingdom, tax sparing credits are available in respect of tax saved as a result of tax incentives given in Cyprus on interest paid, provided the loan was made for the purposes of promoting development and in respect of investment allowances on capital expenditure for specific types of investment.

Yugoslavia

There are tax sparing credit provisions in respect of tax that would have been payable but reduced or waived under the legal provisions of either contracting State for tax incentives.

The tie-breaker clause

Another way in which Cyprus can prove an invaluable tax-planning vehicle is through the tie-breaker clauses introduced in the Double Taxation Treaties it has concluded.

Let us take the Cyprus–UK Treaty as an example.

The UK legislation (Section 249–251 FA 1994) regulates the tax treatment of UK registered dual resident companies. The Inland Revenue has ruled that in order for the dual residency provisions to apply, a Double Tax Treaty must contain a tie-breaker clause for dual resident companies under which residency is awarded as being in the territory with which the United Kingdom has concluded the Treaty. A country that meets these criteria is Cyprus.

The Double Tax Treaty between Cyprus and the UK states in Article 4(i): 'For the purposes of this Convention, the term 'resident of a contracting state' means any person who, under the laws of that State, is liable to tax therein by reason of his [or her] domicile, residence, place of management or any other criterion of a similar nature'.

On this basis, a UK company that establishes a branch in Cyprus and is managed and controlled from Cyprus will be dual resident as contemplated by Section 249 (i) FA 1994.

Article 4(3) of the Double Tax Treaty between Cyprus and the UK states: 'Where... a person other than an individual is a resident of both Contracting States, then it shall be deemed to be a resident of the

Contracting State in which its place of effective management is situated.'

Therefore, a UK company that establishes a branch in Cyprus and has its place of effective management in Cyprus is UK non-resident for tax purposes and is resident for tax purposes in Cyprus. This structure is very popular as it combines the prestige and reliability associated with a UK entity with low corporation tax and access to a rich network of Double Tax Treaties as applicable in Cyprus.

Double Tax Treaties – the future

Double Tax Treaties will no doubt continue to encourage investment between territories. As Cyprus continues to add to its panoply of fiscal incentives to attract foreign investment, it will certainly continue negotiations for the expansion of its already rich network of Double Tax Treaties. Already, the Cyprus Republic is currently negotiating over 20 new Treaties, while several others are being renegotiated following changes in the political situation of the correspondent territories.

2.5

Cyprus Double Tax Treaties: Summary of Withholding Taxes

Peter G Economides, Chairman, Totalserve Management Ltd and Senior Partner, PG Economides & Co.

Notes:

(1) 15 per cent if received by a company holding directly less than 25 per cent of the capital.

(2) 15 per cent if received by a company holding directly less than 10 per cent of the capital.

(3) 10 per cent if received by a company holding at least 25 per cent of the capital of the paying company. However, if German corporation tax on distributed profits is lower than on undistributed profits and the difference between the two rates is 15 per cent or more, the withholding tax is increased from 10 per cent to 27 per cent. In all other cases the withholding tax is 15 per cent.

(4) 15 per cent if received by a company holding directly less than 25 per cent of the capital.

(5) 5 per cent if received by a company controlling less than 50 per cent of the voting power.

(6) If received by a company controlling less than 10 per cent of the voting power, thus entitled to refund of excess Advanced Corporation Tax deducted in the UK. If company controls more than 10 per cent of the voting power, it is not entitled to the refund.

(7) 15 per cent if received by a company controlling less than 10 per cent of the voting power.

(8) Nil on literary, dramatic, musical or artistic work.

(9) Nil for literary, artistic or scientific work, film and TV royalties.

(10) 5 per cent on film and TV royalties.

(11) Nil if paid to a government or for export guarantee.

(12) Nil if paid to the government of the other state.

(notes continue on page 87)

Table 2.5.1

COUNTRY	RECEIVED IN CYPRUS						PAID FROM CYPRUS					
	Dividends (%)		Royalties (%)		Interest (%)		Dividends (%)		Royalties (%)		Interest (%)	
Austria		10		0		0		10		0		0
Belarus	(20)	5		5		5	(20)	5		5		5
Belgium	(4)	10		0		10	(4)	10		0	10	
Bulgaria	(24)	5		10	(25)	7	(24)	5		10	(25)	7
Canada		15	(8)	10	(11)	15		15	(8)	10	(11)	15
China		10		10		10		10		10		10
Czech and Slovak Republics		10	(9)	5	(12)	10		10	(9)	5	(12)	10
Denmark	(1)	10		0	(13)	10	(1)	10		0	(13)	10
Egypt		15		10		15		15		10		15
France	(2)	10	(10)	0	(13)	10	(2)	10	(10)	0	(13)	10
Germany	(3)	15	(10)	0	(12)	10	(3)	15	(10)	0	(12)	10
Greece		25		0		10		25		0		10
Hungary	(4)	5		0	(12)	10		0		0	(12)	10
India	(2)	10		15	(12)	10	(2)	10		15	(12)	10
Ireland		0	(10)	0		0		0	(10)	0		0
Italy		15		0		10		0		0		10
Kuwait		10	(9)	5	(12)	10		10	(9)	5	(12)	10
Malta		0		10		10		15		10		10
Mauritius		0		0		0		0		0		0
Norway	(5)	0		0		0	(5)	0		0		0
Poland		10		5		10		10		5		10
Romania		10	(9)	5	(12)	10		10	(9)	5	(12)	10
Russia	(21)	5		0		0	(21)	5		0		0
Singapore		0		10	(26)	10		0		10	(26)	10
South Africa		0		0		0		0		0		0
Sweden	(4)	15		0	(12)	10	(4)	10		0	(12)	10
Syria	(17)	0	(18)	15		10	(17)	0	(18)	15		10
Thailand		10	(23)		(22)	15		10	(23)		(22)	15
United Kingdom	(6)	15	(10)	0		10	(6)	0	(10)	0		10
United States	(7)	10		0	(14)	10	(7)	0		0	(14)	10
CIS countries		0		0		0		0		0		0
Yugoslavia		10		10		10		10		10		10
All other countries	(16)		(16)		(16)		(19)	0	(15)	10		25

(13) Nil if paid to the government of the other state, in respect of bank loans, in connection with the sale on credit of any industrial commercial or scientific equipment or any merchandise.

(14) Nil if paid to a government, bank or financial institution.

(15) Nil if royalties are on literary, artistic or scientific work including films, TV films or radio broadcasting.

(16) At the rate applicable in accordance with domestic Law.

(17) 15 per cent if received by a company holding less than 25 per cent of the capital of the paying company.

(18) 10 per cent on copyright of literary, artistic or scientific work including cinematography films and films or tapes for TV or radio broadcasting.

(19) Dividends paid by Cyprus local companies to foreign shareholders are exempt from withholding tax irrespective of treaty requirements.

(20) 5 per cent if the total investment exceeds EUR 200,000. If the investment is less than EUR 200,000 then: 10 per cent if the beneficial owner holds more than 25 per cent of the share capital of the paying company or 15 per cent if holding is below 25 per cent.

(21) 10 per cent if the total investments in the capital of the company is less than USD 100,000.

(22) 10 per cent if it is received by any financial institution (including an insurance company).
10 per cent if such interest is paid in connection with the sale on credit of any industrial, commercial or scientific equipment.
10 per cent if such interest is paid in connection with the sale on credit of any merchandise by one enterprise to another enterprise.
Nil if paid to a government of the other state.

(23) 5 per cent of the gross amount of the royalties for the use of, or the right to use, any copyright of literary, dramatic, musical, artistic or scientific work, including software, cinematograph films or films or tapes used for radio or television broadcasting. 10 per cent of the gross amount of the royalties received as consideration for the use of, or the right to use, industrial, commercial or scientific equipment or for information concerning industrial, commercial or scientific experience. 15 per cent of the gross amount of the royalties received as consideration for the use of, or the right to use, any patent, trade mark, design or model, plan, secret formula or process.

(24) 10 per cent if the recipient owns less than 25 per cent of the share capital of the company paying the dividends.

(25) Nil if paid to or guaranteed by the government of the other state or a statutory body thereof, or to the National Bank.

(26) 7 per cent if received by a bank or other financial institution.

Dividends, interest or royalties are not subject to any withholding tax when paid by a Cyprus International Business Company.

Part Three

Legal Environment

Legal Environment and Framework

Demosthenes Mavrellis, Consultant, Chrysses Demetriades & Co. Law Office

Foundations

The Constitution of Cyprus is one that follows the doctrine of strict separation of powers. The president, who appoints and presides over the deliberations of the Council of Ministers, is the head of state and government and heads the executive branch. The number of ministers is constitutionally capped at 10, but in practice there are 11, including the Minister of Education, who was not appointed under the Constitution. The ministers are not members of and are not answerable to the legislative branch. Other than a certain number of actions that are specific to the president, all decisions are taken by the Council of Ministers, which has the residual executive power (deciding by a majority vote).

All legislative power rests with the House of Representatives, which has the power to legislate on all issues. The composition of the House currently provides for 80 members. Of the 80 members only the 56 Greek-Cypriot members currently sit in the House, since the Turkish-Cypriot members have refused to sit in the House since the inter-communal conflicts of the early 1960s. All financial bills must be enacted by the Executive Branch and then be approved by the House.

Judicial power is the exclusive preserve of the Courts. The Courts of First Instance are the District Courts, and the Supreme Court, which also sits as a Constitutional Court, hears all appeals. All Supreme Court judges are appointed by the president and cannot be removed, unless in a manner prescribed in the Constitution, until they reach retirement age. The Supreme Court appoints all district judges, and it is the only body that can remove them. There are currently 11 members of the Supreme Court.

The president has a veto power over all bills passed by the House pertaining to international relations, defence and security issues, which may be exercised over the whole of the bills or parts thereof. Furthermore the president has the power to refer any bill to the House for reconsideration. The House then has a period of 15 days to reconsider the bill. If the House persists in its decision, the president is obliged to publish the bill in the Official Gazette within 15 days, thus giving it the force of Law. The president also has the right to refer any bill to the Supreme Court on grounds of constitutionality. The Supreme Court will then advise the president on the constitutionality of the bill, in whole or in part, and if there are no constitutional impediments, the parts of the bill that abide by the Constitution are published and become Law.

The Cyprus Constitution reflects the European Convention of Human Rights (ECHR) in its text almost verbatim. Therefore rights as understood by the most liberal democratic traditions are so guaranteed. The Courts also follow the jurisprudence of the European Court of Human Rights and are bound by its decisions. Individuals also have the right to petition the European Court of Human Rights having exhausted all recourse within the domestic legal system. Strict adherence to the decisions of the European Court of Human Rights and subsequent changes in the Law to mirror those decisions, have ensured that Cyprus has been able to adopt the most contemporary views on rights and social policy.

The Legal Framework

Cyprus follows a system of English Common Law with Civil Law modifications.

Common Law and Equity, and English Court Procedure, as well as laws passed by Westminster and the colonial administration prior to 1960 form the crux of the Cyprus legal system. Further legislation passed by the House ever since usually follows the spirit and method of the Common Law. It is remarkable that the Cyprus Companies Law (Cap 113) is virtually identical with the English Companies Act of 1948, although it has been slightly modified to reflect various (but by no means all) changes made on the English Companies Act since, especially those that have been promulgated to abide by European Union directives. Contract Law follows that of India as codified by the British colonial government, whereas Evidence Law is identical to English Law prior to the Civil Evidence Act of 1994.

Continental Law influence can be found in the fields of Constitutional and Administrative Law. Article 146, which gives a general right of recourse to the Supreme court in respect of any complaint against any decision, act or omission by a governmental or quasi governmental body or person acting in such a capacity exercising an executive power contrary to the Constitution or to any law or made *ultra vires*, is virtually the same as the Greek relevant article and can claim descent from Civil Law ancestry. The Article 146 procedure is very useful when challenging the imposition of any tax or duty or the compulsory acquisition of land. In this respect it can be said that the Supreme Court acts as an administrative court in the mould of the French *Conseil D'Etat*. Decisions of Greek, French and German courts are followed unless the Supreme Court has ruled on such matters.

Constitutional Law on the other hand, given the nature of the State, follows that of the United States where one finds more developed jurisprudence dealing with separation of powers.

Whereas there were provisions within the Constitution giving the Orthodox Church exclusive jurisdiction over family matters in respect of the Greek Cypriot community and to Turkish Civil Law over family matters pertaining to the Turkish Cypriot Community, these have been recently abolished during the 1990s and Family Courts have been created which now decide cases involving family issues. These Courts mainly follow Civil Law (Greek) concepts.

Section 29 of the Cyprus Courts of Justice Law 14 states that every court in its exercise of Civil or Criminal Jurisdiction shall apply (in the following order):

- the Constitution, the laws made thereunder and any other law becoming applicable by the Court;

- the laws in force prior to independence, insofar as those are not inconsistent with the Constitution;

- the Common Law and the doctrines of Equity, save insofar as other provision has been or shall be made by any law and so long as not inconsistent with the Constitution;

- the laws and principles of vakf (Turkish Religious Properties) (not applicable after 1974);

- the Acts of Parliament of the United Kingdom, applicable to Cyprus before independence but subject to similar qualification as above;

- the law applied by the High Court of Justice in England in exercise of its admiralty jurisdiction before independence, as may be modified by any Cyprus law.

It follows that in any matter governed by the aforementioned provisions or by laws enacted in the spirit of Common Law decisions of the English High Court and other Commonwealth jurisdictions are considered and have a persuasive effect unless the Cyprus Courts have ruled in such matter. The doctrine of *stare decisis* applies and Cyprus Courts follow English procedure.

Effects of accession to the European Union

Following accession of the island to the EU in May 2004, the Union's *acquis communautaire* will be fully incorporated into Cyprus Law. To make this possible the authorities in Cyprus have incorporated over 80,000 pages of laws and regulations into domestic law, a process which continues to ensure that all necessary remaining legislation is in accord with that of the EU. Cyprus has ranked first among the candidate countries in the race to fully adopt *the acquis*. Post accession, all new Commission Regulations will have a direct effect on Cyprus, as will all Directives, which, although directly effective, will have to be incorporated into domestic law.

The impact of accession cannot be underestimated since it will abrogate any distinction between a Cypriot person, natural or legal and any such person from another EU country. It is expected that this development will lead to more and more companies and people moving to the island and taking advantage of its extremely favourable taxation and strategic business.

3.2

Legal Dispute and Arbitration Proceedings

Demosthenes Mavrellis, Consultant, Chrysses Demetriades & Co. Law Office

The Courts

As the legal system in Cyprus is based on that of England and other Commonwealth jurisdictions as far as Criminal and Civil cases are concerned, it follows that any person familiar with that system will not find it hard to recognize in the Cypriot dispute resolution system, a framework that is familiar, predictable in its outcome, trustworthy and versatile. Criminal and Civil Procedures are largely based on that of England, as it was at the time of Cyprus' independence in 1960. Some modifications, such as the absence of the right of trial by jury, evolved to reflect specific needs arising out of realities in Cyprus. The concept of Equity is also incorporated within the Cypriot legal system.

The administration of justice in Cyprus is governed by the Constitution and the Courts Legislation of 1960-No.3 1998. The judicial framework is comprised of the District Courts and the Supreme Court. The District Courts are the courts of first instance in civil cases and criminal cases involving possible custodial sentences of less than three years. Crimes that are punishable with more than three years in custody are dealt with by the Assizes Court. The Supreme Court acts as an appeal court for both civil and criminal proceedings and maintains original jurisdiction in admiralty cases.

The hierarchy of the District Courts starts at the level of the president of the Court and moves downward to senior district judge and district judge. District judges can hear cases in which the claim is limited to CYP 25,000 and senior district judges can hear claims of up to CYP 50,000. The litigation process can be slow, taking about three years to complete in most cases, but it is not overwhelmingly expensive as in other similar jurisdictions.

The principle of *stare decisis* or precedent is followed in Cyprus courts. That means that the Courts feel obliged to stand by their own decisions and to follow the decisions of the Supreme Court, which is in itself bound by its own rulings. Along with the Constitution, statutes passed by the House of Representatives, subsidiary legislation and all those British colonial laws that were maintained following Independence, the corpus of the Courts' decisions (case law) forms the body of Cypriot Law. In addition to that, English decisions prior to independence also form part of the case law and new decisions of the Superior Courts of England and other Commonwealth jurisdictions can have a persuasive effect on a Cypriot Court. The application of a solid system of judicial precedent allows potential litigants to feel, at most times, confident about the outcome of a dispute and encourages trust in the judicial system.

The Courts have the capacity to award common law damages as well as a range of equitable remedies such as specific performance and injunctions. In general costs will follow the event, meaning that the loser will have to pay the winning party's costs.

The Foreign Judgements (Reciprocal Enforcement Law) (as amended by law 130/2000 and now renamed 'Law concerning certain Decisions of Courts of Commonwealth Countries') (the 'Law') provides powers to the Council of Ministers to apply the provisions of the Law, reciprocally, to the judgements of any country that enforces judgements given in the Cypriot Courts. Decisions of the English Courts, Commonwealth Courts and courts of those countries that are signatories to bilateral treaties of judicial assistance in criminal and civil law matters with Cyprus are enforced by the Cypriot Courts by way of registration, as prescribed in the Law. It is expected that following its accession to the EU in May 2004, Cyprus will incorporate the Brussels Convention for the recognition of judgements between EU courts, as part of the *acquis communautaire*.

Any person can apply to the Courts, within six years of the date of a judgement, to have such judgement registered in the Cyprus District Court by stating the facts on which the foreign judgement was based. The Courts will enforce the foreign judgement as long as it is not contrary to Cypriot public policy, not obtained by fraud and not contrary to the rules of natural justice and as long as the prescribed matters that need to be proven by the Rules of Court are so proven. So long as a judgement is registered and subject to provisions of the Law for having such judgement set aside, any registered judgement shall be of the same force and effect as a Cypriot judgement. Proceedings may be taken on a registered judgement, the sum for which a judgement is registered shall carry interest and the registering Court shall have control over the execution of the registered judgement.

International Arbitration in Cyprus

Under Cyprus Law, International Arbitration is covered by a different law than domestic arbitration. Having understood that the existing framework for arbitration (Law of 1944) allowed for too much judicial intervention in the arbitral process, Cyprus became the second country after Canada to adopt the Model Law on International Commercial Arbitration developed by the United Nations Commission on International Trade Law (UNCITRAL). The International Commercial Arbitration Law of 1987 follows the Model Law almost verbatim, the basic difference being that it incorporates a definition of the word 'commercial' within the corpus of the law.

International commercial arbitration is defined as arbitration between parties that have their place of business in different states. The basic benefit of adopting this new law is that the power of a litigant to ask for the intervention of the Court in any stage of the arbitration, as is the case in the domestic law, is curtailed, thus allowing for a speedy adjudication. The new law, as well as Cyprus' strategic location and availability of reasonably priced, high-calibre, English-speaking professionals, makes Cyprus an ideal place in which one would choose to conduct an arbitration.

As Cyprus is a member of the 1958 New York Convention on the Recognition and Enforcement of Foreign Arbitral Awards it follows that it will recognize any award made in any of the contracting states and will reciprocally have any award granted under the Cypriot Law recognized by those states.

3.3

The Regulation and Supervision of Banking in Cyprus

Central Bank of Cyprus

Introduction

An effective system of banking supervision rests largely on the existence of a suitable legal framework and adequate ongoing supervisory arrangements, focusing both on the assessment of the financial condition and viability of each bank at a micro-level as well as on the maintenance of the safety and stability of the banking system as a whole and the protection of depositors at a macro-level.

Laws relating to banking

The Central Bank of Cyprus Law and the Banking Law are key elements of the institutional legal framework of Cyprus' banking system.

As from 5 July 2002 a new Central Bank of Cyprus Law became effective, repealing the one of 1963. The new Law was enacted in order to comply with the Treaty of the European Union and the statute of the European System of Central Banks. It, *inter alia*, provides for the independence of the Central Bank of Cyprus (CBC), sets price stability as the CBC's primary objective and includes an explicit prohibition of direct financing by the CBC to the public sector. Moreover, according to the new Law, the Monetary Policy Committee, which previously had simply an advisory role, now acquires a decision-making role and assumes responsibility for the country's monetary policy.

The main tasks of the CBC, in order to achieve its objectives as defined in the Law, are as follows:

- to formulate and implement the country's monetary policy;

- to conduct the country's exchange rate policy in consultation with the Council of Ministers;

- to manage the official foreign exchange reserves of Cyprus and to conduct foreign exchange operations;

- to supervise banks in Cyprus

- to promote the smooth operation of payment and settlement systems;

- to perform the tasks of banker and financial agent of the Government of Cyprus.

The power of the CBC to regulate and supervise banks in Cyprus stems also from the Banking Law of 1997. The provisions of the Banking Law (as amended) are largely in line with the European Union Banking Directives and incorporate, to a large extent, the 'Core Principles' developed by the Basle Committee on Banking Supervision, which constitute a global standard for prudential regulation and supervision.

The Banking Law defines banking business and sets out the legal framework within which this may be carried out, describing the minimum prudential standards that banks must meet. Any entity wishing to carry on banking business in or from within Cyprus must obtain a licence from the CBC, which is the licensing authority for banking business. The Banking Law also lays down the minimum authorization requirements that must be satisfied before a banking licence may be granted, including a minimum initial capital of CYP 3 million and 'fit and proper' criteria for both directors and management. The CBC retains discretion, under the Law, to attach any conditions to the licence of a bank or to reject an application for obtaining a licence.

Foreign banks are placed on an equal footing, *mutatis mutandis*, with domestic banks with regard to licensing and regulatory matters. They enjoy national treatment and may provide the full range of banking services.

In addition to the licensing criteria, the Banking Law defines the permissible activities of institutions that are licensed and confines these activities within certain limits in order to avoid the taking of undue risks and maintain adequate financial strength. There are restrictions on credit facilities to individual borrowers, bank directors and 'connected persons' as well as on holdings of immovable property and shareholdings in companies other than those that are doing business integral or closely related to banking. There are also restrictions with regard to the ownership of banks.

The relevant limits are outlined below.

Credit facilities to individual borrowers, bank directors and connected persons ('large exposures')

Lending to a single person or a group of 'connected persons' is restricted to a maximum of 25 per cent of a bank's capital base and the aggregate of all large facilities may not exceed 800 per cent of a bank's capital base. The purpose of these restrictions is to prevent over-concentration of lending.

Moreover, there are limits with regard to the amount of credit facilities granted to directors, which are also expressed as a percentage of a bank's capital base. The aggregate of all these facilities may not exceed 40 per cent, while the total value of any unsecured facilities should be restricted to a maximum of 5 per cent. Banks are also required to ensure that any transactions with related parties are on an arm's-length basis.

Banks' shareholdings

A bank is not allowed to acquire or hold directly or indirectly more than 10 per cent of the share capital of any other company and in the case of a bank incorporated in Cyprus the value of any share capital held in any other company should not exceed 10 per cent and for all companies, on aggregate, should not exceed 25 per cent of the bank's capital base. These limits apply to all investments with the exception of investments in insurance companies and companies that carry out business that is integral to or closely related to banking, provided that such companies are incorporated in Cyprus. The above limits can only be exceeded with the prior written approval of the CBC.

Acquisition and disposal of immovable property

A bank may not acquire or purchase any immovable property except for the purpose of conducting its business, for providing recreational facilities to its staff or for selling the property in the course of satisfaction/settlement of debts due to it. In the latter case, such property must be disposed of within three years of its acquisition.

Limitation on large shareholding in banks

There is also a requirement to seek approval from the CBC for proposed changes in significant ownership or controlling interests in existing banks. Control is defined as beneficial ownership of the bank's share capital, which carries 10 per cent or more of its voting rights.

Trading activity and dealing by a bank in its own shares is prohibited. Furthermore, the Banking Law enables the CBC to define how a bank's capital base is to be measured and to require the maintenance of a solvency ratio as well as a liquidity ratio.

In the exercise of its supervisory role, the CBC is empowered to exchange information and cooperate with overseas supervisory authorities, to arrange trilateral meetings with each bank and its auditors and to have bilateral contacts with the external auditors of supervised banks, if it considers this necessary for the protection of depositors. The CBC may also request banks to submit returns, accounts and other information. Finally, the Banking Law contains extensive measures that the CBC may take in order to bring about timely corrective action when a bank fails to meet prudential requirements or when there are regulatory violations.

Directives issued under the Banking Law

Another important element of the legal and regulatory framework involves prudential regulations issued for the purpose of implementing the provisions of the Banking Law. These are set administratively by the CBC (without the need to amend the Law), thus providing flexibility in adapting supervision to accommodate innovation and new developments in the banking environment.

By virtue of the powers vested in it by the Banking Law, the CBC has issued the following Directives encompassing largely the principles prescribed by the respective Directives of the European Union.

Directive on the monitoring and control of credit facilities to individual borrowers or bank directors and their connected persons

This Directive has been issued for the purpose of implementing the provisions of the Banking Law with respect to large credit exposures.

Directive for the computation of the capital base of banks

In this Directive the CBC prescribes what constitutes a bank's capital base and the method for its computation.

Directive for the computation of the capital adequacy ratio of banks

The Directive prescribes what constitutes a capital adequacy ratio and requires banks to keep a minimum amount of capital in relation to risk weighted assets, as a cushion for absorbing potential losses. This approach deals mainly with credit risks. The minimum ratio to which banks are required to adhere is currently 10 per cent.

Capital Adequacy Directive (CAD)

The Directive sets capital requirements in respect of market risk.

Directive on the layout and the contents of the annual accounts of banks

Banks are required to submit to the CBC and publish accounts in accordance with the layout and the contents prescribed by this Directive.

Directive on cross-border credit transfers

The Directive applies to credit transfers between Cyprus and member states of the EU for amounts not exceeding EUR 50,000 or its equivalent in Cyprus pounds or in the currency of any of the EU member states. It aims at introducing transparency and facilitating the execution of cross-border credit transfers in a fast and efficient way and with a minimum cost.

Directive for the computation of prudential liquidity

The CBC has issued this Directive in order to ensure that banks maintain adequate liquidity by monitoring mismatches between assets and liabilities. Banks are required to report assets and liabilities in prescribed time bands depending on their remaining period to maturity and to contain mismatches within maximum allowable limits.

Directive on the employment of funds derived from foreign currency deposit liabilities

The Directive sets the framework within which banks may utilize the funds emanating from foreign currency deposits from customers. Banks are required to hold a minimum level of assets of instant liquidity in order to ensure adequate liquidity in foreign currencies. In particular, as from 1 March 2003 total assets of instant liquidity (as defined by the CBC) must at all times be at least equal to 75 per cent of foreign currency deposit liabilities from customers.

Directive on foreign currency positions and exposures

This Directive deals with foreign exchange risk management, prescribing limits on banks' positions in relation to their capital base. It stipulates that the net open position in any one currency overnight may not exceed 3 per cent of the bank's capital base (there is a wider margin of 5 per cent for intra-day positions) and the overall aggregate net position in all currencies together may not exceed 6 per cent. (There is a wider margin of 8 per cent intra-day.) Banks are also required to set up appropriate stop loss limits on a daily as well as on a cumulative basis.

Directive on the framework for the evaluation of internal control systems

The Directive provides for the establishment of risk management units as well as Audit Committees.

Supervisory regime

The existing well-developed legal framework establishes the foundations for adequate supervision and allows the CBC to carry out and enforce its responsibilities effectively.

The objective of banking supervision is to ensure that banks are financially sound and not posing a threat to the interests of their depositors. Attention focuses on the individual bank but the soundness and safety of the banking system as a whole is considered equally important so as to minimize systemic risk and retain public confidence. In the exercise of its supervisory role the CBC uses both off-site monitoring and on-site examination.

Off-site monitoring involves the receipt, review and analysis of an extensive range of periodic prudential returns submitted by banks, which cover almost every aspect of their operations. The analysis of this information enables the CBC to monitor each bank's performance and its compliance with the Banking Law and the Directives issued thereunder on an ongoing basis. The process assists in identifying any problems or capturing warning signals or areas of excessive risk in the bank's operations. Any areas of concern revealed through the prudential returns are taken up with the bank involved for remedial action. Off-site monitoring may also trigger off a special on-site examination, where a problem may require further investigation.

On-site examinations are carried out at least once a year at locally incorporated banks and at least once every 18 months at branches of foreign banks. They aim at assessing the current financial condition and soundness of a bank and its future prospects and also at ascertaining compliance with the Banking Law, the Directives and Regulations issued by the CBC and the conditions attached to its banking business licence.

Deposit Protection Scheme

A Deposit Protection Scheme has been in operation as from 1 September 2000, with the aim of protecting small depositors from losses in the event of a bank failure.

A Fund with a separate legal status has been established with contributions from member banks. The Fund is administered by a Management Committee and operates under the auspices of the CBC. Membership is compulsory for all licensed banks unless exemption is granted by the Management Committee.

The Scheme provides for immediate compensation should the CBC or a court decision determine that deposits have become unavailable. The principle of coinsurance exists with compensation amounting to 90 per cent of the total amount of deposits of each depositor up to a maximum of the equivalent in Cyprus pounds of EUR 20,000.

The Scheme currently covers deposits in Cyprus pounds only but it will be extended to cover deposits in euros and other currencies of the EU by the time of Cyprus' accession to the EU.

Cyprus International Trusts

Demosthenes Mavrellis, Consultant, Chrysses Demetriades & Co. Law Office

The basic law that regulates international trusts in Cyprus is the International Trusts Law of 1992 (the 'Law'). Originally, trusts were (and in the case of trusts other than international trusts still are), regulated and governed by the Trustees Law, Cap. 193 enacted in 1955 and based on the English Trustees Act 1925 and by the Doctrines of Equity and Case Law as it was applied in England prior to the independence of Cyprus in 1960. This meant that Cyprus' Trusts Law was outdated, since it was out of line with the developments that had taken place in England and in some other countries.

Therefore, the then existing law on trusts, now applying solely to domestic trusts, had certain disadvantages and could not adequately serve all the needs and demands of those who wished to use an international trust as one of the available instruments in their international tax planning.

With this in mind the Government, as part of a series of measures promoting Cyprus as a financial centre, introduced a new bill, which led to the passing by the House of Representatives of the 'International Trusts Law of 1992'. The Law endeavours to create the necessary environment for foreign investors to establish international trusts in Cyprus, to give freedom of movement of funds and also to remove certain ambiguities as to whether the existing legislation could cover set-ups, such as those that are common in other jurisdictions.

Under the Law, for a trust to qualify as an 'International Trust' the following conditions need to be satisfied:

- The settlor must not be a permanent resident of Cyprus.

- At least one of the trustees must at all times be a permanent resident of Cyprus.

- No beneficiary other than a charitable institution is a permanent resident of Cyprus.

- The trust property does not include any immovable property situated in Cyprus.

One may envisage the possibility of an individual settlor forming a Cyprus Company, the shares of which vesting entirely to him or her and of whom he or she is the sole director, which will act as the sole trustee of the international trust to which the assets of this individual would be transferred.

A settlor is deemed to have the ability to dispose of his or her assets to an International Trust if at the time of such transfer is of full age and of sound mind under the law of the country in which he or she is a permanent resident. The Inheritance Law of the Republic of Cyprus or of any other country shall in no way affect any transfer or disposition made to a Cyprus International Trust and the validity of such transfer shall not be challenged. In the absence of any express provision to the contrary contained in the instrument creating the International Trust, such a trust shall be deemed to be irrevocable by the settlor and his or her legal representatives notwithstanding that it is voluntary.

Notwithstanding provisions of bankruptcy law in Cyprus or any other country, in the event of the settlor's bankruptcy, any transfer of assets made to the International Trust shall not be void or voidable, unless in the case of an International Trust which is voluntary and made without consideration or for the benefit of the settlor, their spouse or children and to the extent that it is proven to the satisfaction of the Court that the trust was set up with the intent to defraud persons who were, at the time the property was transferred to the Trust, the settlor's creditors. The burden of proof to establish intent to defraud lies with any creditors seeking to annul the Trust. Such action must be initiated within two years following any transfer or disposal of assets to the Trust.

The Trust can be valid for 100 years from the date of its creation, whence it will terminate if it has not hitherto been terminated pursuant to a relevant term in the instrument creating it. Charitable and Purpose Trusts are not subject to the rule and may exist in perpetuity.

Subject to the provisions of the instrument creating an International Trust, the trustee will be allowed at any time to invest the whole or any part of the trust funds in any kind of investment wherever the investment is situated and whether or not the funds have already been invested. Any investment made by the trustee may be varied or retain its original state as long as the trustee exercises diligence and prudence that a reasonable person would be expected to exercise in making such an investment.

The applicable law of Trust may be changed to or from the Law of the Republic provided that:

(a) in case of a change from the Law of the Republic to another law, the new applicable law recognizes the validity of the trust and the respective interest of the beneficiaries;

(b) in the case of a change from another law to the Law of the Republic such change is recognized by the applicable law of the trust previously in effect.

Any arrangement varying or revoking the terms of the International Trust or enlarging or modifying the powers of management or administration of the trustees shall not be approved unless the Court is satisfied that such change is for the benefit of the persons applying for it or those categories whose interests are expressly protected under the Law and of any other interested parties.

Subject to the terms of the instrument creating the Trust and absent a Court order mandating any disclosure of information, the trustees or any government officials may not disclose to any person not legally entitled thereto, any information or documents relating to the name of the settlor or beneficiaries, any deliberations pertaining to the manner of exercise of discretionary powers and the reasons for exercising those and also to those referring to trust accounts. Trust beneficiaries may request any documents relating to Trust accounts.

The income of the Trust that is derived from sources outside Cyprus shall be exempt from all taxes imposed in Cyprus and also exempt from Estate Tax, which in any event, since the enactment of the Law, has been abolished for all estates. The stamp duty chargeable for the instrument creating an International Trust will be CYP 250. International Trusts are exempted from the requirements of registration under any law.

Part Four

Establishing a Business in Cyprus

Using Cyprus for International Business

Emily Yiolitis, Director / Legal Consultant, Totalserve Management Ltd

Introduction

International business can be carried out via Cyprus by a number of vehicles, namely:

- an International Business Company now known as the Cyprus Company;

- an International Branch;

- an International Partnership;

- a Cyprus International Trust.

Investors and entrepreneurs will use one of the above vehicles to conduct their international business via Cyprus. What makes Cyprus more attractive and advantageous than some other jurisdictions is the extensive network of Double Tax Treaties that Cyprus has concluded with many countries. It must be mentioned that some of the Treaties which Cyprus has, contain, either in their original text or by virtue of Protocols to the Treaties, anti-avoidance provisions or limitation of benefits articles that may exclude Cyprus offshore entities from the application of the Treaties and in particular with reference to the provisions of the Treaties relating to dividends, royalties and interest. The Treaties that contain anti-avoidance provisions are those of Canada, France, Germany, United Kingdom, United States and Denmark, but such anti-avoidance provisions vary from country to country. Due to the enactment of the new tax legislation, effective from 1 January 2003, and which provides for a unitary tax rate, these provisions will no longer be significant and full benefits of the Treaty in question will apply.

As a rule, Cyprus is a tax efficient intermediary vehicle for investment purposes and has often been used for reducing the overall tax burden of investors who choose to conduct their business via the rich treaty network offered by Cyprus. In fact, investment is often routed from the West to emerging Eastern markets via Cyprus. The structuring is as shown in Figure 4.1.1.

The most popular way of conducting international business via Cyprus is the Cyprus Company.

The Cyprus company

Cyprus companies are limited liability companies incorporated under the Cyprus Companies Law, Cap. 113. Until recently, and more specifically until 31 December 2002, Cyprus International Business companies were taxed at the favourable rate of 4.25 per cent on their profits annually and offered significant tax advantages to expatriate employees. In light of accession to the EU however, there has been a wholesale review of the tax system in Cyprus. The old system of taxation in Cyprus was remittance based. The new system has thoroughly revised the old and replaced it with a system of taxation of worldwide income for Cyprus residents and of Cyprus source income for non-residents.

This means that a company will be taxed if it is deemed to be resident in Cyprus; a company will be deemed to be resident if it is managed and controlled in Cyprus (incorporation per se is no longer

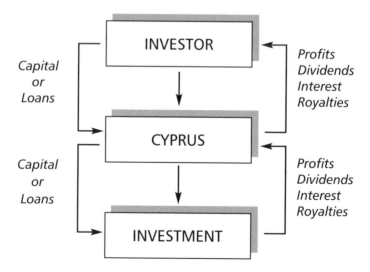

Figure 4.1.1 Cyprus as an intermediary vehicle

sufficient to establish residence); and a company not managed and controlled in Cyprus will be non-resident. Resident companies will be charged to tax on the income accrued or arising from sources both within and outside Cyprus. Non-resident companies will be charged to tax only on Cyprus source income.

The basic impact of the new legislation on International Business Companies (IBCs) is that there will no longer be a distinction between local companies and IBCs and the taxable income of all Cyprus companies will be taxed at the rate of 10 per cent. For the years 2003 and 2004 there is an additional tax of 5 per cent for profits above CYP 1 million.

IBCs established in Cyprus prior to 31 December 2001 and which, during the year of assessment ending 31 December 2001 derived income from sources exclusively outside Cyprus (or were carrying out activities during 2001 and did not receive income by the year end due to the nature of their activities), will have the option to elect to be taxed at the rate of 4.25 per cent for the years of assessment 2003, 2004 and 2005 with the proviso that this election when made is irrevocable, and that the IBC in question will continue to derive income from sources exclusively outside Cyprus. Provided that such an election is made, certain tax exemptions and other beneficial provisions introduced by the new legislation, (such as group relief, tax-free reorganizations, tax exemption on the disposal of shares, etc) will not be applicable.

Contrary to popular belief and despite the increase of the tax rate, the new legislation is expected to foster rather than hinder international business conducted via Cyprus. The new legislation has in fact introduced the possibility of Cyprus companies being zero rated for tax purposes in Cyprus, if they are managed and controlled from abroad. Careful tax planning can ensure that no taxes are payable abroad either.

The special status granted to ship owning and ship management companies is extended to the year 2020. Under this status, profits earned by a Cyprus company that owns ships under the Cyprus flag and operates in international waters are exempt from tax, while profits of ship management companies are taxed at 4.25 per cent unless they opt to be subject to tonnage tax calculated on the tonnage of the ships managed by them.

The main advantages could be summarized as follows:

- Company income tax rate is only 10 per cent on the net profit, which is still an all-European low rate.

- Income in the form of dividends, subject to certain conditions, is not taxed.

- Dividends from a Cyprus company to non-residents bears no withholding tax.

- Expatriate employees pay low tax rates.

- There are no exchange control regulations, and a company may transfer foreign funds in and out of the country at any time without any restriction.

- Obtaining a residence and employment permit is an easy process, once the company meets mandatory requirements.

- There is no estate duty.

- There is no capital gains tax, except on immovable property situated in Cyprus. (The capital gains tax rate on immovable property is 20 per cent on the net profit after allowing for inflation.)

- There is no stamp duty on transfer of shares or other assets.

- There is a tax exemption on profits from the sale of stocks, shares and securities.

The Cyprus International Branch

Section 347 of the Companies Law, Cap. 113 provides for the registration of a branch of a foreign company in Cyprus. The taxation of the International Branch is dependent upon whether central management and control is exercised from within Cyprus. If management and control are exercised from Cyprus, the profits of the branch are taxable at the rate of 10 per cent in the same way as a Cyprus Company. If not, the profits of the branch are not liable to any tax in Cyprus. A strong but not conclusive indication of the place of management and control is where the majority of the directors of the corporation reside, where the board meetings are held and where the general policy is formulated.

The Cyprus International Partnership

According to the Partnership and Business Names Law, Cap. 116, partnerships registered in Cyprus may be either general or limited partnerships. In a general partnership every partner is liable jointly and severally with the other partners (without any limit) for the debts and obligations of the partnership. The limited partnership on the other hand, is a partnership in which at least one of the partners has unlimited liability for the debts and obligations of the partnership, with the possibility that the remaining partners enjoy limited liability. As such, a limited liability company may also be a partner in a limited partnership.

The profits of a Cyprus International Partnership are not subject to any tax in Cyprus.

Trusts

The English Law on Trusts as applied in England prior to the 16 August 1960, as well as the provisions of the Cyprus Trustees Law, Cap. 193, are the applicable laws in Cyprus in relation to Trusts, subject to any existing statutory provisions. In 1992 the International Trusts Law was enacted to provide for the creation of International Trusts in Cyprus.

In Cyprus it is possible to create any one of the following three types of trusts:

- A *'Local Trust'* – The Cyprus International Trusts Law does not apply to such trust which is governed by the English Law and the doctrines of equity as applied in England prior to 16 August 1960, and by the Cyprus Trustee Law, Cap. 193, which is very similar to the English Trustee Act 1925. This type of trust is subject to Exchange Control Law and unless special permission is given by the Central Bank of Cyprus, the settlor as well as the beneficiaries must be residents of Cyprus and the property settled by the trust is subject to exchange control in Cyprus.

- An *'Offshore Trust'* – A trust of this type may be established with the approval of the Central Bank of Cyprus under the provisions of the Exchange Control Law (Note: It is anticipated that The Central Bank will cease to be the competent authority and that the Exchange Control Law will have been repealed prior to entry to the EU in May 2004.) It is legally the same as the 'Local Trust' explained above, but the beneficiaries are persons who are not residents of Cyprus, all the activities of the Trust are outside Cyprus but for some reason (non-compliance with some technical requirement) the Trust does not qualify to be designated as an International Trust. Such a trust will be governed by the same legal provisions as the Local Trust.

- A *'Cyprus International Trust'* – For a Trust to qualify as an International Trust, the following requirements must be fulfilled:
  - the Settlor must not be a permanent resident of Cyprus;
  - no Beneficiary other than a charitable institution may be a permanent resident of Cyprus;
  - the Trust property cannot include any immovable property situated in Cyprus;
  - at least one of the Trustees for the time being must, during the whole duration of the Trust, be a permanent resident of Cyprus.

The income and gains of an International Trust derived or deemed to be derived from sources outside the Republic shall be exempt from all tax imposed in the Republic and no estate duty shall be chargeable in respect of assets belonging to an International Trust. Trust income such as royalties, interest or dividends is exempt from income tax in the hands of the trustees, and the beneficiaries of an International Trust are also exempt from payment of income tax in respect of money received from the trustees. In fact the only payable fee in relation to an International Trust is a one-off stamp duty, currently set at CYP 250.

All things considered, the prospects for international business in Cyprus are promising. Cyprus has managed, via the overhaul of its tax regime, to be the first country within the applicant countries for EU membership to be in full compliance with OECD criteria and the EU Code of Conduct and at the same time, to retain and in certain circumstances increase its competitive advantages as an international business centre. The unitary tax rate will remain attractively low and should not in principle deter investors. On the contrary, it is likely to increase investment if not in quantity, then arguably in quality. The elimination of the tax discrimination currently applicable will better link foreign and domestic businesses, eroding the fence that has hitherto deterred cooperation and openness. The readjustment of revenues from various tax bands has enabled policy makers to create an attractive, all-round more balanced system of taxation. In conjunction with the rest of the advantages of accession (the expected improvement of the political climate, the conditions of macroeconomic stability to be secured by adoption of the euro and membership in the EMU, the liberalization of capital flows from and to Cyprus, etc) all factors point towards an eventual transformation of Cyprus into a regional business centre in which Cypriot vehicles and tax planning via Cyprus will enjoy increased popularity.

Foreign Participation in Cyprus Companies

Demosthenes Mavrellis, Consultant, Chrysses Demetriades & Co. Law Office

Introduction

Cyprus has adopted a relaxed policy towards allowing foreign participation in its economy. Throughout the years it has assisted the establishment of a great number of companies that were offshore in nature and whilst incorporated in Cyprus had the scope of their activities completely outside Cyprus. This happened because of the very low percentage of tax levied on these companies (4.25 per cent) and the existence of a host of Double Tax Treaties between Cyprus and other nations. Because of steps to harmonize Cyprus law with that of the EU, however, such distinction has now been abolished and all companies, whether they be International Business Companies (IBCs) whose operations are exclusively overseas, companies that focus their activities exclusively or to a great extent in Cyprus or IBCs that may develop a mixture of international activity and some activity in Cyprus, are treated the same for taxation purposes. For all companies that were established prior to 2001 and were enjoying the 4.25 per cent tax regime a transitional period until 31 December 2005 is still available.

Due to the very competitive corporate tax regime (10 per cent basic rate of corporate taxation), low individual taxation, strategic location and the wealth of reasonably priced, internationally trained professional talent, Cyprus is increasingly becoming the main regional financial centre in the Eastern Mediterranean; an area of great strategic and commercial importance. Because of Cyprus' European socio-economical structures, coupled with the very privileged relationship Cyprus enjoys with Russia and many Eastern European and Middle Eastern countries, Cyprus is the ideal location for multinational companies to base their operations, arrange their financing and control their interests in the area.

The growth of the services industry, as well as a booming tourist industry, has led to great prosperity in Cyprus and an ever-increasing need for investment on the domestic front. It is projected that in the next few years there will be a need for a significant number of high-investment infrastructure projects, such as marinas, golf courses and theme parks. The abolition of any restrictions in the activities of IBCs will allow these companies, which are already acclimatized with the country, to include domestic opportunities in their investment portfolio. It is anticipated that following the full accession of the island to the EU, a lot of Europeans may choose to make Cyprus their home and take advantage of its extremely high quality of life. That will lead to an expansion of the market place and further investment in real estate and consumer services.

In view of the fact that we are now in the last stages preceding EU accession, the Central Bank of Cyprus has loosened up the restrictions (based on the Exchange Control Law) to direct foreign investment by foreign nationals. This was done by a policy announcement dated 7 January 2002. The main gist of the new policy is to allow individuals or bodies corporate who are resident in a member country of the EU to acquire up to 100 per cent of any business (subject to rules regarding the acquisition of real property by aliens) and to invest in any stocks quoted on the Cyprus Stock Exchange without restriction, save in the case of banks, where non-Cypriots are not allowed to own more than 50 per cent of the equity. Restrictions for persons who are not residents of the EU are listed below.

Formation and operation of companies

The formation and operation of companies is governed by the Cyprus Companies Law, which is basically the same as the English Companies Act 1948. The law is about to be amended to take into consideration all the new EU directives. Cyprus International Business Companies (IBCs) as well as all other companies (any distinction from now on becoming increasingly irrelevant) are limited liability companies incorporated under the Cyprus Companies Law, Cap. 113. The case law attached to the Companies Law is that of England up to 1960, and the thinking behind more recent decisions of Cypriot Courts reflects English and Commonwealth legal jurisprudence.

Companies are formed after an application is filed with the Registrar of Companies and a fee is paid. Each company must have a Memorandum of Association stating its powers and objectives and Articles of Association, which are for all intents and purposes the by-laws of the company. For each company at least one shareholder and one director are required. Bodies corporate may be directors of Cyprus companies. The company must have a secretary, who need not be a resident of Cyprus, and just one shareholder is sufficient. No bearer shares exist, but nominees may be used with the approval of the Central Bank of Cyprus. Bank references for the beneficial owners must be provided to the Central Bank of Cyprus. Any information given to the Central Bank is, in accordance with the provisions of the relevant law, kept confidential.

Prerequisites for the approval of applications by the Central Bank

For companies incorporated in EU countries or controlled by natural persons resident in an EU country there are no restrictions as to the scope of their activity and all privileges relating to local companies apply, as is explained above.

As a rule all applications by non-EU nationals for the formation of a company that will have all its activities outside Cyprus will be approved as long as they are not contrary to public policy. All other proposals for investment within Cyprus may be approved if they abide by the following restrictions, which are industry sector specific and are listed in a Central Bank policy paper dated February 1997.

As regards the primary sector (agriculture, animal husbandry, forestry, etc), only 49 per cent foreign participation is allowed and the minimum investment should be CYP 100,000. All applications are examined by the Central Bank in conjunction with the Ministry of Agriculture.

In the manufacturing sector, foreign participation of up to 100 per cent is allowed but any investment exceeding CYP 750,000 must be made in consultation with the Ministry of Commerce, Industry and Tourism.

In the services sector foreign participation is allowed in a wide variety of fields, some requiring a minimum investment of CYP 50,000 and others requiring an investment of CYP 100,000. Details of specific requirements are listed in two appendices to the Central Bank's policy paper. The Central Bank also has the right to approve foreign participation to the level of 24 per cent, even if the indicative levels of investment are not satisfied.

Restaurants are subject to a minimum level of investment of CYP 125,000 and require a foreign contribution of at least CYP 60,000. The investment must be geared toward high-quality service and management.

There is a predetermined maximum allowable level of foreign participation for the following:

- For the local banks whose shares are quoted on the Cyprus Stock Exchange, the maximum allowable participation for non-resident foreigners and Cypriot non-residents is 15 per cent. Of this, no more than 6 per cent may be owned by non-resident foreigners. The participation of each non-resident individual or corporation is restricted to a maximum of 0.5 per cent of any one company's issued capital. All this is subject to the Central Bank's right to approve larger percentages of foreign participation if deemed necessary.

- For tourist projects (such as hotels, leisure complexes, tourist villas, etc) the percentage of foreign participation is determined in consultation with the Ministry of Commerce, Industry and Tourism. Currently 49 per cent is allowed in hotels and other primary tourist projects, whilst 100 per cent may be allowed in supplementary tourist projects such as marinas and golf courses.

Applications for participation in other sectors of the economy are decided on the particular characteristics of each application.

4.3

Shipping and Ship Management

Costas Georghadjis and Antonis Taliotis, Deloitte & Touche

Introduction

The year 2002 was a milestone in Cyprus' history. The country concluded its Accession Negotiations with the EU in 2002, signed the Accession Treaty on 16 April 2003 and will join the EU on 1 May 2004.

The accession has secured the future of the Cyprus Shipping Industry, with the EU approving the Cyprus shipping safety standards and tax framework. The prospects of Cyprus developing into an even greater shipping centre are now better than ever.

Cyprus shipping is a major industry for the Cyprus economy, contributing around 2 per cent of GDP and employing more than 5,000 people.

Responsibility

Responsibility for the development and administration of merchant shipping in the Republic lies with the Ministry of Communications and Works. The relevant authority within the Ministry is the Department of Merchant Shipping, which is based in Limassol and is responsible for the registration of ships, administration and enforcement of local legislation and international conventions, marine safety, marine environmental protection (with regard to ships' operations), maritime training, certification of seamen, control of shipping, investigation of marine casualties, labour disputes on board Cyprus ships, and other related activities.

Legislation

The registration of ships under the flag of Cyprus is governed by the Merchant Shipping (Registration of Ships, Sales and Mortgages) Laws, which are based on the British Merchant Shipping Acts. The two other principal merchant shipping laws are the Merchant Shipping (Masters and Seamen) Laws and the Merchant Shipping (Fees and Taxing Provisions) Laws.

Cyprus has also ratified all major international conventions on prevention of sea pollution, maritime safety, training and certification of seamen and limitation of shipowners' civil liability in cases of oil pollution damages. It has also ratified all major conventions on maritime labour standards.

Ownership of Cyprus ships

Under merchant shipping law the following persons may register a ship under the Cyprus flag, as long as they own more than one-half of the shares of the ship:

- Cyprus nationals;

- a corporation established under the Companies Law and having its registered office in Cyprus;

- provided permission is granted by the Council of Ministers, a corporation established in another country in which the controlling interest is with Cypriot nationals.

A ship owning or ship management entity may be registered in Cyprus as:

- a limited liability company;

- a general partnership where the liability of all the partners is unlimited or a limited partnership and where all except one of the partners have their liability limited to their capital contribution to the partnership;

- a branch of an overseas company.

Formation of a shipping/ship management entity

Any non-Cypriot owner wishing to register a ship under the Cyprus flag must incorporate a company in Cyprus, which will either acquire the ship in its name or bareboat charter the ship for the purposes of parallel registration under the flag of Cyprus. The registration of such a company requires:

- Central Bank of Cyprus approval if the shipowner is a non-EU resident.
- Approval of company name by the Registrar of Companies. Names which are too general or which are similar to existing names used by other entities are not permitted.
- Preparation and filing with the Registrar of Companies of two principal constitution documents:
  - the Memorandum of Association, which states the company's name, its business objects, its limited liability status and the amount of its nominal share capital;
  - the Articles of Association, which regulate the company's internal management and the rights of its members among themselves.

The registration of a ship management company in Cyprus is subject to the same requirements applicable for ship owning companies. Additionally the Central Bank requires a reference letter from a commercial bank on the financial standing and integrity of the applicant.

Shareholders, directors, secretary and registered office

Every company must have at least one shareholder (either individuals or legal persons) and at least one director and a statutory secretary. The company must also have a registered office in Cyprus.

Registration of ships

A ship not exceeding 15 years from the date its keel was laid, owned by a qualifying person, can register in the Cyprus Register of Ships provided it complies with the relevant legislation and regulations.

A ship older than 15 years may also be registered, provided it complies with certain additional requirements, which must be fulfilled concurrently with the submission of the application for registration and must be complied with at all times while the vessel remains registered, irrespective of any subsequent transfer of ownership. Ships older than 15 years registered under the Cyprus Registry are subject to inspection by the Department of Merchant Shipping.

Provisional registration

Provisional registration is possible under the Cypriot Merchant Shipping legislation for ships that at the time of registration are situated at any port outside Cyprus.

The provisional registration period is six months, but an extension for an additional three months can be obtained. The application for provisional registration must contain certain information, such as the basic specifications of the vessel and the flag it carries at the time of application, the details of the Cyprus company which will own the vessel (including the name under which the vessel will be registered, its type, year of build and gross tonnage), the name of the classification society recognized by Cyprus with which the ship is entered and the intended area of trading. In addition the applicant vessel must have an agreement for the clearance of accounts with a recognized Radio Traffic Accounting Authority. Furthermore, the place where the vessel will be at the time of her provisional registration must be communicated to the Registrar of Cyprus Ships prior to the provisional registration as well as the name of the consular office where the owners wish to effect the provisional registration of the vessel.

At the time of provisional registration, fees, tonnage tax for six months, radio station fees and fees for the issuance of the provisional certificate are payable (see separate paragraph on fees payable). For extending the provisional registration period for an additional three months, one-half of the registration fees and tonnage tax are payable.

Permanent registration

Permanent registration in the case of a ship under provisional registration must be effected before the six months' (nine months if extension has been secured) provisional registration elapses. The application for permanent registration must be accompanied by the following: a certificate of deletion from the previous register, a copy of an agreement with a recognized Radio Traffic Accounting Authority, copies of the ship's statutory certificates, certificate of survey, Cyprus tonnage certificate and/or international tonnage certificate, and a duly verified ship's carving and marking note.

The certificate of survey and the Cyprus tonnage certificate (or the international tonnage certificate) must be issued by a recognized classification society.

Once the application procedure is completed and the relevant fees have been paid the Registrar of Cyprus Ships registers the vessel in the Cyprus Registry.

A vessel that was under a provisional registration and whose permanent registration is effected before the provisional registration period has expired is not subject to any additional fees, except for the fee for the issuance of the certificate of permanent registration in the Cyprus Registry.

Parallel registration of ships

Under the merchant shipping laws of Cyprus, parallel registration of ships can be effected with more than 20 countries whose legislation is compatible with that of the Republic.

'Parallel-in' registration is used when a ship under a foreign flag is bareboat chartered to a Cyprus shipping company. The registration is valid for a period fixed by the Minister, usually two years, but may be extended for further periods.

The initial registration fees are 20 per cent higher than those applicable for a provisional or permanent registration. In cases where the ship is deleted from the current registry and reregistered for the benefit of the same charterer the registration fees are reduced by 50 per cent. Otherwise the vessel is subject to the same fees applicable to Cypriot vessels (see separate paragraph on fees payable).

'Parallel-out' registration is used when a ship under the flag of Cyprus is bareboat chartered to a non-Cypriot company and registered in a foreign register.

A vessel under parallel-out registration is subject to the same fees applicable for any Cypriot vessel, with the exception of fees for the issue or renewal of a radio licence (see separate paragraph on fees payable).

Registration, change of name, deletion

The Cyprus Registry is now the sixth largest in the world and on accession by Cyprus to the EU it is estimated that it will represent 25 per cent of the whole EU fleet. It will also be the only 'Open Registry' in the EU; in other words it will be possible for non-Cypriots to register ships under the Cyprus flag, provided the conditions set out in the paragraphs 'Ownership of Cyprus ships' and 'Formation of a shipping/ship management entity' are complied with.

A vessel may change its name on application to the Registrar. Seven days must elapse from change of name to submission of application to register. A Cypriot vessel is automatically deleted from the Registry as soon as more than half of the shares in the ship pass on to a non-Cypriot. The deletion procedure is only completed once any registered mortgages and/or other encumbrances are discharged.

Mortgages of ships

Mortgages of ships should be recorded in the Cyprus Register of Ships and additionally with the Registrar of Companies, where the shipowner is a company. The Cyprus law relating to ship mortgages is similar to the English law; in that it affords full protection to mortgagees and has become one of the deciding factors in attracting ships from all over the world.

Manning of Cyprus ships

Manning of Cyprus flagged ships is governed by the Merchant Shipping (Masters and Seamen) Laws, the International Convention of Standards of Training, Certification and Watchkeeping for Seafarers and the Merchant Shipping (Composition and Number of Crew) Regulations.

Officers of a Cyprus ship are not required to hold a certificate issued by the Cyprus Government to perform duties on board, provided they are in possession of a valid certificate of competency issued by another country with which Cyprus has a bilateral agreement.

Every Cyprus ship is required to secure a document of safe manning by the Department of Merchant Shipping.

Exchange control

Ship owning and ship management companies, owned by non-Cypriot residents are not subject to any exchange control restrictions. (It is expected that exchange control restrictions currently applicable for Cypriots will soon be abolished.)

Fees payable by Cyprus ships

Fees payable by Cyprus ships compare very favourably with those payable under other well-known international flags; for example in many instances they are well below those payable under the Liberian or Panamanian flags. Reductions on the annual tonnage taxes payable on ships whose management is exercised by a Cyprus ship management company are available under the current legislation.

A summary of the current fees in Cyprus Pounds (CYP) is set out below:

Tonnage tax

Ships other than passenger ships
Tonnage tax is calculated based on the following formula:

(basic charge + gross tonnage increment) x age multiplier

where the basic charge is CYP 100.

Gross tonnage is determined as follows:

For every unit of gross tonnage up to 1,600 units	CYP 0.26
For each unit between 1,601 and 10,000 units	CYP 1.16
For each unit between 10,001 and 50,000 units	CYP 0.06
For units of gross tonnage in excess of 50,000	CYP 0.04

The age multiplier is determined as follows:

For ships up to 10 years of age	0.75
For ships between 11 and 20 years of age	1.00
For ships over 20 years of age	1.30

Passenger ships
Double the fees applicable for other ships

Registration of ships

Ships other than passenger ships

For every unit of gross tonnage up to 5,000 units of gross tonnage	CYP 0.10
For each unit between 5,001 and 10,000 units of gross tonnage	CYP 0.08
For units of gross tonnage in excess of 10,000	CYP 0.04
Minimum fee	CYP 125
Maximum fee	CYP 3,000

Passenger ships

For each unit of gross tonnage	CYP 0.15
Minimum fee	CYP 250

Registration transfer or transfer of interest in a amortgage

For each unit up to 10,000 units of gross tonnage	CYP 0.02
For every additional unit over 10,000	CYP 0.01
Minimum fee	CYP 30

Discharge of mortgage

No fees

Transfer of ownership

For each unit up to 10,000 units of gross tonnage	CYP 0.02
For every additional unit over 10,000	CYP 0.01
Minimum fee	CYP 30

Deletion of ships from the Register

No fee

Radio Station fee

Fee for permit for installation and operation of wireless telegraphy and/or

telephony station on board	CYP 10
renewal of radio licence	CYP 10

Other fees

Examination of application for registration	CYP 15
Examination of application for change of name	CYP 15
Approval of change of name	CYP 80
Provisional certificate of Registry	CYP 10
Carving and marking note	CYP 10
Transcript of registry	CYP 10

Taxation

Shipowners, ship managers and crewmembers can take advantage of taxation incentives offered not only by domestic legislation, but also through the wide and increasing network of Double Tax Treaties of Cyprus. These are outlined below.

Shipowners

Exemption from any Cyprus income/corporation tax on:

1. the income of a shipowner of a Cyprus ship from the operation of such ship in any shipping enterprise between Cyprus and ports abroad or between foreign ports (the operation of a ship includes the chartering of a ship);
2. dividends that are paid directly or indirectly from profits of ships as per (1) above;
3. no Defence Fund Contribution is levied on dividends paid by ship owning companies;
4. no capital gains tax on the sale of the ship or on the sale or transfer of the shares of a ship owning company;
5. reduction on tonnage taxes where a Cyprus ship management company manages the ship.

Ship managers

Under current tax legislation, ship managers:

1. are subject to a special ship management tax calculated at one-quarter of the rates applicable for tonnage tax;
2. may elect to be taxed under the Income Tax Law instead at the rate of 4.25 per cent on the taxable profit determined in accordance with international accounting standards;
3. are not subject to Defence Fund Contribution is levied on dividends paid by ship management companies;
4. are not subject to capital gains tax on the sale of shares of these companies.

Crew earnings

The earnings of the crew of a Cyprus ship are exempted from Cyprus income tax and social security contributions. In addition, non-Cypriot crewmembers may enjoy total tax exemption if provided for by the Double Taxation Treaties of Cyprus and the domestic legislation in their home countries.

Publication of information

Ship owning companies do not have to file their financial statements with the Registrar of Companies, but they do have to file details of their registered shareholders, issued share capital, directors and secretary. An annual return, required to be filed with the Registrar of Companies, updates this information with any changes.

Part Five

Property Ownership and Living in Cyprus

5.1

The Cyprus Real Estate Market and Foreign Investment

Antonis Loizou, FRICS, Chartered Surveyor, Senior Partner, Antonis Loizou & Associates, Chartered Surveyors

General

Cyprus has a highly active property market at a level that is disproportionately high by comparison to the overall size of the local investment market. The reasons for this are mainly the lack of alternative investment opportunities of a profitable nature in Cyprus, the relatively high returns that property investment has shown in the past, the limited risk that prevails in local real estate, the serious interest that European buyers and investors have shown in Cyprus and, more recently, the pending accession of the island to the EU (May 2004).

Returns

The Cyprus property market lends itself to both large- and small-scale property investments. Returns from property development have historically shown an average of between 15 per cent and 25 per cent p.a. on the total invested capital or a return approximating to 20 per cent to 30 per cent p.a. on personal capital invested. As to annual returns from rental income in relation to the current value of an investment (ie not its historic cost) a figure between 6 per cent and 8 per cent p.a. can usually be achieved. These levels of return, when compared with alternative forms of investment in Cyprus, are very attractive, but what is more important, is that such investments have limited downside risk, as the capital appreciation of real estate is almost certain, having ranged between 3 per cent and 7 per cent p.a. over the past 10 years.

So far Cyprus has been spared from the periodic recessions in property markets that appear in other, more advanced, economies and as such, local prices, at the worst, tend to remain stable. Unlike those in Europe, however, the Cyprus real estate market is far from perfect. As a generality, it can be said, without contradiction, that whenever there is reduced demand, property owners simply withdraw their property from the market, thereby limiting the supply and so ensuring the prices for property remain stable. As intimated, this situation is commonplace in Cyprus, since the attachment of an owner to his or her property is a very important personal matter. In short, local owners will only dispose of their property at what they think is the 'right' price; otherwise they simply will not sell. With this in mind, it will be realized that very few people are willing sellers, even at prices that are over and above prevailing market rates; an attitude which has been integral to the creation of the ongoing positive market trend over the last 30 years.

Foreign demand

As mentioned, the Cyprus property market has proved popular with both local and foreign individuals, whereas investments by foreign firms have been restricted by numerous laws and regulations. Foreign investors may purchase just one house, land not exceeding 4,000 sq. m, offices for their business (unlimited) and share capital in local real estate companies of up to a maximum of 15–25 per cent. Nevertheless, and despite these restrictions, foreign investment in real estate has risen very fast from CYP 14 million in 1975 to CYP 250 million in 2002, an average increase of 62 per cent, which to some is quite alarming. Moreover, the volume of interest doubled between 2000 and 2001 and again between 2001 and 2002. Such investment, at this point in time, is confined primarily to retirement or holiday home acquisitions, being more than 90 per cent of the total, with office acquisitions by offshore companies accounting for the remaining 10 per cent.

As of today, Cyprus has not attracted serious real estate investors such as property developers, whether alone or in joint venture with a local partner, but this is expected to change quickly after accession to the EU and the subsequent lifting of restrictions on real estate acquisitions by foreigners.

Cyprus, in terms of foreign retirement and holiday home purchases, is considered one of the three most popular Mediterranean destinations for European middle-income groups. Little Cyprus, with a population of only 700,000, competes with large Spain, of 40 million people and even larger France. Why then is Cyprus popular with foreigners?

Reasons for Cyprus' popularity

The primary reasons for Cyprus' popularity and the increasing interest in real estate acquisition on the island are:

- *A very low crime rate* – The fast increase in the incidence of crime in many larger countries has caused investors to seek safer areas in which to reside, such as Cyprus. Security is especially important to the aged and the retirement markets, and is now the top consideration amongst investors as opposed to the cost of acquisition, which was the case in the past. Cyprus recognizes it cannot compete with Spain, Italy and France in terms of investment opportunities and attractions but that it can do so in terms of its lower crime rate, drug problem, protection rackets and other criminal activities. To put this in perspective, and despite recent isolated incidences of crime, mainly in the tourist areas and at odd hours, the rate of increase of local crime is very low. Based on official statistics, crime in Cyprus has increased over the last 10 years at an average annual rate of 7 per cent, but, nevertheless, the island's crime rate is 6 per cent of that in the United Kingdom, 10 per cent of Germany's and 30 per cent of that in Portugal and Ireland.

- *Business efficiency and communications* – The European approach to everyday business and the country's excellent communication system, which enables instantaneous contact at a touch of a button with the outside world, are both major attractions to foreigners. According to detailed research, Cyprus is the third most advanced country in the world in terms of telecommunications and has telephone charges that are the lowest in the EU.

- *Language and friendliness* – Easy communication with the locals, most (80 per cent) of whom speak English, and the possibility of corresponding with Governmental Departments in that language, allied to the level of professionalism and the hospitality of the people is an added bonus for many.

- *Cost of living* – The relatively low cost of living in the past, compared with much of Europe, has been of further benefit and, although the last few years' inflation has eroded this advantage, major items, such as rents, entertainment and eating out, remain at relatively low levels by comparison. However, inflation is expected to reach 3–4 per cent during 2003, slightly above the EU average. The standard of living is high, reaching 70 per cent of that of average EU members, whereas per capita income approximates to USD15,000 and the cost of living is about 60 per cent of the average of EU members.

- *Strong currency* – The relative strength of the Cyprus pound and its close relationship with the euro is a further attraction for foreign investors, especially those from Europe and will be particularly so once Cyprus has become part of the EU in May 2004 and ultimately the Euro zone (by 2009).

- *Security of title* – The land registration system in Cyprus, the security of title and the protection of ownership that it is offered are further benefits. The holder of a title or a party to a property sales contract is secured by the Government and is further protected by the local Courts. Property ownership is considered a sacred investment in the country and there has not been even one incident of compulsory acquisition of real estate, other than for the development or construction of public projects. It should be noted also that in Cyprus, the custom that prevails in some jurisdictions of ownership by possession does not exist, so ensuring enhanced security for foreign and local investors alike.

Limitations on foreign acquisitions

Foreigners buying property in Cyprus must obtain the Council of Ministers' Approval, which is generally given routinely to European individuals (but not companies), provided they can prove that they earn more than CYP 12,000 p.a. (per couple) in their own country and that they have no record of serious crimes. Once approved, foreign owners of local property may become permanent residents and have unlimited length of stay in the country for themselves and their family. During this stay the property can be used only by the purchaser and his or her family, but cannot be leased or exploited as a business (other than for leases longer than 28 days and the tenants must be local residents). After a period of 10 years of residence over an aggregate total of 13 years, an application may be lodged for obtaining local nationality with all the same benefits permitted to existing Cypriots. Thus, buying real estate is one way to stay on the island and to obtain a Cyprus/EU passport. This situation is unique to Cyprus and is especially important to non-EU members since it provides a way to become an EU citizen.

Joining the EU (+5 years)

With the joining of the EU and the ultimate removal of restrictions by the Cyprus Government for EU nationals and companies in regard to real estate acquisition, which will occur by 2009, a large increase in demand in the local property market is anticipated. Large European investment and property development companies are expected to seek investment on the island, much as they have done in Spain, Portugal and, more recently, in Greece.

Demand for suitable land and property will likely increase sharply and initially land prices will, in all probability, more than double in seaside areas, with choice plots possibly increasing three to four times. Similar seaside locations in popular areas of Spain and Portugal are now double the price of similar properties in Cyprus. This would seem to indicate there is strong potential for capital appreciation by both speculators and developers.

Concurrently, the lifting of the restrictions in relation to work and the setting up of businesses, which is already quite easy for EU members, will likely attract a new, younger generation of purchasers, especially from EU countries. This whole new market is thought to be considerably larger than the holiday home and retirement market. Furthermore, marked potential is also foreseen from the other 10 countries that are acceding to the EU along with Cyprus, especially those which have little sun and no coastline.

Locations to buy

In seeking real estate investment in Cyprus the following locations are deemed likely to be the most rewarding:

- Land near to or on the beach.

- Land suitable for division into building plots.

- Development of holiday and retirement homes for foreigners including old people's homes coupled with medical care.

- Apartment development for permanent-resident rental.

- Investment in golf projects, commercial marinas, care centres and quality sports centres.

- Education and hospital facilities. Although of a different nature, investment in these sectors has a very strong property element. Considering Cyprus' proximity to the Middle East, there is deemed to be strong potential for investment in high-technology private hospitals to cater to its 200 million Arab neighbours, providing a form of medical centre in the region similar to that in Israel. Similarly, the new law on higher education has increased the demand for private colleges and universities providing education to both local and foreign students. This relatively new activity has attracted more than 10,000 foreign students in just three years, with a large unsatisfied demand remaining, especially from the Far East, including China, the Arab countries and India.

New potential investors

Local property developers feel that Cyprus is as yet an undiscovered investment destination for people from many European countries. In the past people have tended to think that foreign interest comes only from the United Kingdom and, like with the tourist industry, major efforts have been directed towards that market to the exclusion of others. This is not altogether surprising as Cyprus has strong connections with the United Kingdom and because British nationals find it easy to deal with Cyprus.

Bearing in mind interest rates in Switzerland, Cyprus enjoyed serious interest from that country and also from Sweden, resulting in a substantial increase in real estate sales levels by investors from both countries, reaching levels close to those by UK residents within a very short period of time.

As at mid-2003 promising new client countries include Germany, the Netherlands and Belgium, in addition to other European nations. However, market penetration in Europe is adversely impacted by the level of commissions payable in Cyprus to foreign agents from 5 per cent to a maximum of 8 per cent, whereas for other markets (eg Spain) commissions exceed 10 per cent.

The Eastern European market is another matter altogether. Cyprus, regrettably, appears to survive on the misfortunes of others and as it was helped by the Lebanon crisis in 1975–76, so it attracted heavy interest from Yugoslavia/Serbia in 1990 and 1992 and from Russia (and other eastern bloc countries) since 1993–94. A strong demand still prevails.

A short sectoral overview of property investment and development

Residential

The residential market is the strongest sector catering to both local and foreign investors. The sector covers sales of building plots, individual housing and apartment development, and permanent and holiday homes, whether near the sea or in the mountain resorts. Extended financing facilities for housing from 10 to 30 years repayment, which were first introduced in late 2002, have enlarged the housing market and ensured the doubling of demand over the last two years (2002–03). This trend is expected to continue over the next 3 to 5 years.

Within this category falls the holiday home and retirement home market. Both categories have strong local and foreign potential, with approximately one in six Cypriots owning a holiday home in addition to ownership by foreigners. Statistically, 60 per cent of the foreign residential demand comes from the United Kingdom and the remaining 40 per cent from other countries, with a substantial proportion being from Russia and Yugoslavia.

Locals prefer the eastern part of Cyprus which is a more family-oriented location, being close to Nicosia, whereas foreigners prefer Paphos (60 per cent), Limassol (20 per cent) and Larnaca (15 per cent), in preference to eastern Cyprus (5 per cent).

Commercial/retail

This is a saturated market at present, with Cyprus having more shops per capita (approximately six times more) than any other EU country. As a result the demand for retail premises, other than in tourist locations, is slow.

Office

The office market has a three-year cycle in Cyprus. At this point in time this market is passing through a depressed period and is not expected to revive until after 2005, even though EU membership could well increase demand for office space, especially in Nicosia, being the capital. There are, however, opportunities to buy land as of mid-2003 and to secure building permits to be ready for the next increase in demand.

Industrial

This sector is restricted to building land for industrial uses, since most industrial users prefer to buy their own plot and erect their own industrial building to their own specifications. However, given the size of the island, and the short distances between the main centres, this type of development is not restricted solely to defined locations.

Impact on the property market from a possible settlement to the Cyprus problem

Recently moves have been made to achieve a solution to the Cyprus problem based on a bi-communal federation. The developments are rapid and it is hoped that a solution may be found over the coming two years, and possibly sooner given the Republic's accession to the EU in May 2004.

Any resolution is likely to upset the prevailing state of the property market since it must also resolve the property issue in the Turkish held areas and the resettlement of its inhabitants, who are now refugees. At the same time, the solution will almost certainly attract added investment from abroad, since some investors have been discouraged by the present situation.

Nevertheless, it is difficult to project how the market will behave, since most of the market's reaction will depend on the nature of the solution. It is expected, however, that for an initial period of two to three years after a solution is put in place the market will remain stable, even though the sale of property by returning refugees and new developments in the currently Turkish-held areas will have their effect. Considering, in addition, the anticipated increased demand by both local and overseas investors, this adjustment period is not expected to surpass that two to three year time frame.

Taxation

- Corporate profits are taxed at 10 per cent.

- Investment income from dividends and profit on the sale of securities is exempt from tax.

- Repatriation of profits from Cyprus companies to non-residents is free from any withholding tax.

- No time restriction on carrying forward tax losses.

- Group relief provisions.

- Numerous exceptions.

- If domiciled in Cyprus no estate duty is payable on worldwide and local property. This is a most important item for wealthy individuals due to the double taxation agreements that Cyprus has with most countries, including Russia.

- VAT is not charged on property.

Property taxation

Table 5.1.1 Transfer fees payable depending on a property's value at the time of transfer

Value	Fees
Up to CYP 50,000	3%
CYP 50,001–CYP 100,000	5%
Over CYP 100,000	8%

Table 5.1.2 Immovable property tax (per annum and based on 1st January 1980 valuations)

	Per thousand
Up to CYP 100,000	zero
CYP 100,001–CYP 250,000	2 0/00
CYP 250,001–CYP 500,000	3 0/00
Over CYP 500,000	3.5 0/00

Capital gains

Subject to numerous exceptions and indexation, a 20 per cent charge is levied on a profit. A CYP 50,000 tax-free allowance is made for a private residence and CYP 10,000 for any other property. The effects of this tax are limited due to the indexation system that prevails.

Indicative property prices

Table 5.1.3 Residential premises

Location	2-bed flats	3-bed flats	2/3-bed bungalow with pool	3/4-bed villa with pool
Paphos	CYP 65,000	CYP 75.000	CYP 150.000	CYP 200,000
Limassol	CYP 58,000	CYP 70,000	CYP 140,000	CYP 200,000
Nicosia	CYP 60,000	CYP 75,000	CYP 150,000	CYP 230,000
Paralimni	CYP 33,000	CYP 38,000	CYP 150,000	CYP 180,000
Larnaca	CYP 45,000	CYP 53,000	CYP 150,000	CYP 180,000

Table 5.1.4 Residential values

Property type	Rental value
Offices	With all modern facilities CYP 600–CYP 1200/sq.m.
Shops	CYP 1000–CYP 3000/sq.m. of building
Industrial	CYP 250–CYP 350/sq. m of building
Land	
Residential	CYP 100–CYP 150/sq. m
Touristic	CYP 80–CYP 220/sq. m
Office/Commercial	CYP 400–CYP 600/sq. m

5.2

The Acquisition of Immovable Property by Aliens in Cyprus

Demosthenes Mavrellis, Consultant, Chrysses Demetriades & Co. Law Office

The acquisition of immovable property (land and buildings) by aliens in the Republic of Cyprus is regulated by the Immovable Property Law, Cap. 109 of 1936 as subsequently amended and modified. The purpose of the Acquisition (Aliens) Law is to protect the local population from extensive and disproportionate ownership of land by aliens and to avoid any artificial rise in prices that may price the local population out of the market. It also serves to protect local businesses from competition and exploitation by large foreign undertakings. Despite the law, however, a lot of immovable property in Cyprus has passed through foreign ownership, especially in the form of holiday homes, apartments and small building sites.

The market in real estate has picked up since the war of 1974. This is because of the Government taking a relaxed attitude towards granting immovable property acquisition licences to aliens, especially as regards residential and office properties. This is in accordance with the Government's general philosophy of promoting Cyprus both as a tourist destination and as a regional financial centre. Foreign ownership of land has increased manifold since the 1970s because of the growth of the offshore companies on the island. Executives who have arrived in Cyprus to work for these companies have more often than not sought to acquire their own little 'place in the sun', given Cyprus' excellent Mediterranean climate, its modern amenities and the hospitable nature of its people. There has also been development of office space, and a lot of international companies have invested in state-of-the-art office complexes. In addition to this there has also been a great interest in acquiring retirement homes on the island, especially among pensioners from northern countries. Consequently, because of all the aforementioned reasons it can be said that any alien applying for a licence to acquire immovable property should not run into any particular trouble.

The Law forbids the acquisition of immovable property by an alien otherwise than with the permission of the Council of Ministers. This power has now been delegated to the relevant District Officers. Acquisition by succession is freely allowed by the Law.

Acquisition means not only outright purchase of property by aliens but leases of immovable property that exceed 10 years, acquisition of shares in a Cyprus registered company that owns immovable property in Cyprus, if such acquisition would turn the company into an 'Alien Controlled Company' as described below and the creation of a trust that gives an alien beneficial ownership of property or a company as described below.

An alien is defined as:

- a natural person who is not a citizen of the Republic (it is expected that following Cyprus' accession to the EU in May 2004, the term alien will not include a citizen or a company of any country that is a member of the EU);

- a company that is controlled by alien persons;

- a trust for the benefit of an alien person.

For the purposes of this Law a company controlled by aliens means any undertaking:

- whose board of directors is comprised of 50 per cent or more alien persons;

- in which 50 per cent or more of the voting power is exercised directly or indirectly by aliens;

- in which more than 50 per cent of its shares belongs to aliens;

- that has, at the time of the acquisition of the immovable property, through its Articles of Association or any other constitutional document, granted to an alien rights to determine that the operation of the undertaking will be controlled by such alien. A trust beneficial to an alien means a trust that allows beneficial ownership of the immovable property to an alien.

If the area of land acquired is one necessary for a dwelling house or business premises and is smaller or equal to 2,670 sq. m (exceptionally but quite frequently, the area can be stretched to 4,000 sq. m) then the licence will generally be granted in all bona fide cases.

If the acquisition of land for the purpose of building a dwelling house or business premises exceeds 4,000 sq. m, the licence granted is subject to terms, restrictions, preconditions and criteria as set by the Council of Ministers and approved by the House of Representatives (Regulation 374/90). In summary, the Regulations provide for a timetable that needs to be followed when building on the designated property, that the cost of developing the property be paid in foreign exchange, that taxes and duties to the Republic are settled and that any development is in accordance with the licence.

The procedure followed is an application to the District Officer by the alien wishing to acquire immovable property. The application needs to be accompanied by the following items:

- a Government Survey Plan of the property;

- a copy of the title deed;

- a copy of the contract of sale;

- a floor plan of the residence (if the subject property is an already existing building);

- the square footage of the property;

- statement of the applicant's finances;

- copies of passports of the applicant and spouse (showing only the picture page and the stamps indicating entry to and exit from Cyprus);

- marriage certificate;

- copy of residence permit and any work permit;

- application on form Comm. 145;

- in case the applicant is a company, or the applicant is a company shareholder, the certificates of registration of shareholders, directors and registered offices;

- a copy of the Articles of Association and information regarding its activities and its staff, Cypriot and foreign, together with their National Insurance numbers.

5.3

Living in Cyprus

Lewis Scudder

In a nutshell, and reflecting no bias at all, Cyprus is a pleasant place in which to live and work. A person coming from foreign parts can quickly slot into it. Foreigners who find themselves isolated and alienated usually have only themselves to blame. A Westerner need not confront difficult issues of culture shock or lifestyle, and one coming from the Middle East finds much that will be familiar. Cyprus is a 'melting pot' and always has been. Yes, the island Republic has its unique characteristics, but they reveal themselves at an easy tempo and are more frequently refreshing than jarring. Given an incentive and a chance to express it, Cypriots are a friendly and accommodating people.

The flavour of Cyprus is that of an ancient place. Archaeology has laid bare a human record dating back to before 7000 BCE. Once people started to sail the open waters, Cyprus, the Mediterranean's third largest island, attracted all who came and went upon the seas – Minoans, Egyptians, Phoenicians, Mycenaean Greeks, Romans and Byzantines. Each touched its personality. Its copper mines gave Cyprus its name, but the ancient world also knew Cyprus to be a garden island, a place of refuge and peace. It is a 'pocket-sized' archaeological and historical treasure house full of gems.

Cyprus' character has been shaped by several waves of influence since Byzantium left its lasting imprint. The island was ruled by a Latin West for almost four centuries (1191–1570). It began with Richard the Lionheart (who, in a brief reign, garnered St George for England) and ending with the Lusignan exile kings of Jerusalem and the Venetians. They exerted every effort to repress the island's Greek and Orthodox heritage. Still not far beneath the surface, the trauma of those days has shaped the island. One suspects that Cypriot-Orthodox unease with the island's indigenous Muslims lies not so much in their being Muslim – they having emerged during the three centuries of sloppy Ottoman rule (1570–1878) – as in the fact that they were once Catholics.

A now-Protestant Britain resumed control of Cyprus in 1878 and ruled it until 1960. The protracted civil conflict leading to independence incubated many of the island's present political difficulties. The fledgling Republic of Cyprus struggled with ethnic polarization between minority 'Turkish' and majority 'Greek' segments. Its strategic significance reasserted itself with the Cold War, and overt and covert Great Power meddling in the island's internal affairs exacerbated ethnic tensions. In 1974 an abortive coup attempt by a Greek army faction stimulated the Turkish army to occupy the northern third of Cyprus. The island was divided. Whole neighbourhoods and villages were shifted – Greeks going south; Turks going north – and the violence and acrimony that accompanied this has left deep wounds. Anyone living on the island will soon become aware that, current reunification efforts notwithstanding, this inter-communal tension will take a long time to heal.

Nearly eight centuries of shoddy and alien foreign rule left Cyprus a poor country. The island exported people worldwide. Inherently an industrious and inventive people, Cypriots still remember days when meat was a rare treat and affluence was something other people had (often at their expense). But the body blows of the 1974 war stimulated Cypriot resilience and enterprise into overdrive. Furthermore, the Lebanese civil war brought a massive infusion of refugee capital onto the island in the 1970s. Especially on the southern part of the island, new projects were launched, agriculture expanded (witness a burgeoning and internationally respected wine industry), highways were built, and tourism was vigorously cultivated. From knowing need on every level of life, within a generation Cypriots have pulled themselves out of poverty and into an era of prosperity. It is a remarkable success story.

Southern Cyprus, today, is obviously a prosperous democracy. The network of well-made and well-posted roads ties this part of the country together. Goods and services move efficiently. Crime is rare, and walking the streets even at night is not considered risky. Public transportation continues to be underdeveloped, but the entrepreneurial spirit long ago evolved a system of service taxis that connect the major cities. (It takes some research, but once discovered it shows itself to be inexpensive and efficient.)

Communications, particularly over the last ten years, have improved dramatically. Efficient telephone and Internet services are available even in remote villages. With the main seaport in Limassol and international airports in Larnaca and Paphos, transportation of people and goods is well handled. The main cities of Nicosia, Limassol, Paphos and Larnaca are growing centres of enterprise, with modern business facilities and pleasant accommodations.

A feature of Cypriot life that strikes anyone new to the island is tourism. It is everywhere, and Cypriot tourists themselves are part of the picture. Tourist hotels and vacation apartments are a prominent feature of the main coastal cities and the mountain resorts. They come in all grades and are generally clean and well cared for. Water is safe to drink. One hardly ever hears of the sort of gastrointestinal complaints common to other tourist destinations. Cypriots jealously protect their reputation for scrupulous cleanliness, and one may eat their lush salads with gusto. Pubs, nightclubs, cafes and restaurants of every description dot the landscape, offering options for both ethnic and international cuisine and entertainment. In the summer, doubling the island's population, the beaches and highways are full of enthusiastic tourists who arrive pale and leave with a painful-looking cooked lobster hue, having gotten their money's worth (and more!) of fun in the sun.

For some years Cyprus has offered itself as a retirement haven and many expatriates (primarily British) have taken advantage of incentives offered. Unlike other countries in the region, where foreign ownership of property is severely restricted, in Cyprus foreigners may purchase property and build homes. This fairly openhanded Cypriot attitude and the heretofore relatively low cost of living account for a large expatriate population of permanent residents. While provisions for foreign ownership of land are likely to liberalize even further after Cyprus fully integrates itself into the EU, the cost of living will increase (as it has already been doing) with the addition of the 15 per cent VAT the EU requires and other market forces that will come into play.

Having noted the inter-communal tensions, it is worth remarking here that tourism could not thrive were those tensions overtly expressed. In fact, both the island's 'North' and its 'South' have a vested interest in keeping tensions cooled, since tourism is essential for both. For Cypriots themselves, the tensions are always very much in mind, but for the foreign visitor and even the foreign resident they can be almost subliminal.

This remarkable sense of business-like proportionality has contributed to making Cyprus a good place from which to do business. Cyprus has profited from the collapse of Beirut as the region's business hub. Cypriot enterprise has done its best to capitalize on that windfall advantage. Offshore companies thrive on the island. They find its proximity to Eastern Europe and to the Middle East (without most of the Middle East's limitations and inconveniences) a genuine 'plus'. Convenient access to both Israel and the whole Arab world has meant that business meetings and conventions can be held on Cyprus that cannot otherwise be organized. Again, this is a windfall advantage that Cypriot businessmen and hoteliers know how to use.

When one sets up housekeeping in Cyprus there are certain things that become apparent. Over the past decade or so the Western-style mega-store has made its appearance. This has meant that the family-owned business has suffered and lifestyle has been affected. Customarily, Cypriots have cherished a laid-back and informal lifestyle. Wednesday and Saturday afternoons, for instance, are times when businesses close down and people take well-earned leisure time off. While that continues to be a pattern, the faster-paced, price-slashing (not to say greedy) newcomers, for whom Wednesday and Saturday afternoons are neither sacred nor necessary, are threatening that tradition. The upshot of this new pattern, however, is that almost all modern products – from food of all nations to apparel from around the globe, and from electronics of all descriptions to the very latest household appliances – are readily available at affordable prices.

In times past visitors and residents alike could be heard complaining about the monochrome offerings in restaurants and hotel dining rooms. Generic Greek-style cuisine was all there was, and even stabs at offering something more 'exotic' came out tasting much the same. More recently, the taste and coloration of what is on offer has changed dramatically. Cyprus can now boast of its offering a genuine cosmopolitan flavour to life.

This has gone hand-in-glove with the importation of foreign labour into almost all sectors of the economy – from entertainment and the service sector to household staff, and from technology to construction and agricultural labour, and everything in between. From being an exporter of people, Cyprus has become a net importer, and this has had both negative and positive effects. Negatively, of course, the presence of a large expatriate servant population has alienated many Cypriots from significant sectors of the productive economy and their cultural identity has also been affected. As has happened elsewhere, it is creating a two-tier society, particularly as Cypriots express rising expectations and decline to accept certain kinds of work. One of the positive effects, however, is that those coming to reside on the island and who require (or desire) domestic assistance can find it readily available.

While public education and university education on the island may leave much to be desired, Cypriots have availed themselves of a highly developed private education system that has grown up somewhat like Topsy. They have pursued university education overseas, returning home with top-flight credentials and a vision for making the best of what they now have at hand. The foreigner coming to Cyprus with young children, therefore, has access to good British-curriculum English-language schools. Decent English-language newspapers are published on the island, and most matters can be transacted in English, although those foreigners who acquire even a smattering of Greek are enthusiastically applauded.

An anxiety for anyone moving overseas is health care. Cyprus is a very healthy place in which to live, enjoying a good climate and copious amounts of fresh air. The provision of medical services is also well attended to. Professionals at all levels practise medicine with a high degree of competence, and their services are frequently noted to be substantially below the cost of private medicine in Europe and the United States. Only for the most exotic conditions does one need to consider travelling off-island. It is certainly useful to be covered by good health insurance, but that is true anywhere in the world.

A question people ask is whether they will find places in which they may worship. Here it must be noted that the Greek Orthodox Church of Cyprus, which traces its origins to St Paul's first missionary journey, is dominant and its influence can be felt both in religious life (Cyprus is peppered with fascinating monasteries and every village has its parish church) and in the civic life of the country. In an age when national churches have been urged to adopt ecumenical perspectives, the Church of Cyprus has bid welcome to other Christian religious expressions bearing responsible credentials. Parishes of Anglican/Episcopalian origin are to be found in all the major cities and serve an increasingly wide range of Protestant needs. Catholic churches, particularly of the Latin and Maronite rites, are also found in those cities. Even Coptic Orthodox churches are now established in both Limassol and Nicosia. Muslims will find at least one central mosque in each major city.

But Cyprus, like other countries in the region, has experienced a growing number of less-coherent religious expressions ranging from free-form evangelical or charismatic Protestant gatherings to Jehovah's Witnesses, Mormons, and Seventh-Day Adventists. Not surprisingly, this unsettling cacophony elicits an occasional backlash on the part of the established church. Nonetheless, Cyprus customarily maintains its democratic poise with respect to religion. Whatever one's religious predilections, if they are not too exotic, one is likely to find some accommodation.

In summary, Cyprus is an interesting and comfortable place in which to live, work and raise a family. This is true both for those whose perspective is long-term and for those who foresee a more limited stay. Its history is varied and colourful; its people are welcoming and creative; its future appears to be bright and stable. It will continue to be a bridge between East and West, a feature that, as it comes into the EU, will become ever more useful for businesses and other enterprises.

Part Six

Financial Environment

Banking and Finance in Cyprus

Sofronis Eteocleous, Manager, Economic Research & Planning, Laiki Bank

Introduction

Banking in Cyprus has a history of over 140 years. It is well developed, stable and has the leading role in financial intermediation. Under the new Central Bank of Cyprus law, which came into effect on 5 July 2002, the main tasks of the Central Bank are the following:

- the supervision of banks;
- the definition and implementation of monetary policy, including credit policy;
- the conduct of exchange rate policy;
- the holding and management of official international reserves;
- the promotion, regulation and oversight of the smooth operation of payments and settlement system;
- the performance of the tasks of banker and financial agent of the Government;
- the participation as a member in international monetary and economic organizations.

Although small in size compared to their international counterparts, Cypriot banks operate as fully-fledged universal banks, offering a wide range of products and services. Banks in Cyprus can be divided into four categories: commercial banks, specialized credit institutions, cooperative credit institutions and international banking institutions.

Commercial banks

At the end of 2002 there were 11 banks offering their services through a network of 484 branches, which correspond to around 0.7 of a branch per 1,000 inhabitants. Compared to the average of EU countries, which was below 0.5 of a branch per 1,000 inhabitants in 2001, it is evident that there is a high degree of branch density in the Cyprus market.

All commercial banks in the sector are privately owned, with no governmental participation in their capital. Of the 11 commercial banks five are locally incorporated – Bank of Cyprus, Cyprus Popular Bank, Hellenic Bank, Universal Bank and Co-operative Central Bank; four are foreign controlled – Alpha Bank, National Bank of Greece (Cyprus), Commercial Bank of Greece (Cyprus) and Société Générale (Cyprus); and two are operating as branches of foreign incorporated banks – Arab Bank and National Bank of Greece S.A. Four of the locally incorporated banks are public companies quoted on the Cyprus stock exchange; the exception being the Co-operative Central Bank.

The way the sector has developed over the years, with competition leading to rationalization, coupled with some takeover activity, has led to the creation of three large banks: the Bank of Cyprus, the Cyprus Popular Bank and the Hellenic Bank. These three banks at the end of 2002 accounted for 66 per cent of domestic banking assets, 71.8 per cent of lending and 67.9 per cent of deposits (of both commercial banks and specialized credit institutions).

Until a few years ago, commercial banks earned the largest part of their income through traditional banking services, such as retail, commercial and corporate banking. The rapid changes in the economic environment and the increasing competition, however, forced banks to expand and diversify beyond the boundaries of traditional banking. Banks have expanded to other financial services, like private banking, insurance, investment banking, underwriting of issues of capital, asset management and stock brokerage, either through the setting up of subsidiaries or through acquisitions. Both the range of products and the standard of services offered compare well with those of developed countries.

Recognizing that the domestic market offers limited opportunities for further growth and expansion, the Bank of Cyprus, the Cyprus Popular Bank and the Hellenic Bank have placed particular emphasis in recent years on the geographical diversification of their activities through overseas expansion. Greece has been the target market for all three, where many branches and subsidiaries have been set up. In addition, two of these banks have also set up branches in the United Kingdom and Australia, where the Greek community has a strong presence. The internationalization of operations is of strategic importance to these banks and is likely to intensify in the forthcoming years. Their efforts so far have had a positive impact on their growth and profitability.

Specialized credit institutions

There are currently three specialized credit institutions – the Cyprus Development Bank, the Housing Finance Corporation and the Mortgage Bank of Cyprus – offering their services through a network of seven branches as of end 2002.

The Cyprus Development Bank is a government-controlled company, established in 1963 to act as a catalyst for economic and social development. The Government's stake at the end of 2002 was approximately 88 per cent. The bank's activities aim at strengthening business entrepreneurship and competitiveness and supporting the expansion and intensification of value-added projects. Its core activities comprise banking and consulting.

The Housing Finance Corporation is also a government-controlled institution. It accepts deposits and provides loan facilities for housing, mainly to low- and middle-income households.

Lastly, the Mortgage Bank of Cyprus, which is a subsidiary of the Bank of Cyprus, provides medium- and long-term financing for housing, real estate development and industrial projects.

Structure of the consolidated balance sheet of domestic banks

Total assets of domestic banks (commercial and specialized) grew from CYP 6.9 billion (166 per cent of GDP) in 1996 to CYP 15.5 billion (251 per cent of GDP) in 2002 (see Table 6.1.1). This level is comparable to the average of the EU countries, which stood at 264 per cent of GDP in 2000.

Advances are the major assets of the banks, accounting for 53.2 per cent of total banking assets at the end of 2002. Lending between 1996 and 2002 grew at an average annual rate of 13.2 per cent, reaching CYP 8.3 billion, which was equivalent to 134 per cent of GDP. The level of bank credit is comparable to that of the United Kingdom, which stood at 131 per cent of GDP at the end of 2001. This is attributed to the protracted period of fiscal deficits and the accommodative monetary policy followed since 1974, as well as to the fact that the capital market in Cyprus is less developed. Excluding bills discounted, the bulk of credit (86.8 per cent) in 2002 was in local currency (see Table 6.1.2).

Table 6.1.1 Balance sheet of commercial and specialized banks (CYP million)

Assets	2002	% share	Liabilities	2002	% share
Balances with Central Bank	1,422.7	9.1	Deposits	11,997.9	77.1
Local cash	54.8	0.3	*Demand*	*1,087.8*	*7.0*
Foreign assets	3,169.8	20.4	*Savings*	*278.6*	*1.8*
Local investments	1,709.7	11.0	*Time*	*10,631.5*	*68.3*
Government	*1,345.1*	*8.6*	Foreign liabilities	505.3	3.2
Private	*364.5*	*2.4*	Capital & reserves	1,836.0	11.8
Advances	8,283.7	53.2	Other liabilities	1,229.4	7.9
Other assets	927.9	6.0			
Total	**15,568.6**	**100.0**	**Total**	**15,568.6**	**100.0**

Source: Central Bank of Cyprus

Regarding liabilities, customer deposits are by far the major liability of the banks, accounting for more than 77 per cent of total banking liabilities at the end of 2002 (see Table 6.1.1). Deposits grew from CYP 5.7 billion (138 per cent of GDP) in 1996 to almost CYP 12 billion (194 per cent of GDP) in 2002. Unlike advances, deposits are more evenly distributed among local and foreign currency. At the end of 2002, 67.9 per cent of deposits were in local currency and 32.1 per cent were in foreign currency (see Table 6.1.2).

With respect to the sectoral composition of credit, the loan portfolio of banks is well diversified (see Table 6.1.3). The bulk of credit at the end of 2002 (97 per cent) went to the private sector and only 3 per cent to public institutions. Personal and professional loans, which include loans to financial services companies, to individuals for the purchase of shares, hire purchase and credit cards, accounted for 42.9 per cent of total credit. Foreign and domestic trade loans accounted for 19.5 per

Table 6.1.2 Advances and deposits in local and foreign currency (CYP million)

	Advances		Deposits	
	2002	% share	2002	% share
Local currency	7,184.1	86.8	8,142.2	67.9
Residents	*7,146.0*	*86.3*	*7,437.7*	*62.0*
Non-residents	*38.1*	*0.5*	*704.5*	*5.9*
Foreign currency	1,092.4	13.2	3,855.7	32.1
Residents	*785.1*	*9.5*	*351.2*	*2.9*
Non-residents	*307.3*	*3.7*	*3,504.5*	*29.2*
Total	**8,276.5**	**100.0**	**11,997.9**	**100.0**

Source: Central Bank of Cyprus

cent of total credit, while loans with respect to the building and construction industry represent a share of 14.5 per cent. It is worth noting that in recent years the share of credit to the manufacturing sector has exhibited a declining trend. In 2002 the share of credit to the manufacturing sector was 6.8 per cent, compared with 12.5 per cent in 1995, which reflects the declining importance of manufacturing in the Cyprus economy. A declining trend, but not of the same magnitude, is exhibited by the tourism sector.

Loans are adequately secured with tangible collateral, mainly real estate. Each bank reviews the quality of its portfolio regularly in order to determine the level of provisions to be made for bad and doubtful debts. The adequacy of these provisions is examined thoroughly by the Central Bank.

Capital adequacy

All banking institutions, commercial and specialized, are subject to the capital adequacy requirements prescribed by the Central Bank, to which they are obliged to adhere. The minimum capital ratio required stands at 10 per cent, which is slightly higher in comparison to the 8 per cent recommended by the Basel Committee and the respective EU directive. At the end of 2001 the capital adequacy ratio in the banking system stood at 14 per cent, well above the minimum requirement, while for individual banks the ratio varied between 11.7 per cent and 21.9 per cent.

Table 6.1.3 Sectoral distribution of bank credit

Sector	1995 CYP m	% share	2002 CYP m	% share
Public institutions	82.5	2.4	248.5	3.0
Agriculture	82.8	2.4	112.9	1.4
Mining	13.9	0.4	27.0	0.3
Manufacture	430.6	12.5	560.8	6.8
Transport & communications	42.5	1.2	136.3	1.6
Foreign & domestic trade	842.2	24.5	1,614.6	19.5
Building & construction	566.0	16.5	1,198.9	14.5
Tourism	378.7	11.0	819.5	9.9
Personal & professional	982.4	28.5	3,558.0	42.9
Bills discounted	22.0	0.6	7.2	0.1
Total	**3.443.6**	**100.0**	**8,283.7**	**100.0**

Source: Central Bank of Cyprus

Cooperative Credit Institutions

Cooperative Credit Institutions, which comprise Cooperative Credit Societies and Savings Banks, make up another important category of entities engaged in banking activities in Cyprus. Unlike, however, commercial and specialized credit institutions, cooperatives are mutually owned, non-profit organizations established to serve their members and the local communities. In addition, their activities are confined to the core banking services, loans and deposits, and their supervision is assigned by law to the Commissioner of Cooperative Development. At the end of 2002 there were 363 registered cooperatives, most of which are located in small villages – a figure of around 0.5 institutions per 1,000 inhabitants.

Cooperatives have witnessed a significant growth in recent years (see Table 6.1.4). Their total deposits between 1996 and 2002 grew at an average annual rate of 10 per cent, reaching CYP 3.5 billion (57 per cent of GDP) at the end of 2002. Total advances over the same period grew at an average annual rate of 7.1 per cent to almost CYP 2.7 billion (43 per cent of GDP). At the end of 2002, in terms of local currency deposits and lending, cooperatives had a share of 30.1 per cent and 27.1 per cent, respectively.

With respect to the loan portfolio of cooperatives, credit is allocated to four different sectors: housing, personal and professional, agricultural and other. The bulk of all lending, more than 50 per cent, goes to the housing sector.

International Banking Institutions

This group of banking institutions currently comprises 30 banking units, of which 28 are International Banking Units (IBUs) and two are

Table 6.1.4 Cooperative Credit Institutions – total deposits and advances

	Deposits CYP m	% change	Advances CYP m	% change
1996	1,976.2	9.7	1,838.0	11.3
1997	2,188.1	10.7	1,991.2	8.3
1998	2,416.3	10.4	2,132.8	7.1
1999	2,570.6	6.4	2,410.2	13.0
2000	2,821.5	9.8	2,483.9	3.1
2001	3,109.0	10.2	2,519.0	1.4
2002	3,513.0	13.0	2,672.0	6.1

Source: Central Bank of Cyprus

Administered Banking Units (ABUs). IBUs/ABUs were originally confined to dealings in foreign currencies with non-residents. As from 1 January 2001, and in the context of financial liberalization, these institutions are permitted without restriction to grant medium- and long-term loans or guarantees in foreign currencies to permanent residents. It is expected that in the future these banking institutions will be permitted to carry on additional activities including the taking of deposits in local currency. All distinctions between domestic and offshore banks will be eliminated by 31 December 2005.

IBUs are required to operate as fully staffed units and can take the form of a branch or a subsidiary of a bank already established in a foreign jurisdiction. There are currently 24 branches and four subsidiaries. ABUs are required to carry on banking business in their own name, but their day-to-day administration is carried out on their behalf by another bank, which must be already licensed by the Central Bank of Cyprus to operate in or from within Cyprus. The total assets of IBUs and ABUs at the end of May 2002 stood at CYP 5.5 billion, of which 36 per cent represented claims on banks, 32 per cent advances, 26 per cent investments and 6 per cent other assets.

Concluding remarks

The environment in which Cypriot banks operate has changed immensely in the past couple of years, due to the process of harmonization with the *acquis communautaire*. The most important changes relate to the introduction of a regime of floating interest rates, the gradual abolition of restrictions on capital movements and the adoption of the freedom of establishment and the freedom to provide services. These changes have altered fundamentally the business environment and created new opportunities and challenges for banks.

The new environment has increased competitive pressures and potential risks. Competition is expected to intensify even further as a result of EU accession and the complete liberalization of capital movements. The key challenges for banks in the new environment are to improve their operational efficiency whilst addressing staff costs. Diversification of earning capacity, strengthening of risk management systems, exploitation of technology, promotion of Internet banking, improving quality of service and continuous development of human resources are becoming more imperative.

The outlook for Cypriot banks is positive. They are adequately capitalized and financially sound and have shown in the past they have the ability to adapt to changing conditions.

Anti-money-laundering Measures in the Banking and International Business Sectors

Central Bank of Cyprus

The Prevention and Suppression of Money Laundering Activities Law (the Law), enacted in 1996, places special responsibilities upon banks and financial institutions. Banks, as well as other persons engaged in financial business, are required to adhere to prescribed procedures for customer identification, record keeping and internal reporting, as well as to ensure that employees handling financial business are aware of their obligations under the Law and receive adequate training designed to assist them in recognizing money-laundering transactions. They are also required to appoint fully qualified persons as 'Money Laundering Compliance Officers'. Failure to comply with these requirements amounts to an offence punishable with imprisonment, a fine, or both.

The Law designates the Central Bank of Cyprus as the competent supervisory authority for all banks operating in Cyprus and has assigned to it the responsibility for ensuring a bank's due compliance with the provisions of the Law.

In this respect, the Central Bank of Cyprus' requirements have been embodied in a relevant 'Guidance Note' issued to both domestic banks and international banking units, under the provisions of the Law. These requirements are:

- Banks should seek and obtain satisfactory evidence of a customer's identity at the time of establishing an account relationship and prior to the execution of any banking transactions.

- The identification of both personal and corporate customers should be made by obtaining documents issued by reputable sources; for natural persons this includes a national identity card, a passport or, for example, utility bills and, for corporate customers certificates of incorporation, or other documents such as a Memorandum and Articles of Association.

- In the case of corporate customers, other than public companies listed on recognized stock exchanges, customer identification aims at verifying the identity of the natural persons who are the company's ultimate beneficial shareholders and controllers and, in all cases, the identity of all signatories to an account. (Such procedures do not imply that companies may not have nominee shareholders as provided under the Cyprus Companies Law).

- Banks may open accounts for bearer share companies provided that:
  - the bank takes physical custody of the bearer share certificates;
  - the identity and background of the beneficial shareholders is ascertained;
  - the business introducer of the account, such as a lawyer or accountant, confirms, at least once every year, that the company's capital base and shareholding structure has not been altered.

In the case of accounts in the name of trusts and nominees of third persons, banks are required to establish the identity of all settlors and true beneficiaries and the person(s) on whose behalf the nominee is acting.

Banks are prohibited from accepting cash deposits in foreign currency notes from a customer or group of connected customers in excess of USD 100,000 or equivalent per calendar year without the prior written approval of the Central Bank of Cyprus.

Banks have been instructed to keep a copy or references of a customer's identification documents as well as supporting evidence and records that will enable an investigator to retrace the path of criminal proceeds. Furthermore, when banks are effecting the transfer of funds by electronic means (eg by SWIFT), they are required to identify the names, addresses and account numbers of both the ordering and beneficiary customers.

All banks in Cyprus, both domestic and International Banking Units, are required to submit to the Central Bank of Cyprus a monthly statement of cash deposits and transfers of funds under which the following are reported:

- all cash deposits in Cyprus pounds in excess of CYP 10,000 in the case of domestic banks, and in foreign currencies in the case of both domestic banks and International Banking Units, in excess of USD 10,000;

- all unusual funds transfers in excess of USD 10,000 or equivalent;

- all their customers' incoming and outgoing transfers, and not only unusual such transfers, in excess of USD 500,000 or equivalent;

- the total turnover of customers' accounts whose cumulative annual inward and outward transfers exceed USD2 million;

- a list containing particulars of customers' cash deposits in foreign currency notes in excess of USD 100,000 or equivalent for which the Central Bank's prior written approval has been obtained.

Furthermore, all banks are expected to keep computerized accounting systems so as to enable them to identify immediately all cash deposits in excess of the limits set.

The Central Bank of Cyprus has also been appointed by the Council of Ministers under the provisions of the Law to act as the supervisory authority for all persons involved in the provision of international non-banking financial business from within Cyprus – international financial services and trustee services companies as well as managers and trustees of international collective investment schemes. A 'Guidance Note', similar to that applicable to banks, has been issued by the Central Bank under the Law to cover customer identification and record keeping procedures, staff training policies and the duties of 'Money Laundering Compliance Officers'.

In the non-banking and non-financial international business sector, the Central Bank operates a strict regulatory framework aimed at eliminating the abuse of the sector by criminals. Non-banking and non-financial international business enterprises authorized under Cyprus' Exchange Control Law are required to:

- divulge the names of their beneficial owners to the Central Bank of Cyprus;

- submit bank references on behalf of their beneficial owners from banks located in the owners' home countries;

- prepare and submit annual accounts to the Central Bank of Cyprus, after they have been audited by Cyprus-based accountancy firms;

- file with the Central Bank a confidential annual return which provides information on the company's directors, expatriate employees, financial highlights, analysis of local expenditure and local presence details;

- obtain temporary residence or employment permits for their expatriate employees, which can be revoked if expatriates are discovered to be involved in unlawful activities.

Cyprus' Anti-money-laundering Laws and Procedures have been assessed by a number of international bodies including:

- The Council of Europe in 1998, which concluded that Cyprus should be highly commended for the generally sound and comprehensive manner in which it adopted measures in line with international standards and should be congratulated for the very comprehensive legal framework put in place. The report noted also that Cyprus' anti-money-laundering system compares favourably with others in place in larger countries that are members of the Financial Action Task Force (FATF).

- The FATF, in its report in June 2000, which recognized that the anti-money-laundering system of Cyprus was in line with international standards and excluded Cyprus from the published list of 'non-cooperative jurisdictions'.

- The International Monetary Fund (IMF), whose report in August 2001 indicated unequivocally Cyprus' high level of banking supervisory and regulatory standards applied to the international banking and financial services sectors.

6.3

Insurance in Cyprus

Sofronis Eteocleous, Manager, Economic Research and Planning, Laiki Bank

Introduction

The sector is, as in most countries, divided into life and general (non-life) insurance provided both by separate and composite companies. At the end of 2002 there were 42 companies licensed to transact business, of which 29 were local and 13 were non-local. The Office of the Superintendent of Insurance, under the Minister of Finance, supervises the functioning of all insurance companies.

The industry witnessed a significant growth in 1999, due to the stock exchange boom, during which the total premium income written increased by 113.5 per cent to CYP 436.5 million (see Table 6.3.1). During the period 2000–02 the continuous decline in share prices had an adverse impact on the sector. The life business was particularly hit, owing to the limited demand for single premium policies. Total premium income written in 2000 declined by 25.4 per cent, while a further 19.7 per cent decline was recorded in 2001. Total premiums written by local companies in 2001 accounted for 85.6 per cent of the market, compared to only 14.4 per cent written by non-local companies.

Despite the decrease observed, the insurance industry plays a significant role in economic activity. Total insurance premiums in relation to GDP in 2001 reached 4.4 per cent, a figure that places Cyprus in thirty-first position in the global insurance industry. In comparison to the EU average (9 per cent) it is evident that there is room for further growth in the market. Total premiums per capita amounted to CYP 385.8 in 2001 (see Table 6.3.2), a figure that is well below the EU average (CYP 1,220) but which nevertheless places Cyprus in thirtieth position in the international insurance industry.

It is also important to note that insurance companies are a major institutional investor. Total investments held by insurance companies as at the end of June 2001 stood at CYP 887.5 million (see Table 6.3.3), which was equivalent to 15.1 per cent of GDP. This figure, however, is

Table 6.3.1 Insurance premiums

	1997	1998	1999	2000	2001
CYP m					
Life premiums	98.6	111.1	338.7	219.2	144.5
Non-life premiums	87.2	93.3	97.8	106.5	117.0
Total	**185.8**	**204.4**	**436.5**	**325.7**	**261.5**
% change					
Life premiums	12.3	12.8	204.7	–35.3	–34.1
Non-life premiums	9.2	7.0	4.8	8.9	9.9
Total	**10.9**	**10.1**	**113.5**	**–25.4**	**–19.7**
% of GDP					
Life premiums	2.2	2.3	6.7	4.0	2.4
Non-life premiums	2.0	1.9	1.9	1.9	2.0
Total	**4.2**	**4.3**	**8.7**	**5.9**	**4.4**

Source: Insurance in Cyprus 2001: Directory and Statistical Information

Table 6.3.2 Density of insurance (CYP)

	1997	1998	1999	2000	2001
Life premiums per capita	149.8	167.6	508.0	326.6	213.2
Non-life premiums per capita	132.6	140.7	146.7	158.7	172.6
Total premiums per capita	282.4	308.3	654.7	485.3	385.8

Source: Insurance in Cyprus 2001: Directory and Statistical Information

well below the EU average recorded in 2001 (52.7 per cent). In terms of the investments held by insurance companies in equities, these accounted for 4.9 per cent of the stock market's capitalization.

Lastly, it is important to note that in 2002 the new Insurance Companies Law was passed, which brought Cyprus into full compliance with the EU directives on insurance. The new insurance

Table 6.3.3 Investments of insurance companies, June 2001 (CYP million)

	1997	1998	1999	2000	2001
Total investments	369.4	434.1	518.8	1.084.4	887.5
Investments to GDP	8.5	9.2	10.4	19.2	15.1
Investments in equities	59.6	75.4	100.5	467.0	280.2
Share in market capitalization	5.7	6.3	4.2	4.7	4.9

Source: Insurance in Cyprus 2001: Directory and Statistical Information

legislation envisages stricter supervision and is expected to improve the environment in which insurance companies operate.

Life insurance

In 2002 there were 12 companies licensed to transact life business, of which ten were local and two were non-local. From 1999 onwards, developments in the life insurance market have been directly related to the substantial fluctuations recorded in share prices. Life premiums in 1999 recorded an increase of 204.7 per cent (see Table 6.3.1). In contrast, the tendency in 2000 and 2001 was negative, as life premiums declined by 35.3 per cent and 34.1 per cent, respectively. As a result, the share of life premiums to total premium income dropped from 67.3 per cent in 2000 to 55.2 per cent in 2001. In 2001 life premiums written by local companies accounted for 88.8 per cent of the market, while non-local companies accounted for the remaining 11.2 per cent. The ratio of life insurance premiums to GDP decreased from 4.0 per cent in 2000 to only 2.4 per cent in 2001 (see Table 6.3.1). The same ratio in the EU stood at 5.9 per cent. Life premiums per capita amounted to CYP 213.2 (see Table 6.3.2), while the EU average stood at CYP 803.5 in 2001.

Currently there is great concentration in the life sector, mainly from bank-controlled insurance companies. In 2001 the three largest companies, Laiki Cyprialife, Eurolife and Universal Life, accounted for 75.8 per cent of total life premium income. The top five companies accounted for almost 89 per cent of the life insurance market. Bank-related insurance organizations wrote 57.2 per cent of life premiums, compared to 61.9 per cent in 2000.

Life class investments represent the main part of the total investments made by insurance companies (see Table 6.3.4). At the end of June 2001, total investments by life insurance companies stood at CYP 795.9 million, compared to CYP 959.4 million a year earlier, which in relation to GDP amounted to 13.5 per cent. Investments in equities account for the largest part of the portfolio of life insurance companies (33.9 per cent), followed by government bonds (18.8 per cent).

Non-life insurance

The general insurance sector comprised 30 companies in 2002, of which 19 were local and 11 were non-local. In contrast to life premiums, non-life premiums have been growing steadily during the past few years (see Table 6.3.1). The total non-life premiums between 1997 and 2001 grew at an average annual rate of 8 per cent, reaching CYP 117 million in 2001 (2.0 per cent of GDP). The same ratio in EU

Table 6.3.4 Breakdown of investments, June 2001 (CYP million)

	Life	Non-life	Total	% share
Equities	270.3	9.9	280.2	31.6
Government bonds	149.7	20.9	170.6	19.2
Corporate bonds	18.7	3.6	22.3	2.5
Bank deposits	98.0	43.9	141.9	16.0
Overseas investments	110.9	5.6	116.5	13.1
Real estate	34.1	3.8	37.9	4.3
Policy loans	91.7	–	91.7	10.3
Mortgages	21.8	–	21.8	2.5
Central Bank	0.7	3.9	4.6	0.5
Total	**795.9**	**91.6**	**887.5**	**100.0**

Source: Insurance in Cyprus 2001: Directory and Statistical Information

countries stood at 3.07 per cent. As a result of the increasing non-life business, the share of non-life premiums to total premium income improved from 32.7 per cent in 2000 to 44.8 per cent in 2001. In 2001 non-life premiums written by local companies accounted for 81.7 per cent of the market, while non-local companies accounted for the remaining 18.3 per cent. Per capita premium amounted to CYP 172.6 (see Table 6.3.2), while the EU average stood at CYP 417.1 in 2001.

The general insurance sector is less concentrated than the life sector. The top three non-life companies, Laiki Insurance, General Insurance of Cyprus and Minerva Insurance, controlled 34.7 per cent of the non-life premium income in 2001, while the top five controlled 46 per cent. Bank-related non-life insurance companies wrote 45.2 per cent of general insurance premiums, compared to 46.4 per cent in 2000.

Non-life insurance business comprises six different classes (see Table 6.3.5). The motor vehicle insurance business is the most important class of general insurance, although its share in terms of premiums declined from 52.8 per cent in 1997 to 45.3 per cent in 2001. Motor is also the most competitive class, with 25 companies active in the business. In terms of concentration, the ten largest companies offering motor insurance services controlled 73.5 per cent of the premium income in 2001. Fire insurance and accident and health insurance are also important classes of non-life business, representing 18.1 per cent and 16.9 per cent of the general business premiums written during 2001.

Concluding remarks

The insurance sector has faced a difficult environment over the past three years. This is mostly attributed to the sharp decline of share

Table 6.3.5 Non-life premiums by class

	1997	1998	1999	2000	2001
CYP m					
Motor	46.0	47.7	48.5	51.9	53.0
Fire	15.1	16.3	17.0	18.8	21.1
Accident & health	11.9	13.1	15.3	16.2	19.8
Employers' liability	4.9	5.2	5.0	5.1	5.9
Marine, aviation & transit	4.4	5.3	5.8	7.7	9.4
Miscellaneous	4.9	5.7	6.2	6.8	7.8
Total	**87.2**	**93.3**	**97.8**	**106.5**	**117.0**
% share in total					
Motor	52.8	51.1	49.6	48.7	45.3
Fire	17.3	17.5	17.4	17.7	18.1
Accident & health	13.7	14.0	15.6	15.2	16.9
Employers' liability	5.6	5.6	5.1	4.8	5.0
Marine, aviation & transit	5.0	5.7	5.9	7.2	8.0
Miscellaneous	5.6	6.1	6.4	6.4	6.7
Total	**100.0**	**100.0**	**100.0**	**100.0**	**100.0**

Source: Insurance in Cyprus 2001: Directory and Statistical Information

prices and the extremely competitive market. Nevertheless, the prospects for the insurance sector are promising. The new insurance legislation, which is in line with the EU directives and became effective from January 2003, has strengthened the regulatory framework. The process of consolidation is expected to start sooner rather than later as there is a proliferation of small insurance companies and it is considered essential that bigger and stronger economic entities are created more able to cope with the increased competitive pressures that will emerge as a result of EU accession.

6.4

The Cyprus Development Bank

The Cyprus Development Bank

Introduction

Cyprus Development Bank (CDB) is an internationally respected financial institution, dedicated to offering clients the kind of personal, interactive service that goes beyond traditional banking and financing, to include strategic business advice and technical support. Its mission is to be a differentiated banking institution.

CDB commenced operations in 1963 as a wholly government-owned entity. Even though government owned, it has always retained a considerable degree of autonomy. Today, its shareholders are the Cyprus Government (88 per cent) and the European Investment Bank (12 per cent).

When CDB was established, its purpose was to promote the economic development of Cyprus through the mobilization and allocation of scarce human and capital resources. To this end, it aimed at establishing or restoring and strengthening the competitiveness of the sectors it supported. Its focus has traditionally been corporate entities, existing or new, from all productive sectors of the economy.

During its initial years, CDB provided financial support, primarily in the form of long-term loans and equity capital. It was the first bank in Cyprus to provide seed capital and equity participation to a number of Cypriot companies and to act as a catalyst and facilitator in their growth. Later, consultancy services were introduced and were directed towards helping clients to solve a wide variety of problems in the fields of project management, new business development and strategic management.

Today, CDB provides a broader range of financial instruments and corporate finance services. Its comprehensive range of products and services includes corporate banking, project finance, equity finance, strategic and business advisory services, treasury products and services as well as asset and portfolio management. In providing this array of products and services, the Bank always ensures a commitment to a long-term business relationship with each client, from initial concept to final implementation and beyond.

In addition to providing finance and advice to the business sector, CDB has pioneered innovative projects in the areas of the environment, information technology and education. It also cooperated with scientific and business associations for carrying out research, primarily into economic and financial subjects. Moreover, it has contributed to the broader social and cultural life of the island, selectively providing financial support to activities of its particular interest. Indicatively, it has sponsored the publication of literary works, seminars and symposia as well as sports events.

The first ten years

During the first ten years of its operation, CDB mainly financed projects in the manufacturing and tourism sectors. Following the Turkish invasion of Cyprus in 1974, which paralysed the local economy, CDB had to write off 47 per cent of its loans and about 30 per cent of its equity investments and faced a perilous future.

The Cyprus Government, recognizing that the Bank had an important role to play in reactivating the Cyprus economy, introduced special measures for restoring CDB's creditworthiness under the title 'Scheme of Arrangement of May 1996'.

Financial assistance and support to viable small scale manufacturing industries was one of the basic objectives of CDB after the Turkish invasion. In collaboration with the Ministry of Commerce and Industry, the Bank established a specialized section within the organization to deal with the financing and related problems of these enterprises.

Steady growth and profitability

The years between 1976 and 1986 were significant years in the evolution and further growth of CDB in its dual role as a development and a financial institution. In line with its corporate philosophy of constantly re-examining and adapting its functions to accord with market needs, CDB adopted a liberal lending policy and expanded its technical and managerial consultancy capability.

The value of loans approved rose sharply through the 1970s and 1980s and profitability was restored. Additional professional staff were recruited and new activities were introduced.

More specifically, in 1984, a separate division was established within the Bank to channel its traditional consultancy services and spearhead growth into new areas of management consultancy. The wide range of assignments undertaken by CDB's consultancy division in subsequent years covered feasibility studies, project and construction management, market and strategic planning, business appraisals, corporate turnarounds, management audits, asset valuations and executive recruitment.

The consultancy services offered by the Bank contributed substantially to the restructuring and modernization of both the hard and soft infrastructure of the Cyprus economy, thereby enhancing the competitiveness and efficiency of private enterprises and public sector entities, whilst also assisting in the internationalization of the former.

In the early 1980s, the Bank took various initiatives in regard to the establishment of a stock exchange in Cyprus; it was involved in the completion of the draft Enabling Law 'to provide for the development of the Securities Market in Cyprus and the establishment and operation of the Cyprus Stock Exchange', which was submitted to the Government for consideration and appropriate action. In 1982, the Cyprus Investment and Securities Corporation (CISCO), a project conceived and actively promoted by CDB, was incorporated as a joint venture between the Bank of Cyprus (Holdings) Limited, the International Finance Corporation (an agency of the World Bank) and CDB.

Developing and diversifying

By the mid-1980s, CDB had branched out into other new fields, the most important being the establishment of a centre, initially called the Small Business Activity Unit, for providing services to small- and medium-sized enterprises (SMEs).

It is internationally acknowledged that SMEs form the backbone of every economy and in this Cyprus is no exception. It is estimated that 99.7 per cent of all businesses on the island are in this category (applying the EU definition for SMEs, ie those companies employing less than 250 employees). Through its SME Centre, CDB has been providing total solutions to small- and medium-sized enterprises all over Cyprus, including the provision of fixed-term loans and equity and the taking of deposits.

In 1985, further developments took place including the formation of new activities to handle the Bank's equity and venture capital operations as well as the identification and development of business opportunities.

Consultancy and management services at the forefront of activities

During the 1990s, CDB provided valuable consultancy services to semi-governmental organizations and municipalities and executed a number of studies and government projects, including harmonization studies on behalf of the Cyprus Government for five important sectors of the economy: industry, air transport, shipping and maritime, telecommunications and postal services. Information technology (IT) was also an area of intense activity, as CDB carried out a study on the development of a national IT strategy for Cyprus, co-sponsored by the UNDP.

In 1990, Novasys Information Services Limited was established by the Bank to offer specialized information technology services to the Government and the business community. One of the important assignments completed by Novasys was the computerization of the operations of various government departments. Novasys also undertook computerization work for Cyprus Airways and the Cyprus Stock Exchange and was involved in the development and provision of a wide range of software applications in the region.

Focusing on maintaining the balance between development and environment, CDB established the 'Enalion Environmental Management Centre', in 1991. Enalion was involved in environmental impact studies and ecosystem analysis, as well as in studies on air pollution and waste management. For about five years, it offered advice to both the private and the public sectors and was involved in environment-related research in Cyprus, as well as in research projects in the other countries bordering the Mediterranean, through a number of EU-funded programmes.

In the early 1990s, CDB established the Cyprus International Institute of Management (CIIM), a postgraduate business school of the highest standard. CIIM's objective is to enhance management capabilities not only in Cyprus but also in the wider region of Eastern Mediterranean and thus contribute to the upgrading of business competitiveness.

The European Investment Bank (EIB) acquires a 5.5 per cent share of CDB

The specialized nature of CDB's business made it essential to maintain a sound and strong capital base by adding new share capital. Therefore, in 1991, CDB ceased to be 100 per cent government owned, as the European Investment Bank acquired a 5.5 per cent of its Bank's share capital. The EIB's participation increased to 12 per cent at the end of 1996.

Preparing for Europe

In view of Cyprus' intended accession to the EU, the Bank established the EC Centre in 1992, aimed at linking local businessmen with their counterparts in Europe. To facilitate these efforts, it became the financial intermediary for the EC International Investment Partners Scheme (ECIP), which it operated successfully for ten years. Moreover, CDB was linked with BC-Net, a computerized system of the European Commission, identifying counterparts for a wide range of business dealings within the EU and in a number of third countries. Additionally, during the period between 1992 and the late-1990s the Bank became involved in a large number of European programmes as a consultant, promoter or partner in the areas of technology, environment and education.

In anticipation of Cyprus' entry into the EU and of client needs post-EMU entry, the Bank has been offering, since the mid-1990s, a wide range of foreign currency loans, predominantly Euro-denominated, as well as investment products in foreign currencies, for retail and institutional investors, including capital guaranteed bonds, mutual funds and hedge funds.

A period of diverse achievements

During the last ten years, CDB strengthened its international network of banking and other institutions with a view to investing and providing services, not only in Cyprus but also on an international level.

One of its biggest ventures abroad was the establishment of the Investment Bank of Kuban (IBK) in 1999, with 25 per cent participation by the European Bank for Reconstruction and Development (EBRD). The aim was to assist the development of the region of Krasnodar through financing of private initiatives, as well as infrastructural works and projects.

Another significant international assignment, delegated to CDB by the European Commission in 1999, was the restructuring of the Palestinian Development Fund (PDF) and its upgrading to a bank.

Since 1998, the centre of interest has been Greece, where CDB, mainly in the form of joint ventures with local investors and leading international banking institutions, invested in several projects in the sectors of tourism, consultancy, IT and telecommunications. CDB also financed Cypriot companies wishing to expand their operations to Greece.

In addition to being active internationally, CDB continued to develop new capabilities in Cyprus. A new business unit, Project

Financing, was set up in 1996 to cater for the need for structured finance and to preserve and further enhance the excellent track record which CDB had built over the years in the assessment of project risk and the financing of major capital investment projects. Project finance was provided to new projects in the public as well as the private sector. The recent trends towards changing the methods in which the public sector undertakes and finances capital investment projects, such as the Private Finance Initiative (PFI), have brought to the fore CDB's expertise in project risk assessment and its capability to play a leading role in arranging competitive packages for the financing of public sector projects.

For the last ten years and as part of its consultancy services to the public sector, CDB has been supporting the Government in its efforts to strengthen Cyprus' telecommunications activities and to transform the island into a regional centre. Specific assignments included, amongst others, the review of the Government's telecommunications policy and the assessment of the viability of regional telecommunications satellite systems for the provision of mobile communication and broadcasting services to Central and Eastern Europe, the Middle East and Africa. These projects were carried out in cooperation with international organizations in the fields of telecommunications, banking and the satellite industry. More recently, the Bank also participated in HELLAS-SAT Consortium Limited, a Greek/Cypriot joint venture that owns and operates a telecommunications satellite system.

From a development bank to a corporate banking institution

Today, after 40 years in operation, CDB continues to maintain the corporate culture of a small bank, with emphasis on person-to-person banking.

The expansion of its range of products and services is gradually transforming it into a corporate banking institution tailored to business customers' individual requirements. In the very near future, CDB proposes to introduce additional commercial banking services, integral to its existing portfolio of corporate products and services. Furthermore, the Bank will continue to provide specialist advice and focused fund management services for institutional and corporate investors.

CDB is widely recognized as a differentiated bank, which offers financing solutions to major corporates and institutions for the execution of pioneering large projects, as well as to active SMEs with modest resources. Given its expertise and extensive experience, the Bank is in a position to assess each investment individually and determine its potential, prior to designing customized and highly competitive financial products, which are differentiated in terms of duration, repayment and structure, compatible with the clients' financial needs, means and abilities.

In today's liberalized marketplace, the pursuit of competitiveness is a burning issue, not just locally but globally. Recognizing this, the Cyprus Development Bank seeks to guide and direct clients towards internationalization, primarily by financing Cypriot companies wishing to expand their operations outside Cyprus, be it in Greece, Europe or the Middle East.

Adhering strictly to commercial disciplines and best international practice, CDB will continue to consolidate its role as an influential bank in Cyprus, offering a comprehensive range of services to the local and international business community.

6.5

Cyprus Securities and Exchange Commission

Dr Marios Clerides, Chairman, Cyprus Securities and Exchange Commission

Introduction – legal framework

The Cyprus Securities and Exchange Commission (the Commission) in its present form was created in April 2001, with the enactment of the Securities and Exchange Commission legislation that came into force in June 2001. The law set up the commission as an independent government body and has entrusted it with the supervision and regulation of the Cyprus capital market.[1]

Duties, responsibilities and powers

The main duties and responsibilities of the Commission emanate from the above mentioned legislation and include, among others, supervision and control of the operation of the Cyprus Stock Exchange and of the transactions carried out on the Exchange.

The Securities and Exchange Commission legislation, together with other capital market legislation (legislation on insider trading, the regulation of collective investments schemes, investment services, initial public offerings and anti-money-laundering legislation), also place on the Commission duties to combat and investigate insider trading, license and supervise the operation of collective investment schemes, license and supervise the providers of investment services, supervise the activities of public companies (including closed-ended investment companies) from the point of publication of the prospectus through to their ongoing obligations (publication of accounts, disclosure and use of accounting standards). Lastly, but not least, the

---

1. The Commission was operating under a much more restricted regime emanating from the Stock Exchange legislation.

Commission monitors the capital market for market manipulation, money laundering and other activities detrimental to the good order of the market.

In order to be able to carry out its duties the Commission is empowered to undertake investigations, assign to approved auditors audits of companies subject to the Commission's control, call witnesses, collect information necessary for the exercise of its statutory responsibilities, obtain documents, issue bye-laws, impose fines and to cooperate and exchange information with other supervisory and enforcement bodies or agencies both in Cyprus and overseas.

Organizational structure

The commission is run by a five-member board, two of which, the chairman and vice-chairman, are full time executive members while the remaining three are non-executive. Additionally, the Central Bank of Cyprus has an observer on the board.

The commission is organized on a functional basis reflecting its key responsibilities with units responsible for:

- the licensing and monitoring of investment firms (basically, brokers, fund managers and own account traders);

- the licensing and monitoring of collective investment schemes;

- supervising listed companies from initial public offering to oversight of their ongoing, continuing obligations;

- market monitoring and enforcement (which carries out investigation for breaches of capital market legislation).

All these units are supported by an internal legal department, which is also responsible for the legal drafting of Commission bye-laws, amendments to the existing legislation and the introduction of new laws and regulations.

The Commission is manned by 35 personnel, who are mainly accountants, lawyers and economists.

As part of the process of joining the EU, Cyprus' legal and supervisory framework has been reviewed on behalf of the EU by other EU Capital Market Commissions to ascertain both the degree of harmonization and the competence of the Commission to perform its duties. The SEC was found to be fully harmonized and well able to fulfil its obligations in accordance with the framework laid down by the EU.

Current and future issues

The primary challenge that the Commission is currently facing is completion of the reformulation of the legal framework of the capital markets in Cyprus, in line with a 'blueprint' accepted by all interested parties – both market participants and political parties. The 'blueprint' separates completely the roles of the Securities Commission and the Stock Exchange. Under this framework the Commission assumes all the supervisory functions of the capital markets in Cyprus while the Stock Exchange assumes the organizational functions – trading systems, central depository, market organization (main market, parallel market and unlisted securities).

The entry of Cyprus to the EU has placed extra 'burdens' on the Commission to maintain the Cyprus capital market framework in line with the ever-changing EU framework, as Europe proceeds to integrate its financial markets further and further and to impose consistent regulation and supervision Europe-wide. The Commission already has, along with the rest of the newly acceding countries, observer status in the CESR (Committee of European Securities Regulators), the European body responsible for shaping the European Capital Market regime, and is expected to become a full member on Cyprus' joining the EU on 1 May 2004.

The longer term issue is that of a 'Single Financial Services Regulator' for Cyprus along the lines observed recently in Europe, with the regulators of banks, capital markets and the insurance sector merging into one overall financial market regulator, as the boundaries of what used to be three distinct markets become increasingly blurred and as market participants evolve ever increasingly into financial conglomerates.

6.6

The Cyprus Stock Exchange

The Cyprus Stock Exchange

The Cyprus Stock Exchange (CSE) commenced operations as a legal entity in the form of a public corporate body on the 29 of March of 1996 by virtue of the Cyprus Stock Exchange Laws and Regulations, which had been passed by the House of Representatives in 1993 and 1995 respectively.

The CSE is a regulated Exchange where all transactions of corporate and public securities are carried out. The securities that are traded include shares, warrants, corporate bonds (straight and convertible), treasury bills and government bonds. The main participants in the market are the Members of the Stock Exchange (stock brokerage firms), the listed issuers and the investors (institutional and private). The market is supervised by The Cyprus Securities and Exchange Commission (SEC).

The CSE aims to be a leading stock market in the region and to further expand into the wider European and international environment, to attract foreign investors and companies for listing and to be an advanced, developed and promising market based on strong foundations and modern infrastructure.

During the seven years since its establishment, progress has been rapid and unexpected for a newly established organization beginning from an almost zero base. In numerical terms the CSE commenced operations with 42 listed companies in 1996 and by the end of 2002 that figure had grown to 153, while market capitalization had risen from CYP 1,039,229,731 in 1996 to CYP 2,723,002,136 in 2002.

2002 can be characterised as a year of important developments and intense activities for the CSE as new legislation and amendments to the existing Stock Exchange Law and Regulations were passed, all in the context of harmonization with the relevant EU directives and continuously changing international developments.

Furthermore, within the framework of ongoing upgrading, the CSE, in September 2002, issued the Code of Corporate Governance for the

Cyprus Stock Exchange. The aim of the Code is the strengthening of the monitoring role of the Board of Directors, the protection of small shareholders, the adoption of greater transparency and the provision of timely information, as well as the safeguarding of the independence of the Board of Directors in their decision making. While the Code is voluntary for listed companies it is fully recognized that Corporate Governance rules and regulations form the main pillars of trust in mature markets and are very important for the stabilization and development of the CSE.

Among earlier important developments in CSE activities was the launching on 2 December 2000 of the entirely new index FTSE/CySE20, which was prepared in cooperation with the FTSE International organization. The Index, which was developed according to international standards, consists of the 20 most tradeable listed shares with the biggest market capitalization and with adequate free float of their shares and can be used in the future for trading of derivatives products. The CySE20 is comparable also to corresponding international indices and offers to investors a very good picture of the trend in the underlying listed securities. Also, in June 2003, the FTSE Med 100 Index was officially launched to represent the performance of the largest companies quoted on the markets of the Eastern Mediterranean region. Initially, the markets covered comprise Cyprus, Greece and Israel. The euro is the base currency of the Index, which is suitable also for derivatives trading.

Integral to the CSE's development and modernization was the introduction on 23 July 2001 of a fully computerized system, consisting of a Central Registry and a Central Depository, thereby computerizing all clearing and settlement procedures. As a result all securities are dematerialized and all transfers of securities, as well as any corporate actions, are run through a central electronic system at the Stock Exchange.

A further development over the last three years has been the strengthening of the relationship and links between the Cyprus and Athens Stock Exchanges specifically in regard to the ongoing exchange of know-how, technology issues, matters such as the establishment of a derivatives market in Cyprus and the dual listing of securities on the two Stock Exchanges. This was an integral step in the further improvement and development of the CSE in the framework of attaining strategic synergies with other Stock Exchanges.

The intense and dynamic presence of the CSE in the Cyprus economy is unquestionable, especially as a vehicle for attracting productive resources. Looking to the future the CSE seeks to broaden its horizons and to take its place within the mature markets of Europe.

Part Seven

Marketing in Cyprus

7.1

Advertising and the Media in Cyprus

Vasilis A P Metaxas, Managing Director,
Pyramis DDB

Introduction

It is a common axiom that the history of advertising is the history of mass media. Nowhere is this truer than in Cyprus. After languishing behind its European counterparts for the better part of the twentieth century, advertising on the island finally came of age in its last decade. This was, in the main, due to a media explosion.

Early steps

One cannot really talk of advertising in Cyprus until after independence in 1960, when the first agencies started to appear. They were not really ad agencies in the European mould; one should rather call them design shops. This reflected the media realities: Cyprus had only one TV channel and one radio station; both state-owned. They accepted advertisements, but the technology of the time imposed format limitations: film for TV and high-band magnetic tape for radio. While commercials for the latter could be produced locally if one had the money for actors/singers and a recording/mixing studio's fee (as likely as not the studio was the one maintained by state radio), there were no commercial film production facilities available. The closest source for this was Athens. Given the poor economy of the Republic's first decades, this meant that only the wealthiest advertisers, such as banks, could afford to have their own TV commercials. Other businesses, if they wanted moving images, had to rely on their foreign principals for ready-made material.

The solution that the vast majority of advertisers resorted to in order to have a TV presence was what became known as a 'slide': a still image complemented with words and music extolling the virtues of the featured product or service. Audio was looked after by journalists doubling as copywriters and, in reality, was no more than a typical radio script of the time. But the picture was key – possibly worth more than a thousand words to the general populace then – and for this you needed a good designer.

Good designers also came in handy given the third media category of that era: newspapers. Printing was coarse, but then, as now, Cyprus had a healthy complement of dailies. It is no wonder then that the advertising agencies were heavily reliant on artists for their services.

To be fair, media scarcity was not the sole reason that advertising agencies did not offer more than graphics with the occasional radio script thrown in. The market structure also played a part. It might come as a surprise to anyone used to European markets but in Cyprus, to this day, there are very few multinationals present. Their products or services have traditionally been available through exclusive local agents/distributors. As a consequence, the rigorous marketing disciplines and practices of the multinationals – and the resulting demands on advertising agencies – were until recently things of lore.

It might be argued that, should the multinationals have been present, they would have infused the market with competitive practices that would have brought about – among others – a multimedia environment. This would, in turn, have forced agencies to develop along the lines of their European counterparts. This is interesting speculation, but the fact remains: the picture remained relatively unchanged until practically the end of the 1980s.

The catalytic '90s

One of the Government's first steps after Cyprus' application for EU accession was to liberate the airwaves in 1989. Almost immediately the first private station, 'Radio SUPER', sprung up. Inexperience told, and it was to close down less than two years later having run in the red for most of its brief tenure. But it secured a glorious place in the island's media history as the first of all the private stations that were to follow, many of which proved to be quite successful.

In the same year, 1989, another earth-shattering change took place: the state TV company – still the only one on the island – upgraded its equipment to accept commercials in U-matic format. Video production being considerably cheaper than film, this meant that, suddenly, many smaller advertisers could afford their own TV commercials. It wasn't long before the 'slide' became an item of the past. It wasn't missed.

If anyone had been missing the signs, late-1992 heralded the new era, when the first private TV channel started broadcasting. 'LOGOS' (the 'Word'), belonged to the Church and beat everybody to the path. It wasn't successful; the public as it turned out had no taste for movies where all scenes with a hint of gender interaction had been censored. But, like Radio Super before it, LOGOS TV marked a new beginning. LTV followed in early 1993, then ANT1 and SIGMA; all broadcasting nationally. By 1996, regional channels started appearing. By necessity, viewer surveys were not long in coming.

The '90s also saw the emergence of magazines. The first to solidify a footing were TV Programmes guides, but a booming economy and more leisure time resulted in a host of general and specialized periodical publications by the end of the decade. Lastly, outdoor advertising appeared and, after a shaky start, now seems entrenched.

Suddenly, after three decades of being essentially commission agents, advertising agencies had to earn their money differently. With so many media partitioning the consumer's attention, clients had to spend more; they were now asking questions: where to advertise, how much, when, why? At the end of the day: how to have effective advertising.

The need for strategic communication planning, relevant and original creative expression, professional media planning and buying had arrived. Sadly, not all agencies could cope with the new set of rules. Those that adapted and survived are worthy of the title advertising agencies.

The ad agencies

Although the industry has come a long way in a short time, the reader should not look for the modern break-up of advertising services in Cyprus. In most of the Western world, clients expect to work with an agency for strategy/creative and go to specialized independents for media and below-the-line services. This is not yet the case in Cyprus (and it is doubtful it will be in the foreseeable future). All agencies are a one-stop shop. This is not as bad as it might seem, given the size of the market. It is even an advantage for businesses stationed abroad; it is arguably more efficient to communicate with one and the same team for all one's needs.

Excluding highly specialized services, such as public relations and interactive, all serious agencies in Cyprus are able to look after most clients' needs. Even where they cannot help, such as in implementing a research programme for example or building an exhibition stand, they will almost certainly help in seeking out a suitable supplier. For a fee, they can undertake to plan, organize and even supervise such projects, and this is something to consider if business dictates an absence from Cyprus for extended periods.

How to find an agency

If one has no referrals, there are a number of sources available at Cypriot embassies and consulates around the world (see Appendix 2: Useful Addresses and Telephone Numbers). The telephone directory is the obvious place to start, but if one wants to be more selective, the bigger agencies are listed in the 'Cyprus Services Directory', published bi-annually by OEB (the Employers and Industrialists Federation). Locally, one may contact the advertising practitioners' professional body, the 'Cyprus Ad Agencies Association', filed under the country's Chamber of Commerce and Industry. Founded in 1983 to promote the ad industry's standards, it has somehow failed to make an impact. Still, its secretary will gladly provide interested parties with a list of the association's members.

In choosing an agency, the first rule holds: have they responded quickly to the initial expression of interest? After that, it is not a bad idea to contact their clients for references; no client would risk losing credibility with a fellow businessman, even if a stranger. When meeting an agency, do not ask them just what they have done for other clients; ask them what they can do for you. Presentations of agency credentials can and tend to drag on.

Is size a factor? Yes and no. Media returns in Cyprus are to a degree an outcome of an agency's volume (of course, being a good paymaster is equally important, not all agencies are); a bigger agency will probably be able to secure a better media deal. On the other hand, unless a sizeable budget is available, the business will probably be more important to a smaller shop – with the resulting benefits. In the end, this is very much a question of the person who will be primarily responsible for handling the account. Ask to see him or her and get to know them.

Is previous experience a factor? Again, yes and no. It is reassuring to know an agency has worked with like products or services before; they should know pitfalls to avoid. But 'knowledge' might result in sterility of ideas too; a less-experienced outfit may prove more creative through lack of preconceived notions about what 'works' and what doesn't.

Sadly, there are no advertising industry competitions in Cyprus yet. It is therefore pointless to look for an agency that has won awards, either for creativity or effectiveness. The same goes for rankings, an agency-selection stepping stone in Europe and the Americas. Really, what one is left with is fundamentals such as history, client list and billings. Agencies are not required to publish figures and they don't, but any serious agency will gladly divulge its numbers so long as the interested client signs a confidentiality agreement. Given that the total market has an estimated value of USD 40 million, any agency that bills more than USD 3 million should be a reliable partner.

Lastly, a note on international advertising networks. By the end of the 1990s almost all were present on the island in one way or the other, with most of the top ten agencies now being connected to a network. The question of whether to choose a 'network agency' or a strictly local one rests on one's specific requirements. If, however, a potential client opts for the former, he might want to make sure that the agency in question is at least partly owned by the network. If, on the contrary, the international connection is only an affiliation, even one of many years standing, it might well be that the international standards anticipated are not there.

Media

The dominant presence on the island is DIAS Group. Owned by the Hadjicostis family, journalists by tradition, DIAS boasts an almost full complement of media. Its TV channel, SIGMA, is clearly the most popular, as is one of its radio stations, PROTO. But this honour it shares with RIK 3, a state station, and the only one to avoid the onslaught of private media.

The second most popular channel is ANT1, with programming connections to its namesake in Greece. Then comes MEGA, with even stronger ties to the Greek channel of the same name. At a distant fourth sits CyBC, the state TV. Once mighty, it has now been reduced to the role of an extra. Although it is the only broadcasting corporation to sport two channels, 'I' for information and 'II' for entertainment, it is very much devoid of advertising and relies on state aid for its survival.

One would do well to consider in one's plans LTV, the country's only Pay-TV channel broadcasting over the airwaves (not cable); by the latest estimates it boasts an impressive 18 per cent penetration of households, almost all ABC1. There is no cable TV in Cyprus and satellite TV has not as yet made significant in-roads. The material all channels accept is Beta SP.

Unless one is in a B2B line or needs to address messages strictly to older, educated men, TV in Cyprus cannot be ignored. With more than two sets per household and daily average viewing approaching three hours, it is by far the country's dominant medium. Again no official figures exist, but it is estimated that wholly three-fifths of all paid advertising is channelled through television. The category's popularity resulted in years past in 'ad clutter' deemed unacceptable. Finally the Radio-Television Authority had to step in and enforce the EU quota system of ad-time per broadcasting hour. It has taken the better part of the last three years to overcome the problem but stiff monetary penalties on deviators means that now one's ad is no longer lost in the crowd.

TV ad volume is nevertheless still big. To help agencies with TV planning, AGB entered the country in early 1998. Using a people-meters sample of 350 households and being monitored by an outside controlling body, it provides ratings information daily. All serious agencies are subscribers to its data; through it they can provide advertisers with numerous reports, such as competitive expenditure and strategies.

If any category has truly boomed it is the one of radio. The two foremost general-audience stations have been mentioned, but there are scores of others catering to more targeted listeners, even one for women (Radio *'Athina'*). The material all stations accept is CDs. Unfortunately, there is no reliable listener research available, but any serious agency will provide guidance on one's needs.

The newspapers category has somewhat declined in recent years, understandably perhaps in view of the proliferation of other media. Still, *Phileleftheros*, the oldest and still leading daily, sells close to 25,000 copies on weekdays and more than 50,000 every Saturday. This is quite an amazing ratio in terms of the island's population, compared to similar figures abroad. Other important papers are *Politis*, an independent, and *Simerini* and *Haravgi*, reflecting right- and left-wing parties' views respectively. Colour insertions are available but not on all days. Print quality tends to lag behind that of Europe. One thing to remember is that newspapers in Cyprus are read predominantly by males.

Mention must be made of foreign-language papers. The most important, *Cyprus Weekly*, comes out every Friday. Selling a healthy 15,000 copies, it caters largely to the island's foreign population. Papers and magazines in languages other than English are also published on the island, but publication dates tend to be erratic and circulation figures suspect.

As mentioned previously, magazines abound on the island. In contrast to the dailies they are an excellent medium to send an unhurried message to women and the younger generation. Unfortunately, official sales figures are available neither for magazines nor dailies; an effort a few years ago to establish an auditing body along the lines of the British ABC came to nought. But the good news as of 2003 is that, finally, reliable readership data is available for both of these media categories. Again, the surveys are carried out by AGB. Although not all agencies have subscribed to them, those that do are able to provide professional planning featuring the GRP, Reach and OTS indices.

Material accepted by print media is film and colour separations. It is a good idea to complement separations with a dry proof. This is no guarantee that the ad colours will be attained, but it helps one to ask for a free reprint in case of gross deviation.

Outdoor advertising used to be the poor relative. Available only on municipal sites and buses, it was run by civil servants and was left relatively wanting. In the mid-'90s, however, private companies started to offer outdoor sites of much better quality and at competitive prices. This prompted another explosion with the result that by the beginning of the twenty-first century all roads, rural as well as urban, were flooded with signs. Public outrage developed, in no small part fuelled by the environmentalists. Finally the matter was taken to Parliament, where, after numerous heated debates, legislation coding outdoor ad signs usage was passed in early 2003. Enforcing it will mean many sites will be torn down as illegal. The two players that seem certain to remain are ADBOARD and MEGA PANEL. Both offer attractive locations and a full complement of sign types, from pavement raquets to huge highway pisas, lighted or not. Material is accepted on a CD.

Following its international boom, the Internet quickly became popular in Cyprus too. As of 2003, it seems that close to 150,000 users exist. This is quite a substantial number given the country's population. Local sites, however, are not huge favourites: excluding a sports site most users surf abroad. It is thus questionable whether it pays to advertise on Cyprus Internet, even discounting the very low banner charges.

Compensation

The million-dollar question: how much to pay? Well, it is up to the client really – but a word of advice: do not drive too hard a bargain. No agency will knowingly accept a losing proposition, so if it turns out that one has squeezed too much, the agency may try to find other ways to stay in the black. In the best case scenario, service will suffer.

Keeping an agency motivated is even more crucial, given that a client will probably be out of the country most of the time. Additionally, the deals the agency will strike for any client, whether media or otherwise, are greatly dependent on its zest. And *that* any client wants to be high.

As a general guide it is suggested that a fee of 10–12 per cent is agreed on net media cost to cover strategic planning, account handling and media services. This, of course, presupposes the availability of a media budget. If one is not available and one's needs lie mostly elsewhere, a project consultancy and handling fee might be the best answer. In any case, creative and production work are paid for separately. Wages are not very high in Cyprus and services are consequently cheaper than in Western Europe. Expect to pay CYP 20 per hour for good creative work. For production, 10–15 per cent on supplier's cost should cover sourcing, planning, organization and supervision of material to be produced. In fact, this range of percentages holds good for any outside job an agency will undertake for a client. VAT currently stands at 15 per cent but if the invoiced party is outside Cyprus it is waived.

Summary

Advertising in Cyprus really came of age in the 1990s. This followed a media explosion, sparked by the liberation of the airwaves following the country's EU application. Developments were fast and furious, resulting in the creation of a multimedia environment and professional ad agencies. In contrast to Europe, agencies are one-stop shops, combining strategic planning and creative with media services. What they cannot handle in-house, agencies will take to a suitable partner. Almost all international ad networks are present in Cyprus, though most through affiliations. The country's dominant medium is TV, well represented by four national channels and one pay-TV channel. Their operations are controlled by a semi-governmental authority. There are numerous radio stations, national and local, and many established newspapers and magazines. Outdoor advertising, recently legislated, complements the mass media picture. All in all, one is able to target one's audience quite successfully. Media planners are aided by AGB, providing daily viewership data and quarterly readership figures. Suggested agency compensation for planning, creative and media services is 10–12 per cent on net media cost. If no media budget is available a project fee may be agreed. Creative is charged separately: expect to pay CYP 20 per hour for good work. For production, or any kind of need not covered above, 10–15 per cent on supplier's cost should cover sourcing, planning, organization and supervision of work.

7.2

Public Relations in Cyprus

Christina Pissi Patsalides, Director, Christian Alexander Public Relations & Event Planning

Background

The Cyprus business market is steadily becoming more sophisticated and therefore more demanding with regards to the field of communications. The island's forthcoming accession to the European Union is a major factor leading the public and private sectors to seriously consider investing in public relations (PR). This in turn has brought about the evolution of high standard PR and event management companies.

The business environment is changing so rapidly that engaging in PR is no longer a light affair but rather is recognized as crucial to any organization, more and more of which in Cyprus require the advice of PR professionals in terms of developing and applying a communication strategy that will depict the desired image of their organization.

With the upcoming competition in all the sectors of the economy, local organizations are realizing that PR is a job to be undertaken only by true professionals, especially those who have knowledge of all the elements comprising the marketing mix equation.

This major turning point in the perception of PR as a stand-alone profession has occurred only over the last five years. For many years PR was considered solely as a function to be executed by the marketing department and even then the person involved had little more than responsibility for entertaining guests of the organization or organizing dinners and cocktail parties. PR was also confused with media relations, with many people thinking that PR professionals are the experts who can influence the media to generate positive publicity for them.

As is appreciated internationally, PR is much more than media relations and has a broader role than event management, so the past five years have been very important in the shaping of the role of PR in Cyprus, since greater attention has been paid to it.

The majority of PR professionals in Cyprus entered the field from different backgrounds, such as marketing, advertising, sociology, business administration and certain other fields that are not even related to communications. It is only recently that youngsters have chosen to pursue PR as a profession and this is why most of the local colleges have only recently started to offer a degree in the subject, with the option to obtain a Masters Degree in Public Relations and Communications from well-known universities in Europe and the United States. Professionals who have entered the field during the last 10–15 years usually belong to accredited professional bodies such as the British Institute of Public Relations, the Public Relations Association of Greece or the Public Relations Association of Cyprus.

Overview of the PR market

PR is a profession that needs both focused specialists and generalists. In Cyprus one can find both. There are few independent PR consulting companies although there are some freelance PR professionals. Most large advertising companies have in-house PR departments and they offer total solution services to their clients, and large corporations frequently have in-house PR departments but also hire outside PR professionals when it comes to specific projects, such as communication strategy development, corporate identity improvement or image development.

PR in Cyprus is rarely used in isolation and in most cases is integrated with other marketing disciplines such as advertising and sales promotion. Usually PR campaigns come as a complement or extension to 'above the line' activities or, in some cases, solely to target specific audiences.

PR people in Cyprus, wherever they work, or whoever they work for, are sure to plan, manage, organize and administer as well as to write, edit, even produce. They also research, evaluate, make presentations and liaise with, even train others in their skills.

Large corporations and semi-governmental organizations

Large corporations and semi-governmental organizations have strong teams of communication specialists who undertake all major areas of PR within their own entities. Some corporations take this a step further by establishing a press relations office, which usually employs

one communications specialist and one or more journalists, special-
izing in the area of business of the corporation, such as financial,
medical or fashion.

Independent PR agencies

Independent PR agencies usually have five to ten employees, but
smaller PR companies with two or three employees are to be found.
Due to the size of the Cyprus market, independent PR agencies are few
in number and tend to cover the whole spectrum of PR, as they do not
limit their services to any specific area of expertise.

Such agencies tend to have close business relationships with advertising agencies and in some cases they work side by side on specific
projects. Public Relations companies also employ account executives or
account handlers who are responsible for liaison with clients.

Independent PR consultants in Cyprus are usually asked by clients
to work either on specific projects with clearly defined time frames or
to work on a yearly basis offering continuous support. In the first case
the independent agency's fee is quoted before the project starts and is
usually paid in two or three instalments, depending on the type of
project. In the second case the agency works on an annual retainer fee,
which provides for a 10–15 per cent increase each year.

Some of the key services the independent agencies offer include:

- development of corporate identity;
- communications strategy – planning and execution;
- image and social advertising;
- media relations;
- PR crisis management;
- event management;
- cause related marketing/sponsorships;
- fund-raising activities;
- employee relations and internal communications;
- writing and editing of newsletters and house journals;
- writing and editing of speeches;
- preparation of press releases and articles for distribution to all
  media.

Internal public relations

Internal communication is vital to employee performance and satisfaction. With the business environment becoming more and more
competitive, an increasing number of companies in Cyprus are coming
to realize the importance of internal PR, recognizing that internal
communication must be in line with the corporate communications
strategy. For this reason PR departments of large organizations also
have the responsibility for internal PR, working closely with the
human recourses department. One of the most frequently used tools of
internal PR in Cyprus is the corporate newsletter.

Sponsorships (cause related PR)

In the last decade sponsorships have gained increased attention from
organizations which, without any specific differentiation, have donated
money to different causes. Specifically, it was during the flourishing
period of the Cyprus Stock Exchange that companies realized that
good community relations could have a beneficial impact on the share
price. As time passed corporations came to realize that not all sponsorships add a positive image to their organization and not all donations
add to the company's reputation. As a result, companies have become
more selective recently when it comes to community relations, focusing
more on actions that impact directly on their desired target audiences.
A parallel benefit was also derived by PR companies from the rise in
the Stock market in 1999 and 2000, as it enabled them to become
specialists in stock exchange IPO campaigns.

Sponsorship programmes usually involve culture, sports and
charity. In many cases the organizations make their intentions known
through personal contacts or through a press campaign, but in many
cases cultural groups and organizers of cultural or sports events make
direct contact with companies, suggesting their projects and
requesting financial support. Semi-governmental organizations often
have fairly large amounts available for sponsorships in their annual
budgets, whereas all other organizations usually spend some 10 per
cent of their communications budget in this way.

Local media

PR Professionals, who either work for independent agencies or as part
of a company's in-house PR Department, seek always to attain and
sustain good personal relations with the media. In some cases they are
in contact with their media contacts on a daily basis, but even if this is

not the case, they seek to maintain such good relations with the press, which comprises six Greek daily newspapers, one English daily and two English weeklies, of which one is a financial paper, which they use to their clients' or company's benefit.

Strategic associates

PR professionals in Cyprus are aware that they cannot operate alone and that to best evaluate the market situation of any case on which they are working a number of elements must be combined. One such element is research. There are numerous professional market research companies operating in Cyprus that are familiar with the local environment and offer up-to-date services in the various areas of research.

Professional development

PR professionals in Cyprus recognize that continuing professional development is essential in order for one to keep up to date on developments in the profession. It is for this reason that many professionals attend key conferences, seminars and other events in Greece, Great Britain and Europe. They also become members of the Cyprus Public Relations Association. The Association supports its members by organizing PR seminars, conferences and other events.

The whole area of Public Relations is closely identified with the frontiers of development and change and PR professionals in Cyprus recognize the need to stay abreast of all issues concerning their profession, both in their own interests and, even more importantly, in the interests of the organizations for whom they work.

Conclusion

Public Relations in Cyprus is slowly gaining the priority it deserves and international companies operating or seeking to institute business there can expect to find professionals of a high standard, who can respond positively to client needs and provide the desired services effectively.

Marketing

*Soulla Kellas, Director, Customized Research
and Anna Rita Hadjigavriel, Regional
Director, ACNielsen AMER*

Stages of economic development

Cyprus is a very small economy. With a total population of just under 700,000 (in the free areas) and a working population of around 320,000 it is one of the smallest EU countries.

Until the 1970s, the Cyprus economy was characterized by the prevalence of small family-based enterprises, production of primary commodities, and a relatively unskilled workforce. Business decisions were 'supplier driven', with the main focus being on the product, while marketing was indistinct from selling and distribution.

In the past 20 years Cyprus has experienced significant economic development, driven by a number of factors; legislation, coupled with the island's suitability as a regional hub, attracted a large number of offshore companies. Another factor was the gradual liberalization, which led to increased competition. Additionally, a flourishing tourism industry (currently running at more than 2.5 million arrivals a year) greatly contributed to the growth of the economy.

In parallel with economic development, the Cypriot consumer became increasingly more sophisticated. While on one hand external technologies and products were more systematically imported, on the other, as a result of higher levels of education and travelling/studying abroad, Cypriots acquired access to the global market.

The economic and cultural evolution that Cyprus has experienced in these past 20 years has yielded significant changes in consumer awareness and expectations. As a result, consumers have become increasingly demanding and selective. These consumers are now driving business direction.

Economic evolution and subsequent changes in consumers' expectations have not as yet fully reflected the corresponding development of the marketing function.

Marketing at present

Although consumers are in the driving seat, most companies react to their needs with short-term planning, rather than being proactive and incorporating marketing as an integrated strategic function.

In order to find the reasons for the lack of full adoption of the marketing function, we should look into the characteristics of most Cypriot companies in terms of size, management structure and stage of development.

The latest census of establishments (1995, published by the Department of Statistics and Research, Ministry of Finance) indicates that 56 per cent of all enterprises (in the private and public sectors) employ at most one staff member, 31 per cent employ between two and four, 12 per cent employ between five and 49 staff, and only 1 per cent employ more than 50 employees. As would be expected, the majority of the small private sector enterprises are in trade. Clearly, and in comparison with most EU member countries, there is a large skew towards very small business units.

It is widely evident that quite a number of the companies that have experienced significant growth in terms of size have not experienced a corresponding change in the management structure and culture. Potent and intuitive owners tend to be the main strategy shapers in many such businesses and marketing is synonymous with sales.

Even with the large, non-family-owned companies, it appears that heads of different departments are assigned the marketing function and are acting as sole strategic decision makers, leaving little space to integrated group marketing.

In terms of their stage of development, most companies are importing technologies and/or new product and service ideas rather than creating their own. It is appropriate to mention that very little Research and Development, and therefore pioneering work on new products and services, takes place in Cyprus. This could be largely attributed to the market size, which is very small and limiting, as well as the fact that there is a very small manufacturing sector.

A study run jointly by Harvard University, the Cyprus Development Bank and the Cyprus International Institute of Management in June 2001, using the methodology adopted for the production of the Global Competitiveness Report, provides interesting indications in this respect. More specifically, Cyprus ranked last out of 60 countries evaluated using the same methodology in 1999.

Furthermore, even though the proportion for Research and Development of the GDP had grown from 0.18 per cent (in 1992) to 0.23 per cent (in 1998), it was still low compared to the EU member average of 1.9 per cent in 1997.

The impact of each of the factors outlined above evidently has a negative effect on the development of the marketing function, restricting both its scope and depth.

Possible developments in view of new challenges and opportunities

The years to come will be characterized by important challenges and opportunities for Cyprus. In order to maintain the strong economic performance of the past 20 years companies, primarily in the private sector, will have to show dynamism and clear strategic vision.

Imminent entry to the EU, the increasing openness of world markets, the growing mobility of capital, environmental pressures and resource availability issues, are all elements representing risk and opportunity at the same time.

The already quoted Global Competitiveness Report shows that Cyprus performed fairly well in terms of infrastructure (24th out of 60) and very high on labour market flexibility (18th out of 60). It is evident

Table 7.3.1 Distribution of educational attainment, December 2002 (%)

Country	Source year	% of 25+ year olds with post secondary education
Denmark	1991	19.6
Norway	1990	17.9
Cyprus	1992	17.0
Finland	1990	15.4
Estonia	1989	13.7
Ireland	1991	13.1
France	1990	11.4
Luxembourg	1991	10.8
Slovenia	1991	10.4
Hungary	1990	10.1
Slovakia	1991	9.5
Greece	1991	8.7
Czech Republic	1991	8.5
Spain	1991	8.4
Poland	1988	7.9
Portugal	1991	7.7
Austria	1991	6.1
Italy	1981	4.1

Source: UNESCO Institute for Statistics

Note: not all EU member countries were included in the report. Moreover, countries with data collected earlier than 1981 were excluded.

from Table 7.3.1 that Cyprus has one of the highest educated work-forces amongst European Union states.

Cyprus' strength on human resources and infrastructure, coupled with greater emphasis on research and development (think tanks have already been set up on the island), and focused training, should aid Cyprus to positively face the upcoming challenges.

In the process of change and in view of the significantly larger market, with the entry of Cyprus into the European Union, marketing will have to evolve from the present limited role to a more integrated and sophisticated one.

Market Research

Soulla Kellas, Director, Customized Research and Annarita Hadjigavriel, Regional Director, ACNielsen AMER

An overview vis-à-vis the international scene

Given the relatively low emphasis placed presently on marketing by the business community in Cyprus, it is not surprising that the market research industry turnover is also low, and especially so in comparison to other EU member states (refer to ratios in Table 7.4.1).

It is, however, worth noting that the lower comparative rates of market research turnover may also be attributed to the fact that Cyprus is a very small market, with a largely homogeneous consumer, with fairly predictable behaviour. Most studies, either quantitative or qualitative, tend to be small scale mainly owing to the need for limited sub-sample analysis. The value of such studies is, therefore, low.

More specifically, for 2001 the total market research turnover, encompassing all research types including Retail Measurement services, was estimated at USD 2 million, a 6 per cent increase over 2000.

Cyprus' regional role

What distinguishes Cyprus from most other markets is the role it plays in the regional coordination of research work. Even though market research revenues generated for the Cyprus market (either commissioned by clients based in Cyprus or those based outside) are relatively small, the overall market research industry is large and very active. In other words there is a large volume of research work managed from Cyprus commissioned by clients based out of Cyprus (eg UK, US, France) and with fieldwork in one of the countries of the Middle East, North Africa, Eastern Europe, Sub-Saharan Africa and Central Asian Republics.

Table 7.4.1 Market research turnover figures

Country	MR Turnover (US$ million)*	GDP (US$ billion)**	Ratio***
Original EU Countries (15)	5,842	7,719	756
New EU entrants (Poland, Czech Rep, Hungary, Slovenia, Slovakia, Estonia, Cyprus)	162	317	511
Small EU States (Slovenia, Estonia)	10	17	588
Cyprus	2	8	250

Source: ESOMAR Annual Study of the Market Research Industry 2001 report

* Trade associations and estimates
** IMF International Financial Statistics May 2002
*** MR turnover into GDP and multiplying by a million

Cyprus has assumed this role primarily due to its geographical position, large pool of graduates (most of whom are fully conversant in English), excellent telecommunications structure and regular direct flights to and from most European destinations (this is the result of a very active tourist industry).

This regional role came into play as early as 1962 with the setting up of the first market research agency on the island. The next largest research agency was established in 1982 and the rest in the 1990s, reflecting the increased demand for research in the local market.

It will be appropriate to mention that research revenues by the Cyprus based firms, which include regional coordination, are estimated to be at least seven times those generated in the local market.

The existence of research agencies in Cyprus with access to the whole of the Emerging Markets region has attracted a number of large global research agencies that wished to extend their regional coverage, mainly through acquisitions and affiliations rather than setting up their own facilities. Such companies include ACNielsen, Synovate and GfK.

Size and structure

The research industry in Cyprus could be characterized as a mature industry with a number of research agencies and research buyers (albeit small market research budgets) and highly experienced research staff. Moreover, there is an active market research association (SEDEAK), which was established in 1994 with the key aim to increase awareness of the research function, protect the profession and raise quality standards. In doing so, all members of SEDEAK have fully adopted the ESOMAR Code of Conduct.

There are currently ten research agencies operating in Cyprus, seven of which are members of SEDEAK, and four of which are actively involved in regional coordination. The industry employs close to 500 full time personnel (excluding freelance interviewers). In line with the amount of regional work performed by, primarily, the largest research agencies on the island, it is not surprising that three-quarters of the total research staff are employed for regional coordination.

Before examining the market research structure in greater detail it is important to note that the whole gamut of research services are offered by the research agencies operating on the island. Furthermore, most of the larger research agencies have specialist units for qualitative, quantitative and continuous research and further specializations within these for business-to-business research or for specific industry sectors (most often for telecommunications, finance, media, automotive and pharmaceutical) and/or for branded products (pricing models, advertising development models and so on).

Retail Measurement research is currently offered by three companies. This is a very large syndicated study, which aims at estimating the market size and structure and brand shares of various product categories sold through the retail environment. Among most fast-moving consumer goods clients this is considered to be one of the most important research services.

Research undertaken in the Cyprus market

The structure of the research industry in Cyprus, as estimated by SEDEAK for 2001, is very much in line with the world trends in terms of research expenditure split between domestic and international clients (see Table 7.4.2), research expenditure contribution by the different research types and methodologies (see Table 7.4.3), research expenditure split between studies with consumers or non-consumers –mainly businesses (see Table 7.4.4).

Continuous research (see Table 7.4.3) primarily includes Retail Measurement research expenditure.

In terms of the method of research, face-to-face in-home interviewing prevails. This is in line with most of Europe, Latin America and Asia. Telephone interviewing (including the use of Computer Aided Telephone Interviewing-CATI) can also be undertaken in view of the fact that fixed-line telephone penetration is almost universal. However, studies undertaken via the telephone tend to be shorter and simpler than those undertaken face to face.

Table 7.4.2 Research expenditure distribution (2001)

	Cyprus (%)	Worldwide (%, excluding US figures)
Domestic clients	80	80
Clients from abroad	20	20

Source: SEEDAK

Table 7.4.3 Research expenditure by research type (2001)

	Cyprus (%)	Worldwide (%, excluding US figures)
Ad hoc research	50	60
Quant	*90*	*80*
Qual	*10*	*20*
Continuous research	50	40

Source: SEEDAK

Table 7.4.4 Research expenditure by consumer group (2001)

	Cyprus (%)	Worldwide (%, excluding US figures)
Consumer research	75	80
Non-consumer research	25	20

Source: SEEDAK

As is the case with most markets, the exception being the United States and Japan, online research is still in its infancy in Cyprus, even though in-home Internet connection is relatively high. From a nationally representative study undertaken by ACNielsen AMER in September 2002, among over 800 18-plus year olds, the in-home Internet penetration was estimated at 25 per cent. Internet usage would be higher.

The only area where the structure of the research industry in Cyprus differs from most other markets, is the research expenditure by client sector. Worldwide, the most important source of revenue for the research industry is the manufacturing sector. This does not apply in the case of Cyprus, which has a very small manufacturing sector. In Cyprus, the largest and more frequent research buyers include companies in the trade sector, service sector (primarily finance and telecommunications) and companies in media.

Market research industry developments

Cyprus' entry to the EU will heighten competitive activity, which is expected to have a positive impact on both marketing and market research activities. More specifically, the local research industry is likely to grow at a faster rate. The growth is likely to result from increased demand for research from both local clients and those based within the EU.

Even though regional coordination is likely to decline, as a result of an increasing number of international organizations setting up offices in key countries in the Emerging Markets region in order to be closer to the consumer, Cyprus could be of far greater importance in the coordination of global projects. Such projects are currently managed out of Western Europe. The key parameters include:

- a large pool of very skilled research staff in project coordination;

- manageable time differences from the United States to Japan;

- daily flights to most European destinations;

- good telecommunications infrastructure;

- relatively lower cost of coordination (daily executive rates are likely to be lower than those in Western Europe).

Historically, Cyprus has demonstrated a formidable ability to adapt to new conditions and to overcome difficult situations. The strength of this ability will be decisive in making Cyprus capable of competing in a significantly larger market, with a plethora of sophisticated products and services and becoming an essential bridge between the West and East.

Part Eight

Human Resources Issues

8.1

Compensation, Benefits and Employee Regulations

Michael Antoniou, Head, Industrial Relations & Labour Legislation Department, Cyprus Employers & Industrialists Federation (OEB)

Labour law

Cyprus Labour Legislation has been heavily influenced by English common law and relevant legislation and by the International Labour Organization (ILO) instruments. Cyprus has so far ratified more than 50 ILO Conventions, which, according to the Constitution of the Republic, enjoy the status of laws following their ratification.

In recent years, and in particular since 1 January 2003, a considerable amount of labour legislation has been introduced within the framework of the harmonization of Cyprus law with the *acquis communautaire*. Comprehensive lists of the major pieces of labour legislation in force and all ILO Conventions ratified by Cyprus can be found at the end of this chapter.

In this chapter, brief reference is made to the most important statutory rights of employees of the private sector. Civil servants enjoy special prerogatives, the examination of which lies beyond the scope of this paper.

Employee statutory rights during their employment

An employee of the private sector is entitled to the following statutory rights:

- **Minimum annual leave with pay:** four weeks.

- **Maximum working hours including overtime:** 48 hours per week on average within a reference period of four months. Less hours of work are provided for certain categories of employees such as 'clerks' (maximum 44 hours), shop assistants (maximum 42 hours), young persons (maximum 38 hours).

- **Maximum night work:** eight hours daily on average in a reference period of one month.

- **Weekly rest period:** 35 consecutive hours.

- **Daily rest period:** 11 consecutive hours.

- **Break:** At least 15 minutes.

- **Maternity leave:** 16 weeks per birth, during which the employee receives a maternity allowance from the Social Insurance Fund approximating to 75 per cent of her gross income of the previous year and subject to the terms and conditions provided by the social insurance law.

- **Parental leave:** 13 weeks per birth for each parent until the child becomes 6 years old or 12 in the case of adoption. Parental leave is without pay or allowance.

- **Leave on grounds of emergency family reasons:** seven days per year for urgent family reasons related with sickness or injury of a child, spouse, parent, brother, sister or grandparent. This is also an unpaid leave.

- **Sick leave:** there is no universal statutory right to sick leave. Such a leave up to 24 days per year with pay is provided by special laws only for hotel and catering employees. Nevertheless, a right to sick leave is widely recognized and practised by all employers (for the duration see below in rights under collective agreements). During absence on grounds of sickness, a sick leave benefit is payable by the Social Insurance Fund for six months per year, subject to certain terms and conditions.

- **Overtime pay:** overtime pay is regulated by law only for hotel and catering employees and for shop assistants: the salary plus 50 per cent for overtime work on any weekday, for both categories, and the salary plus 100 per cent on Sundays and public holidays for shop assistants.

- **Public holidays:** public holidays are provided by law only for shop assistants; nine days per year.

- **Minimum wage:** Minimum wage is provided only for shop assistants, clerks, nurse assistants and assistants in kindergartens. It is currently set at CYP 320 on recruitment and at CYP 340 after six months of employment. The relevant Decree is revised in April every year.

- **Rights of information and consultation:** In certain cases employees and/or their representatives, have the right to be informed and/or consulted by the employer prior to him proceeding with any measures affecting the status of the former. This right is provided by several laws, such as the law for safeguarding of employees' rights in case of a transfer of an enterprise, the law on European Works Councils, the law on collective redundancies and the health and safety at work law.

- **Rights of equal pay and equal treatment:** men and women have a right to equal pay for the same work or for work to which equal value is attributed, subject to certain criteria. Furthermore, men and women enjoy equal treatment with regard to employment and vocational training, including access to employment and training and promotion. Finally, part-time workers and fixed-term workers may not be treated in a less favourable way than the comparable full-time and indefinite period workers, respectively, solely because they work on a part-time or a fixed-term basis. Of course, the 'pro rata temporis' principle applies in these cases.

- **Rights under the National Social Insurance Scheme:** See paragraph below on employer and employee contributions.

Employee statutory rights in the event of the termination of employment

- **Redundancy payment:** An employee whose employment is terminated by the employer on grounds of redundancy, is entitled to a redundancy payment by the Redundancy Fund, provided that he or she had been continuously employed by the same employer for at least two years. The payment is calculated as follows: for the first 4 years of service 2 weeks' wages for each year; for the 5th to 10th year of service 2½ weeks' wages for each year; for the 11th to 15th year 3 weeks' wages for each year; for the 16th to 20th year 3½ weeks' wages for each year; and for the 21st to 25th year 4 weeks' wages for each year of service.

- **Compensation:** In case of an illegal dismissal, the employee is entitled to a compensation payment by his or her employer. The compensation is awarded by the Industrial Disputes Court and it may not be less than the payment the employee would have received had he been declared redundant, while it may not exceed two years' wages. Within these two limits, the Court has absolute discretion in its award. It does, however, take into account the length of service, the age of the employee and the loss of his or her career prospects. The compensation awarded is paid by the employer up to an amount that does not exceed one year's wages and any additional amount is paid by the Redundancy Fund despite the fact that it is not a case of a redundancy dismissal.

- **Notice:** In case of termination of employment because of redundancy or because the employee had failed to carry out his or her work in a reasonably efficient manner, the employee is entitled to a minimum period of notice or to payment in lieu. The period of notice is as shown in Table 8.1.1.

- **Reinstatement:** In the case of employers employing more than 19 persons, if the dismissal of an employee was clearly illegal or was illegal and effected in bad faith, the Court may, if in its opinion the circumstances so justify and the employee has so requested, order his or her reinstatement.

- **Re-engagement:** Where an employer who has declared employees redundant wishes, within eight months of the redundancy, to increase again its workforce of the same type and skill, it must give priority in engagement to employees affected by the redundancy, subject to the operational needs of the business.

- **Unpaid salaries in case of employer's insolvency:** Employees dismissed because of the insolvency of their employer may claim unpaid wages of up to three months from the 'Employers' Insolvency Fund'.

- **Termination of employment without any rights for the employee:** In case of a fair/legal dismissal (with the exception of the case of redundancy where the employee receives payment by the

Table 8.1.1 Notice period requirements

Weeks of continuous employment	Period of notice (weeks)
26–51	1
52–103	2
104–155	4
156–207	5
208–259	6
260–311	7
312 or more	8

Note: Neither compensation payment nor notice for dismissal is required in case of a dismissal effected during the probationary period, which is 6 months (extendable up to 2 years by mutual written agreement at the beginning of the employment).

Redundancy Fund), no rights are afforded to the employee (with the exception of the right to notice or payment in lieu in the case of dismissals on grounds of inefficiency). Reasons for fair/legal dismissal are as follows: the employee fails to carry out his or her work in a reasonably efficient manner; dismissal due to *force majeure*, war operations, uprising, act of God or destruction of the plant; termination of employment at the end of a fixed-term contract of less than 30 months' duration; because of the attainment by the employee of the retirement age; or the employee so conducts him/herself as to render him/herself liable to dismissal without notice (eg commission of gross industrial misconduct in the course of his or her duty, commission in the course of his or her duty of a criminal offence without the employer's agreement, immoral behaviour in the course of his or her duties, serious or repeated contravention or disregard of work's rules or other rules in relation to the employment).

Collective agreements and custom

Employee rights under collective agreements or otherwise during their employment

Due to the fact that in Cyprus there is a high unionization density in almost all sectors of the economy, most terms and conditions of employment are regulated through collective agreements. Collective agreements are freely negotiated between trade unions and individual employers or sectoral Associations, usually with the assistance and guidance of the Cyprus Employers and Industrialists Federation (OEB). They usually last for two or three years and despite their not being legally binding, they are adhered to by both parties. Different levels of benefits, starting salaries and pay increases are provided by different collective agreements. Nevertheless, it can be said that the following are in general terms applicable in almost all cases (detailed information may be collected by OEB from members and prospective members):

- **Annual leave with pay:** On top of the minimum of four weeks per year provided by law, leave entitlement in some cases is gradually increased up to five weeks after a certain period of service (normally after 15–20 years).

- **Working hours:** Normal working hours in manufacturing, construction, retail, banking, agriculture, hotel and catering are 38 per week, while in the rest of the services sector it varies between 38 and 40 hours per week.

- **Overtime pay:** Overtime work is compensated on weekdays with 50 per cent additional payment and on weekends and public holidays with 100 per cent additional payment.

- **Weekly rest period:** Sunday is the normal weekly day of rest and since the five-day week is the rule (with a number of exceptions, eg retail), Saturday is, for most employees, a day off as well.

- **Public holidays:** Approximately 15–17 public holidays with pay are observed by all employers.

- **Maternity, parental and emergency leave:** During maternity leave the employer complements the maternity allowance that the employee receives by the Social Insurance Fund and she has full emoluments for either the whole or the largest part of the maternity leave. The other two leaves, parental and emergency, are without payment from any source whatsoever.

- **Sick leave:** The employer complements the sick leave allowance payable by the Social Insurance Fund so as to secure full salary for the employee for a period varying from one to three months per year.

- **Medical treatment:** Unionized employees and their dependants are usually insured for medical and pharmaceutical purposes through Trade Union Funds, where the employer and employee contribute CYP 5 per month each. Non-unionized employees are usually insured with private insurance companies, the cost being divided evenly between the two parties.

- **Provident fund:** The introduction of a provident fund is optional but once established, its operation is regulated by law and its transactions are subject to inspection by the Ministry of Labour. Both employers and employees pay contributions varying between 5 per cent and 7 per cent of each employee's gross salary.

- **Starting salaries:** There is a significant variety of different levels of starting salaries for the different sectors, individual companies and occupations.

- **Salary increases:** Salary increases are provided for by collective agreements and are normally payable every January. They are usually linked to the rate of average increase of the national productivity during the three-year period prior to the expiration of the collective agreement under renewal.

- **Salary scales:** In a very limited number of sectors (eg banking, shipping agents) and individual enterprises, wage scales are in operation and they provide for the payment of an increment to all employees once a year. This increment is estimated at about 3–4 per cent of an employee's salary and it is usually payable on top of an annual salary increase and COLA.

- **Cost of Living Allowance (COLA):** The COLA system is a wage indexation system fully compensating the price index changes biannually and it is applied over and above 'national productivity' salary increases.

  (NB: Wages in money terms in 2001 increased by 5.1 per cent whilst in real terms wages increased by 3.1 per cent. Data for 2002 is not yet available but it is estimated that wages increased in money terms by 5.5 per cent and in real terms by 2.7 per cent.)

- **Several allowances:** Certain allowances are payable to employees, usually as a compensation for expenses incurred or inconvenience suffered by them. Such allowances include the shift allowance, the travelling allowance, the meal allowance and the hazardous work allowance.

Type and validity of employment contract

All types of employment contracts are recognized by law and are valid to the extent that they do not violate existing legislation. The most common type of employment contract is the permanent, full-time for an indefinite period contract. Contracts for part-time work and/or for a fixed-term duration are also used. The provisions of any individual contract of employment or of any collective agreement, save where they are more favourable to the worker, are null and void to the extent that they contravene the provisions of any law in force.

Information to be given to the employee

Under the law concerning the employer's obligation to inform employees of the conditions applicable to the contract or employment relationship, the employer must give to the employee the following information:

- the name and the address of the employer;
- the date of appointment;
- the period of the employment if it is a fixed-term appointment;
- the place of employment;
- the period of notice to be given in case of termination of employment;
- the job content/description;
- the annual leave entitlement;

- the salary and all the fringe benefits;
- the normal hours of daily or weekly work;
- reference to any collective agreement that might be applicable.

The above information may be given in the form of an employment contract signed by both parties, in a letter of appointment signed by the employer or by any other document signed by the employer. This information must be communicated to the employee within one month following the appointment.

Employer and employee contributions

Employer's contributions

PROVIDED BY LAW (% OF EACH EMPLOYEE'S GROSS SALARY)
Social Insurance Fund: 6.3 per cent
Redundancy Fund: 1.2 per cent (16.6 per cent of this contribution finances the employer's insolvency fund)
Human Resource Development Authority (training levy): 0.5 per cent
Social Cohesion Fund: 2 per cent

PROVIDED BY COLLECTIVE AGREEMENTS
Provident Fund: 5–7 per cent
Medical Insurance: CYP 5 per employee per month

Employee's contributions

PROVIDED BY LAW
Social Insurance Fund: 6.3 per cent of gross salary
Professional tax payable to the Local Authority: CYP 3–157 per year depending on annual earnings
Income tax: as from 1 January 2004, income tax will be as follows:

For income up to CYP 10,000: no tax
For income from CYP 10,001–15,000: 20 per cent
For income from CYP 15,001–20,000: 25 per cent
For income in excess of CYP 20,001: 30 per cent

PROVIDED BY COLLECTIVE AGREEMENTS
Provident Fund: 5–7 per cent of gross salary
Medical Insurance: CYP 5 per month
Trade Union contribution (where the employee is a member of a union): 1 per cent of gross salary subject to a ceiling

NB: Under the social insurance scheme, those insured are entitled to the following benefits and allowances: marriage grant, maternity grant, funeral grant, maternity allowance, sickness benefit, unemployment benefit, invalidity pension, old age pension, widow's pension, orphan's benefit, missing persons allowance and employment injury benefit, which includes temporary incapacity injury benefit, disablement benefit and death benefit.

Foreign workers

Shortages in the labour market have been very severe during the last 12 years. This has led since 1991 to the granting of permits to employers for the employment of foreign labour, subject to certain terms and criteria, the most important being the non-existence of a Cypriot willing to fill a vacancy.

Nevertheless, in case a foreigner is legally employed in Cyprus, he or she is entitled to the same benefits, wages, terms and conditions, statutory or conventional, that are applicable to a Cypriot employed by the same employer in the same or similar occupation.

Labour law in force

1 Termination of Employment Law No 24/1967
2 Annual Leave with Pay Law No 8/1967
3 Protection of Maternity Law No 100(I)/1997
4 Provident Funds Law No 44/1981
5 Shop Assistants Law Cap. 185
6 Hotel Employees Regulations
7 Catering Employees Law No 80/1968
8 Minimum Wage Law Cap. 183
9 Protection of Young Persons at Work Law No 48(I)/2001
10 Organization of Working Time Law No 63(I)/2002
11 Part-time Work Law No 76(I)/2002
12 Parental Leave Law No 69(I)/2002
13 Safeguarding employees' rights in the event of transfer of an enterprise Law No 104(I)/2000
14 Collective Redundancies Law No 28(I)/2001
15 Equal Pay for Men and Women Law No 177 (I)/2002

16 Equal Treatment for Men and Women with regard to Employment and Occupational Training Law No 205(I)/2002

17 Social Insurance Law No 41/1980

18 Posting of Workers Law No 137(I)/2002 *

19 European Works Councils Law No 68(I)/2002 *

20 Information by the Employer of the Terms Relating to the Employment Contract Law No 100(I)/2000

21 Protection of Employees' Rights in the event of the Insolvency of the Employer Law No 25(I)/2001

22 Driving and Rest Hours of Drivers Law No 131(I)/2002

23 Health and Safety at Work (framework) Law No 89(I)/1996 and a series of sets of Regulations (more than 20 sets)

* Due to come into force upon accession of Cyprus to the European Union

ILO Conventions ratified by Cyprus

No 11 Unemployment Convention, 1919

No 2 Right of Association (Agriculture) Convention, 1921

No 15 Minimum Age (trimmers and Stockers) Convention, 1921

No 16 Medical Examination of Young Persons (Sea) Convention, 1921

No 19 Equality of Treatment (Accident Compensation) Convention, 1925

No 23 Repatriation of Seamen Convention, 1926

No 29 Forced Labour Convention, 1930

No 44 Unemployment Provision Convention, 1934

No 45 Underground Work (Women) Convention, 1935

No 81 Labour Inspection Convention, 1947 (Exclude Part II)

No 87 Freedom of Association and Protection of the Right to Organize Convention, 1948

No 88 Employment Service Convention, 1948

No 89 Night Work (Women) Convention (Revised), 1948

No 90 Night Work of Young Persons (industry) Convention (Revised), 1948

No 92 Accommodation of Crews Convention (Revised), 1949

No 94 Labour Clauses (Public Contracts) Convention, 1949

No 95 Protection of Wages Convention, 1949

No 97 Migration for Employment (Revised) Convention, 1949

No 98 Right to Organize and Collective Bargaining Convention, 1949

No 100 Equal Remuneration Convention, 1951

No 102 Social Security (Minimum Standards) Convention, 1952

No 105 Abolition of Forced Labour Convention, 1952

No 106 Weekly Rest (Commerce and Offices) Convention, 1957

No 111 Discrimination (Employment and Occupation) Convention, 1958

No 114 Fishermen's Articles of Agreement Convention, 1959

No 116 Final Articles Revision Convention, 1961

No 119 Guarding of Machinery Convention, 1963

No 121 Employment Injury/Benefits Convention, 1964

No 122 Employment Policy Convention, 1964

No 123 Minimum Age (Underground Work) Convention, 1965

No 124 Medical Examination of Young Persons (Underground Work) Convention, 1965

No 128 Invalidity, Old-Age and Survivors Benefits Convention, 1967

No 135 Protection and Facilities to be Afforded to Workers' Representatives in the Undertaking Convention, 1971

No 138 Minimum Age for Admission to Employment Convention, 1973

No 141 Rural Workers Organizations Convention, 1975

No 142 Human Resources Development Convention, 1975

No 143 Migrant Workers (Supplementary Provisions) Convention, 1975

No 144 Tripartite Consultation (International Labour Standards) Convention, 1976

No 147 Minimum Standards in Merchant Ships Convention, 1976

No 150 Labour Administration Convention, 1978

No 151 Labour Relations (Public Service) Convention, 1978

No 152 Occupational Safety & Health (Dock work) Convention, 1979

No 154 Collective Bargaining Convention, 1981

No 155 Occupational Safety & Health Convention, 1979

No 158 Termination of Employment Convention, 1982

No 159 Vocational Rehabilitation and Employment (Disabled Persons) Convention, 1983

No 160 Labour Statistics Convention, 1985

No 162 Asbestos Convention, 1986

No 171 Night Work Convention, 1990

No 172 Working Conditions (Hotel, Restaurants and Similar Establishments), 1991

No 175 Part-time Work Convention, 1994

No 182 Prohibition and Elimination of the Worst Forms of Child Labour Convention, 1998

Industrial Relations

Michael Antoniou, Head, Industrial Relations & Labour Legislation Department, Cyprus Employers & Industrialists Federation (OEB)

Trade unions

Cyprus trade unions are well organized, strong and experienced. The employees in the public sector are practically 100 per cent unionized, while employees in the private sector are unionized at a rate of approximately 70 per cent, making a total density average of about 75 per cent.

There are two main types of unions in Cyprus: Industrial unions that cover a whole industry island-wide, (eg building, metalworking, woodworking, etc) and single enterprise unions that cover a single undertaking or employer (eg Electricity Authority Employees' Union and the Teachers' Union).

There are two major private sector federations, namely the Pancyprian Federation of Labour (PEO) and the Cyprus Workers Confederation (SEK), the latter affiliated to ETUC. Despite their political origins and their ideological differences, the two Unions cooperate between themselves both at the national and branch level. With only a few insignificant exceptions, the two unions submit joint claims to the Employers' Associations or to the individual employer and they jointly conduct the collective bargaining. They have common goals and objectives and in trying to achieve them they use the same methods and tactics, differing only in the degree of emphasis of their approach. Of course, smaller trade unions also exist and they seek – with some success – to play a role in the Cyprus industrial relations system.

Employers' associations

Employers are also organized in industry or branch level associations, most of which are members of the Cyprus Employers and Industrialists Federation (OEB). Most of the association members of the Employers Federation are registered under the Trade Unions Law, which enables them to act collectively and declare lockouts or resort to other industrial action when a labour dispute over interests reaches a deadlock.

The OEB was established in 1960, immediately after independence and since then it has been the acknowledged representative of the Cyprus business community, both nationally and internationally.

OEB comprises 51 sectoral and professional associations from all sectors of economic activity and more than 500 large, individual enterprises of the private and semi-governmental sectors. Its members employ more than 65 per cent of the Cyprus workforce (a percentage that is one of the highest in the world), thus making OEB the most representative employer's organization in the island.

OEB is a member of all national tripartite bodies, committees and fora, either standing or ad hoc, dealing with the formulation of the State's labour and social policy.

OEB is the only Cypriot organization member of the Union of European Employers and Industrial Federations (UNICE) and the International Organization of Employers (IOE), representing every year the Cyprus entrepreneurial community at the annual conferences of the International Labour Organization (ILO).

Recognizing the utopia of the old doctrine that workers and employers have nothing in common, OEB believes that only through harmonious relations with representative and responsible trade unions can marked progress in Cyprus' social and economic affairs be achieved. Despite its differences and constant divergence of opinion with the Unions, OEB was neither formed for nor is it now engaged in a fight against the Unions. Its object is to bring about a healthy balance of power between the two sides.

Collective bargaining

The present state of Cyprus industrial relations does not fully warrant the terminology 'two sides', which is used to describe labour and management. In the sense that there are differences and that each of the parties tries to get for itself and its members a bigger slice of the cake, the terminology is correct. But, in the sense, that both parties cooperate for the achievement of common ends and for the enlargement of the cake, the element of conflict disappears and the two sides merge into one.

What, however, is of still greater importance is the determination of both OEB and the unions to resolve their differences in an amicable manner, by cooperating with each other and by exhibiting a spirit of understanding and conciliation.

Collective bargaining in the private sector is guided by the principles of the freedom of association and the provisions of the Industrial Relations Code (IRC). The IRC is primarily a procedural, non-legally binding gentlemen's agreement, signed in 1977 by OEB and the two major private sector trade unions, and countersigned by the Ministry of Labour and Social Insurance. It lays down several procedures to be followed whenever a labour dispute arises, but adherence to its provisions rests with the good will of the parties. Despite its nature, the IRC has worked effectively since its introduction and has contributed decisively to the preservation of industrial peace in the island.

Around 75 per cent of the workforce is covered by a collective agreement concluded for all sectors or individual enterprises. Agreements are of two or three years' duration and apply to all employees except senior management.

The material needs of their members having been satisfied to a large extent, the Unions have turned their attention to questions concerning safety, health, work and environment. The main concern of the employers regarding claims of that nature is to avoid arrangements that would unduly restrict the freedom of the entrepreneur to run his or her business in an efficient and productive way.

Another area of non-material benefits that the unions are aiming at concerns managerial rights. Issues such as the organizational structure of enterprises, lay-off of personnel and inter-changeability, so far treated only as consultative matters (ie matters for which the final decision rests with the employer) are now the target and unions exert pressure on employers so as to turn them into negotiable matters. So far, unlike the rest of Europe, employers in Cyprus have had flexibility and freedom of action, but now it appears that there will be pressures to impose on the entrepreneur more restrictions through collective bargaining and otherwise.

Bipartite social dialogue in the form of joint consultations at sectoral or national level is also widely practised in Cyprus.

Sectoral-level bipartite dialogue takes place either in standing committees, as is the case in the hotel sector, or, more usually, on an ad hoc basis when serious issues arise. Several national-level and sectoral-level agreements have been reached over the years between the two sides, with the Government either assuming a mediatory role or no role at all.

Tripartite social dialogue

Since Independence, the State's labour, social and economic policy has been formulated by a wide network of tripartite advisory committees. The most important among these committees are the Labour Advisory Body, the Advisory Economic Committee and the Advisory Committee on Commerce and Industry. All training institutions, ie the Cyprus Productivity Centre, the Higher Technical Institute, the Hotel and Catering Institute and the Human Resource Development Authority are run by Tripartite Boards of Management. Also, the Social Insurance, the annual holidays, the redundancy and the employers' insolvency schemes are administered by tripartite boards.

The most important of all the advisory boards is the Labour Advisory Body, which is chaired by the Minister of Labour and Social Insurance. Its terms of reference are to advise the employer on all labour and social issues and to submit proposals and suggestions on legislation. As a rule the proposals in the labour and social fields discussed at the other advisory bodies end up, especially where no consensus has been achieved, for reconsideration at this body in a final effort to reach consensus. As a rule, therefore (with certain exceptions), every piece of social legislation, prior to its submission to the Council of Ministers or the House of Representatives is scrutinized by the body. And despite its purely advisory nature, through the give and take process characterizing its deliberations, results are obtained which have been effective in bringing about, to a certain extent, a balance between the two sides.

ILO conventions and the accession process

ILO guidelines on tripartite cooperation have long been adhered to in Cyprus and have greatly contributed to the practice of social dialogue and socio-economic policy in general. Cyprus has ratified a large number of ILO conventions, including most conventions on the fundamental rights of workers, labour relations and tripartite cooperation (see Chapter 8.1)

The efforts of Cyprus to harmonize its policies with those of the EU has given new impetus to the promotion of social dialogue. More specifically, the Government, in its effort to further encourage sectoral dialogue for accession purposes, has closely involved social partners in the accession policy and, in particular, in the study of draft legislation through tripartite technical committees.

Future perspectives

Accession to the European Union is Cyprus' most stimulating challenge.

Cyprus' European orientation is the country's natural course, deriving from its history of more than 3,000 years, from its culture, and from its values, but also from its democratic tradition and its market economy. While being situated at the eastern edge of the Mediterranean, Cypriots feel profoundly European.

In its accession course to the EU, Cyprus has been, and continues to be, confronted with a number of challenges. At the same time, the accession course offers opportunities for further growth.

The first serious challenge arises from the harmonization effort itself, and it consists of the adaptation of Cyprus' legal and institutional framework and policies with the full volume of the *acquis* in a short period of time. A second challenge arises from the creation of conditions of intensified competition brought about by the changing external environment of Cyprus in general, but which also comes as a result of its accession course. This challenge creates risks for those sectors of economic activity that may not be able to adjust to the new environment. At the same time, the accession course, and also the globalization of the world economy and the further liberalization of international trade, creates new opportunities for growth in view of the unhindered access of Cypriot goods and services to the EU single market and the easier access to third markets which will ensue.

8.3

Human Resources Management

Jacovos Christofides, Human Resources Consultant

Introduction

The information contained in this chapter on the human resources management function and infrastructure in Cyprus is provided in summary form but is complemented with links to Web sites where additional information may be found.

Human resources management is an area of rapid development in Cyprus. With Cyprus' accession to the EU, the expectations of increased competition, stricter guidelines, opportunities for growth and cooperation are causing many organizations, public and private, to focus on the issues of productivity and efficiency, optimization and alignment. Cypriot businessmen have proven to be entrepreneurial and hard working and many Cypriot companies have successfully ventured abroad, exporting products and services to Europe, the Balkans and the Middle East.

Most companies in Cyprus are family businesses, with the owner(s) usually holding the top executive position(s). A current challenge for many companies is to develop a professional management approach and to implement organizational structures at the top that are based on skills and value contribution rather than ownership and personal relationships.

Within the framework of the 'New Industrial Policy of the Government for the Development of High Technology Industry in Cyprus', the concept of incubators for high-technology companies and centres for carrying applied research and development in high-technology fields is being promoted.

All the above make for a very exciting time for human resources management in Cyprus, especially given the various subsidies that are available to companies for the improvement of their human resources function and for employee training.

Foreign businesses interested in setting up operations in Cyprus will find a good environment in terms of human resources management infrastructure.

This chapter comprises three sections, each addressing a major human resources activity: namely, acquiring, managing and developing human resources. Within each section is to be found information, practical advice and links to more in-depth information.

Acquiring human resources

The first HR related action in setting up a business in Cyprus will be to find and recruit employees.

Academic qualifications of the workforce

In general the labour force in Cyprus is well educated. Cyprus has a good elementary and high school education system and most high school graduates go on to colleges, technical schools and universities in Cyprus and abroad, mostly in Greece, United Kingdom, United States, France and Germany. The most popular fields of study are business administration, economics, accounting and engineering. There are a large numbers of post-graduates with MAs, MScs and MBAs. Almost everybody speaks and writes English, although for advanced writing and speaking skills one would have to look for someone who had spent some time abroad. A third language is not uncommon; usually French, German or Italian.

Work experience of workforce
Approximately 73 per cent of the workforce is employed in the services sector, 22 per cent in the industrial sector, and approximately 5 per cent in the agriculture sector. The unemployment rate in Cyprus is low at 4.3 per cent. A breakdown of the workforce by economic activity is provided in Table 8.3.1.

A company looking for employees in Cyprus will not have difficulty locating qualified personnel for most professions. The standard of education of staff available in Cyprus is very high with the Republic having one of the highest numbers of university graduates per capita in the world. Qualified marketing, sales, accounting, and technical personnel can usually be found easily and salaries, in relation to other countries, especially those in Europe, are generally relatively low.

Professions for which it may be difficult to find personnel are:

Table 8.3.1 Labour by economic activity (thousand)

		1995	1996	1997	1998	1999	2000	2001*
A	Wholesale and retail trade; repairs	49.5	50.8	51.9	52.4	52.9	54.2	55.0
B	Manufacturing	44.0	42.2	40.8	39.6	38.0	36.7	37.2
C	Hotels and restaurants	30.1	30.0	29.7	30.0	31.7	33.0	33.2
D	Construction	27.7	27.3	26.9	26.1	26.2	26.5	26.9
E	Agriculture, forestry and hunting	28.7	27.5	25.0	24.8	24.3	23.8	23.4
F	Transport, storage and communication	17.9	18.4	19.1	19.7	20.4	21.4	22.2
G	Public administration and defence; Compulsory social security	18.2	18.6	19.1	19.8	20.7	21.4	22.2
H	Education	13.3	14.2	14.9	15.2	15.7	16.1	17.0
I	Financial intermediation	12.3	12.8	13.2	13.7	15.3	16.0	15.7
J	Real estate, renting and business activities	12.0	12.5	12.9	13.8	14.5	14.9	15.4
K	Other community social and personal services activities	12.1	12.3	12.4	12.5	13.2	14.2	14.5
L	Health and social work	10.3	10.7	11.0	11.2	11.5	12.0	12.3
M	Private households with employed persons	4.0	5.0	5.5	6.1	6.7	7.8	9.2
N	Extra territor, organ and bodies	3.1	3.1	3.0	2.9	2.8	2.8	2.8
O	Electricity, gas and water supply	1.4	1.4	1.4	1.5	1.5	1.5	1.5
P	Fishing	1.1	1.1	1.2	1.3	1.3	1.4	1.3
Q	Mining and quarrying	0.7	0.7	0.6	0.6	0.6	0.6	0.6

Source: Cyprus National Accounts (Statistical Service, Republic of Cyprus)
Note: * Provisional

- *Highly skilled secretarial and administrative personnel* – although there is an abundance of secretarial and administrative personnel, their skills base is low by international standards. Highly skilled candidates exist but they are few and hard to find.

- *Highly specialized experienced technical and engineering personnel* – although many Cypriots have excellent academic qualifications, their work experience in Cyprus is limited by the lack of opportunities for truly high-tech, high-specialization work. Recently repatriated Cypriots however, may have highly specialized technical and engineering work experience.

- *Research and development personnel* – as above as there are very limited opportunities for work experience in this area in Cyprus.

How to acquire staff

Most Cypriot companies advertise vacancies in the popular daily newspapers. Some newspapers have weekly sections focused on career and employment and candidates do tend to look through these special sections as well as in the Saturday and Sunday editions that have the highest circulation and reading rates. English language newspapers are a good resource especially when looking for English speakers or employees of other nationalities residing in Cyprus.

In addition, a number of specialist HR consulting companies offer recruitment services for a fee, and can provide candidates from databases they have built over time, (allowing for time insensitive candidate identification), can offer screening and selection services and even manage the whole recruitment process.

Salary levels
Average salaries are lower in the private sector (CYP 400–450 per month) compared to the public sector (CYP 760 per month), and the public sector in general offers better employment benefits, including work hours from 7:30 a.m. to 2:30 p.m. As a result, for entry-level positions, school leavers prefer work in the public sector. Indications of salary ranges in the private sector are outlined in Table 8.3.2 and Table 8.3.3.

Note that these figures are an indication only, and actual salaries may vary depending on the position, roles and responsibilities, size of company, economic activity, and supply of labour.

Cyprus has a minimum wage, which at present is set at CYP 320 per month.

Table 8.3.2 Starting salaries by academic qualification

Academic qualifications	Years experience	Salary range (CYP)
High school degree	0	350–400
University degree	0	450–600
University degree	2	550–750
Masters degree	0	
Masters degree	3	700–1200
PhD	0	

Table 8.3.3 Salaries by level

Position	Salary range (CYP)
Staff	350–750
Supervisor	550–850
Junior manager	750–950
Middle manager	900–1500
Senior manager	1500–2600
General manager/CEO	2500+

The Human Resources Development Authority (HRDA) of Cyprus offers several subsidies to companies for newly recruited blue- and white-collar employees. These subsidies are linked to initial on-the-job training initiatives and apprenticeships. The HRDA Web site (www.hrdauth.org.cy) has full details of the different schemes.

Employment of foreign nationals

Foreign nationals wishing to take up employment in Cyprus must have a valid work permit under the Aliens and Immigration Law of Cyprus. Work permits for foreign nationals who possess executive positions in international business companies and local companies are relatively easy to obtain through the Labour Department. Executive employees of international business companies must submit applications to the Central Bank of Cyprus. Application for employment visas may be made in either the home or host country.

For non-executive staff positions, the application must go through the District Labour Office. The company must first prove that a Cypriot national does not exist who could fill the position at that time by advertising the position in the local press. This process can take between one and three months to complete.

Foreign nationals may obtain renewable residence permits valid for one year. The number of times the permit may be renewed and the duration of its validity depend on the purpose of the permit.

For scientific and engineering/technical positions, the foreign employee must also apply and register with the Scientific and Technological Chamber of Cyprus.

Managing human resources

Once employees have been hired, a company has to manage them in accordance with local laws and regulations. This section addresses the Cyprus Labour Law, the employment norms, the employment of foreign nationals in Cyprus, and the trade unions.

Cyprus Labour Law

The Cyprus Labour Law has been amended to comply with the EU Labour Law, with the amendments being enforced effective from January 2003. The Ministry of Labour and Social Insurance is responsible for administering the various labour laws and regulations, including minimum wages, hours of work, holidays, vacations, working and safety requirements, trade disputes, industrial relations, equal opportunities and sexual harassment in the workplace.

Terms of employment norms

- Working hours are normally 40 hours per week Monday to Friday for five-day workweeks.

- Employees are entitled by law to a minimum of 20 days vacation a year for employees working five-day workweeks and 24 days vacation a year for employees working six-day workweeks.

- Employers are liable for compensation to an employee for unfair dismissal. The courts make the final decision on compensation on a case-by-case basis, based on the specifics of the case and related precedents.

- Compensation for redundancy of employees is offered from the Redundancy Fund to which all employers make a contribution of 1.2 per cent of the employees' earnings subject to a maximum.

- The employer and the employee contribute 6.3 per cent each of the employee's earnings (subject to a maximum) to the Social Security Fund. Expatriate personnel of offshore and international business companies do not have to contribute to the fund.

- There are 14 statutory holidays during the year as follows:
  - 1 January (New Year's Day)
  - 6 January (Epiphany Day)
  - First Day of Lent
  - 25 March (Greek Independence Day)
  - 1 April
  - Good Friday (Orthodox)
  - Easter Monday (Orthodox
  - 1 May (Labor Day)
  - Whit Monday
  - 15 August (Assumption Day)
  - 1 October
  - 28 October
  - 25 December (Christmas Day)
  - 26 December (Boxing Day)

Remuneration and benefits

Most companies in Cyprus use a basic salary plus bonus remuneration scheme for full-time non-sales employees. Sales employees usually work according to fixed-salary plus commission schemes. Rewards are usually linked to performance only for sales personnel, although performance-related pay schemes for non-sales employees are just now starting to surface in some of the larger companies. Most companies offer a 13th salary at the end of December (Christmas), which is usually part of the agreed remuneration, although in some cases it is given at the discretion of the employer. Other benefits offered by Cypriot companies usually include provident or pension funds and medical plans.

It is generally accepted that overtime work is paid at time and a half, while overtime worked on public holidays and weekends is paid at double time. Wages are usually paid weekly to industry workers and labourers and monthly to service and office workers.

Trade unions

Unions are very strong in Cyprus. Terms and conditions of employment are negotiated either directly between the employee and the employer or through collective bargaining between trade unions and employers' organizations. There are two trade union federations in Cyprus representing the private sector employee unions. These are the Cyprus Workers' Confederation (SEK) (www.sek.org.cy) and the Pancyprian Federation of Labour (PEO) (www.cytanet.com.cy/peo). Public sector employees are represented by the Pancyprian Public Employees Trade Union (PASYDY) (www.pasydy.org) and bank employees have their own union, the Cyprus Union of Bank Employees (ETYK) (www.etyk.org.cy).

The Ministry of Labour and Social Insurance, through its Industrial Relations Service, provides mediation assistance to trade unions and employer associations for the prevention and settlement of labour disputes, in accordance with the law and the Industrial Relations Code.

Human resources management schemes

The HRDA offers a consultancy services subsidy scheme for strengthening of the HR related infrastructure of companies. The scheme provides technical and financial aid for the preparation of an HRM study (by an external consultant) and the implementation of agreed suggestions/recommendations by the company. See www.hrdauth.org.cy for more information.

Developing human resources

Cyprus maintains public elementary and secondary school systems of a very high standard. The educational system is complemented by vocational schools whose main objective is the satisfaction of the growing demand for skilled personnel by the tourism and manufacturing sectors. A selection of good quality private schools exists also in every major town, which address the needs of foreign speaking pupils. These schools offer tuition in English, French, Italian, Armenian and Arabic at very reasonable fees.

Higher education in Cyprus is provided by public and private tertiary level institutions. About 48 per cent of all secondary school leavers continue their studies. Of these, 50 per cent attend higher education institutions in Cyprus and 50 per cent go abroad.

Public institutions

There are six public tertiary level institutions. The University of Cyprus offers courses leading to graduate and postgraduate degrees. The other five entities offer courses at a sub-degree level in various fields of study. These are the Cyprus Forestry College, the Higher Technical Institute, the Hotel and Catering Institute, the Mediterranean Institute of Management and the School of Nursing.

Private institutions

A number of private third level institutions offer one-to-four-year courses in such fields as secretarial studies, business administration, electrical, civil and mechanical engineering, hotel and catering, banking, accountancy and computer studies. Most have registered with the Ministry of Education, to offer specific courses leading to the award of a Certificate/Diploma/Degree. Some of these institutions have registered to offer postgraduate programmes as well.

Continuous education

There is a large number of private and public continuous education training institutions in Cyprus, offering a wide range of training courses on management, technical, vocational and IT-related topics.

Training and continuous education subsidies

The HRDA offers substantial subsidies for training. The subsidies cover training costs for courses attended both in Cyprus and abroad. In addition, the HRDA offers a scheme that subsidizes the creation of an in-company training centre. Companies that pay employer's contributions to the Training Development Fund are eligible for these subsidies.

Conclusion

Those who are interested in doing business in Cyprus will find that the management of human resources will not be a serious problem. Cyprus has an excellent services infrastructure, and its people are hard working, well educated and friendly. The bureaucracy of setting up is no worse than in any other European country and the tax benefits can be substantial.

After all, Cyprus, due to its strategic location, has a long history of acting as host to foreign visitors, businessmen, traders and investors, and, with EU accession looming, the future is challenging and promising. The island is beautiful, the weather is warm and the crime rate is low. This combination of beneficial factors makes Cyprus the perfect place to set up and grow a business.

Part Nine

Appendices

Appendix 1

Useful Information

Passports and visas

All visitors to Cyprus must be in possession of a valid national passport or travel document. Those coming from the EU, Switzerland, Liechtenstein, Norway and Iceland may enter Cyprus with their national identity card, provided it bears a photograph of the holder and the nationality is clearly stated.

Visas are not required by visitors from many countries, but it is strongly recommended that people intending to travel to Cyprus check with their nearest Cyprus embassy, consulate or Tourism Organization office in advance of travel.

Health requirements and medical facilities in Cyprus

There are no vaccination requirements for visitors to Cyprus.

Medical facilities are available at government general hospitals and at private clinics and hospitals.

In case of emergencies, international visitors may receive treatment and assistance free of charge at government hospitals, but outpatient treatment is subject to payment of a prescribed fee.

Airports and airlines serving Cyprus

The main gateway into Cyprus is through Larnaca Airport, which as at mid-2003 is undergoing major upgrading. Paphos is a second international airport, used more for chartered than scheduled flights.

All major European and Middle Eastern airlines and those from Eastern Europe, Russia and the CIS serve Cyprus, as do many charter airlines, especially during the tourist season.

Time

Cyprus is two hours ahead of Greenwich Mean Time (GMT).

Working hours

Government

Monday–Friday 0730–1430

Business offices

15 September to 31 May
Monday–Friday 0800–1300 and 1500–1800
1 June to 14 September
Monday–Friday 0800–1300 and 1600–1900

Banks

September to May
Monday 1515–1645
Tuesday–Friday 0830–1230

June to August
Monday–Friday 0815–1230

In the tourist areas some bank branches either remain open longer or re-open in the afternoon during the tourist season.

Retail shops

1 November to 31 March
Monday, Tuesday and Thursday 0900 up to 1900
Wednesday and Friday 0900–2000
Saturday 0900–1500

1 April to 31 October
Monday, Tuesday, Thursday 0900–2030
Wednesday 0900–1400
Friday 0900–2130
Saturday 0900–1700
Summer afternoon recess 1400–1700

Post Offices

Monday–Friday 0730–1300
Some open in the afternoon in tourist areas.

Petrol stations

Monday–Friday 0600–1900
Saturday 0600–1500
Most have vending machines out of hours.

Public holidays

There are 14 statutory holidays during the year as follows:

- 1 January (New Year's Day)
- 6 January (Epiphany Day)
- First Day of Lent
- 25 March (Greek Independence Day)
- 1 April (Greek Cypriot National Day)
- Good Friday (Greek Orthodox)
- Easter Monday (Greek Orthodox)
- 1 May (Labor Day)
- Whit Monday
- 15 August (Assumption Day)
- 1 October (Cyprus Independence Day)
- 28 October (Greek National Day – Oxi Day)
- 25 December (Christmas Day)
- 26 December (Boxing Day)

NB: Orthodox Easter tends to be one week later than Catholic/Protestant Easter.

In addition there is Green Monday, 50 days before Orthodox Easter, and 24 December (Christmas Eve). (NB: All public services, private enterprises, banks and shops are closed on public holidays although in tourist areas some shops and services may remain open. Banks are also closed on Easter Tuesday but not on Christmas Eve).

Language

The official language of business and with government is Greek but English is widely used in both sectors, including in official communication with government and its agencies. (NB: Turkish is also an official language but is little used in the Republic of Cyprus at this time but will become more prevalent in the event a settlement is reached over the northern area of the island.)

Although most Cypriots do speak English, except perhaps the older generations in the villages, the learning and use of some Greek will always be well received.

It should be noted also that in recent years there has been a move to reintroduce non-anglicized versions of place names. Thus Nicosia is now frequently referred to on such as road signs as Lefkosia and Limassol as Lemesos, whilst Larnaca and Paphos have had their transliterated spelling amended to Larnaka and Pafos.

Climate

Cyprus has long summers stretching from May to mid-October. Daily temperatures in July and August reach as high as 30°C in Nicosia, 27°C on the coast and 23°C in the mountains. Winters tend to be mild, with temperatures averaging 12°C on the coast in January but with some snow on the mountains at that time. Rain can also be anticipated in winter and whilst for some years there was little precipitation, in early 2002 and 2003 the rains were very heavy and were accompanied by thunder and lightning.

The hot weather is generally ameliorated for visitors, as air conditioning is increasingly prevalent in hotels, offices and private homes in Nicosia and along the coastal areas. Many cars now also have air conditioning, but not usually the cheaper hire cars.

Clothing

For most of the summer months light- to medium-weight wear is recommended. In early and late summer the evenings can become slightly cooler and so a warm wrap or light jacket would ensure comfort.

In winter, and especially in the mountains, heavier clothing is recommended. Given the possibility of rain between January and March across the island, a lightweight raincoat would be useful.

Business dress

For most of the year a visiting businessman would usually be expected to wear a suit and tie, as most of his Cypriot colleagues will be so attired. However, the summer months are very hot and so many locals tend to be more casually dressed, often with open-necked shirts and no jackets. Initially, at least, the foreign visitor should continue to wear a tie, if not a jacket.

Ladies are expected to dress smartly for business throughout the year, wearing light- to medium-weight clothes in summer and something a little heavier in the winter.

Business etiquette

Cyprus is becoming increasingly Western in habit and businessmen and women increasingly busy. It is thus the case that it is important to make appointments in advance and to recognize that meetings increasingly tend to be held to schedule. Given the busier lives of many local businessmen a courtesy call in the event one is delayed is always well received.

Money

The currency in Cyprus is the Cyprus pound, which is divided into 100 cents. Banknotes in circulation are in denominations of 20, 10, 5 and 1 pound and coins are 50, 20, 10, 5, 2 and 1 cent.

Although Cyprus becomes a member of the EU in May 2004 it could be 2009 before the euro becomes the official currency.

Credit cards

All major credit cards are accepted throughout Cyprus.

Exchange control

What exchange control presently remains in force, mainly on the movement of capital, is likely to have been removed before 1 May 2004.

Electricity

The electricity supply is 240 volts, 50 Hz.

Most sockets are 13 amp with three rectangular pins, but adaptors are easy to find.

Water

All food products and drinking water are monitored by the health inspectors of the Ministry of Health, as well as by local authorities across the Republic. All drinking water is of a high quality and safe for human consumption. However, local bottled water is readily available in most restaurants and tavernas.

Telecommunications

Cyprus has one of the best telecommunications systems in the whole of the Mediterranean region, which is also the cheapest in Europe. A complete portfolio of services is available, including mobile communications, e-mail and Internet (including broadband).

As at mid-2003 telecommunications are in the process of being liberalized.

Petrol

Leaded and unleaded fuels are readily available at prices increasingly close to those applicable in Europe. Even diesel, which for many years was subsidized to support agriculture, is now increasing in price to nearer that of standard petrol.

Many petrol stations are self-service and after hours many have vending machines that accept local banknotes and all credit cards. All instructions on these are in Greek and English and visitors will find the locals very helpful in case of difficulties.

Local transportation

Taxis

Taxis are readily available and can be hailed on the street or summoned by telephone. All taxis have meters.

Service taxis
There is a system of service (shared) taxis operating between towns and the bigger villages, which are inexpensive.

Buses

There are bus services both within and between towns and between the villages and towns.

Trains

There are no trains in Cyprus.

Car hire

The major car hire companies are all represented in Cyprus and there are also many local firms that will provide cars at substantially lower rates, even during the tourist season. When hiring cars, especially from smaller companies, it is important to ensure the condition and safety of vehicles and that the vehicle is properly insured.

All hire cars have a red registration plate with an alpha-numeric registration beginning with the letter Z.

Traffic and driving

Generally speaking traffic flows freely on the main highways but at certain times of the day quite substantial traffic jams can be anticipated in the main towns. At these times busy locations are frequented by traffic police seeking to enhance the flow.

The speed limit on the main highways is 100 kph. Such roads are subjected to regular police radar checks, especially at times of peak traffic movement. Inside the towns speed limits vary between 60 kph in suburban areas to 50 kph in more built-up areas. Exceeding the speed limit is punishable by a fine.

The wearing of seat belts in the front of a car is compulsory (although many locals will be seen driving without wearing them) and the use of mobile phones whilst driving and drink driving are strictly forbidden.

The overall standard of driving could be higher and thus visitors hiring cars are recommended to proceed with caution.

Television and radio

There are seven national television channels, with many programmes being transmitted in English with Greek subtitles. CyBC2 has an English news programme every evening.

Satellite television is readily available in hotels and for domestic installation from a number of suppliers, enabling the receiving of a substantial number of channels, among them the BBC, CNN and NBC.

There are numerous local, national and international radio stations accessible in Cyprus, including the BBC World Service and The British Forces Broadcasting Service (BFBS).

Newspapers

Local newspapers in English include The Cyprus Mail, published daily except Mondays, The Cyprus Weekly and The Financial Mirror. Most European newspapers are available in Cyprus either late on the day of publication or early the next day.

Weights and measures

Cyprus uses the metric system for both weights and measures.

International clubs

All of Lions International, Rotary, Round Table, Skal, Inner Wheel and Toastmasters International are active in the main centres of Cyprus.

General information

The Greek Orthodox Church maintains a strong influence over life in Cyprus, including over business and tourism. All religious holidays are strictly kept and the likelihood of doing business on one is minimal, so attention to the public holiday calendar is strongly recommended.

Many Cypriots take their holidays during August, the hottest month of the year, and thus negligible progress in any business or private transaction can be anticipated.

Appendix 2

Useful Addresses and Telephone Numbers

Accountants and auditors

Deloitte & Touche
Corner Themistocles Dervis and Florinis Streets
PO Box 21675
1512 Nicosia
Cyprus
Tel: +357 22 360 300
Fax: +357 22 360 400
Web site: www.deloitte.com.cy

Deloitte & Touche
Tax Services
Eftapaton Court
256 Makarios III Avenue
3105 Limassol
Cyprus

and

PO Box 53180
3301 Limassol
Cyprus
Tel: +357 25 857 700
Fax: +357 25 356 010
Web site: www.deloitte.com.cy

Ernst & Young
Nicosia Tower Centre
36 Byron Avenue
PO Box 21656
1511 Nicosia
Cyprus
Tel: +357 22 674 000
Fax: +357 22 677 005, +357 22 677 004
Web site: www.cy.eyi.com

PG Economides & Co
Chartered Certified Accountants
Totalserve House
17 Gr. Xenopoulou Street
PO Box 53117
3300 Limassol
Cyprus
Tel: +357 25 866 300
Fax: +357 25 866 301
Web site: www.pgeconomides.com

Pricewaterhouse Coopers
Julia House
3 Themistocles Dervis Street
PO Box 21612
1591 Nicosia
Cyprus
Tel: +357 22 555 000
Fax: +357 22 555 001
Web site: www.pwcglobal.com

Advertising services

Gremona / McCann Erickson
Corner Kyriakou Matsi Avenue
and Rodou Street
Nadia Court
PO Box 24740
1303 Nicosia
Cyprus
Tel: +357 22 317 373
Fax: +357 22 318 654
Web site: www.gremona-mccann.com.cy

Innovation Advertising – Leo Burnett
90 Ifigenias Street
2nd Floor
Strovolos
PO Box 16058
2085 Nicosia
Cyprus
Tel: +357 22 378 828
Fax: +357 22 378 577
Web site: www.leoburnett.com.cy

Pandora / Ogilvy & Mather
12–14, Kennedy Avenue
Kennedy Business centre
1st Floor, Office 101
PO Box 23683
1685 Nicosia
Cyprus
Tel: +357 22 767 374
Fax: +357 22 767 388
Web site: www.ogilvy.com.cy

Pyramis DDB Advertising Ltd
49 Elia Papakyriakou Street
2415 Engomi
Makedonitissa
Nicosia

and

PO Box 22438
1521 Nicosia
Cyprus
Tel: +357 22 592 232
Fax: +357 22 591 399
Web site: www.ddbcy.com

Airline offices or general sales agents

Aeroflot	+357 22 669 071
Air Malta	+357 22 661 666
Air 2000	+357 22 672 101
Air Slovakia	+357 22 881 222
Alitalia	+357 22 678 000
Austrian Airlines	+357 22 881 222
Balkan – Bulgarian Airlines	+357 22 668 181
British Airways	+357 22 761 166
Cyprus Airways	+357 22 663 054
Czech Airlines	+357 22 678 000
Egypt Air	+357 22 763 777
El Al – Israel Airlines	+357 25 374 180
Emirates	+357 22 375 462
Finnair	+357 22 678 000
Gulf Air	+357 22 374 064
Iran Air	+357 22 881 222
JAT – Yugoslav Airlines	+357 22 374 757
KLM	+357 22 671 616

Kuwait Airways	+357 22 760 921
Libyan Arab Airlines	+357 22 870 000
LOT – Polish Airlines	+357 22 870 000
Lufthansa	+357 22 873 330
Malev – Hungarian Airlines	+357 22 680 980
MEA – Middle East Airlines	+357 22 670 444
Olympic Airways	+357 22 672 101
Royal Jordanian Airlines	+357 22 375 360
Syrian Arab Airlines	+357 22 376 552
Swiss	+357 22 881 222
Tarom – Romanian Airlines	+357 22 375 266

Banks

Central Bank of Cyprus
80 Kennedy Avenue
1076 Nicosia
Cyprus
Tel: +357 22 714 100
Fax: +357 22 378 153
Web site: www.centralbank.gov.cy
e-mail: cbcinfo@centralbank.gov.cy

Alpha Bank Limited
1 Prodromou Street
1596 Nicosia
Cyprus
Tel: +357 22 888 888
Fax: +357 22 773 766
Web site: www.alphabank.com
e-mail: secretariat@alphabank.com

Bank of Cyprus
51 Stasinos Street
Ayia Paraskevi
2002 Nicosia
Cyprus
Tel: +357 22 378 000
Fax: +357 22 378 111
Web site: www.cy.bankofcyprus.com
e-mail: info@cy.bankofcyprus.com

Hellenic Bank
92 Dighenis Akritas Avenue
1061 Nicosia
Cyprus
Tel: +357 22 860 000
Fax: +357 22 754 074
Web site: www.hellenicbank.com
e-mail: Hellenic@hellenicbank.com

National Bank of Greece (Cyprus) Ltd
15 Archbishop Makarios III Avenue
1065 Nicosia
Cyprus
Tel: +357 22 840 000
Fax: +357 22 758 090

The Cyprus Popular Bank
Laiki Group
154 Limassol Avenue
2025 Nicosia
Cyprus

and

PO Box 22032
1598 Nicosia
Cyprus
Tel: +357 22 811 330
Fax: +357 22 811 492
Web site: www.laiki.com
e-mail: info@laiki.com

Business consultancy services

The Philip Dew Consultancy Limited
Julia House
3 Themistocles Dervis Street
Nicosia

and

PO Box 11836
Bahrain
Tel:+973 1770 0886
Fax: +973 1779 0729
e-mail: pdew@batelco.com.bh

Totalserve Management Ltd
Totalserve House
17, Gr. Xenopoulou Street
3106 Limassol
Cyprus

and

PO Box 54425
3724 Limassol
Cyprus
Tel: +357 25 866 000
Fax: +357 25 866 001
Web site: www.totalservecy.com

Chamber of Commerce and Industry

Cyprus Chamber of Commerce and Industry
38 Grivas Dhigenis Avenue and 3 Deligiorgis Street
PO Box 21455
1509 Nicosia
Tel: +357 22 889 800
Fax: +357 22 669 048
Web site: www.ccci.org.cy
e-mail: chamber@ccci.org.cy
There are also local chambers in Nicosia, Limassol, Famagusta,
Larnaca and Paphos.

Chartered surveyors

Antonis Loizou & Associates
68A Kennedy Avenue
1076 Nicosia

and

PO Box 6634
1640 Nicosia
Cyprus
Tel: +357 22 424 853
Fax: +357 22 428 681

Cyprus diplomatic representation overseas

Australia
30 Beale Crescent
Deakin ACT 2600

Canberra
Tel: +612 62 910 832
Fax: +612 62 810 860
e-mail: cyphicom@iprimus.com.au

Austria
20 Parkring
A-1010 Vienna
Tel: +431 51 30 630
Fax: +431 51 30 632
e-mail: embassy2

Belgium
2 Square Ambiorix
1000 Brussels
Tel: +322 73 53 510
Fax: +322 73 54 552
e-mail: cyprus.embassy@skynet.be

Canada (Consulate General)
365, Bloor Street East
Suite 1010
Toronto M4W 3L4
Tel: +1416 94 40 998
Fax: +1416 94 49 149
e-mail: consulcy@istar.ca

China
2–13–2, Ta Yuan Diplomatic Office Building
Liang Ma He Road
Chao Yang District
Beijing 100600
Tel: +8610 65 325 057
Fax: +8610 65 324 244
e-mail: cyembpek@mail.spikice.com.cn

Czech Republic
6 Sibirske nan
Corner Juarezova 2
160 00 Praha 6
Tel: +420 23 114 622
Fax: +420 24 317 529
e-mail: cyprusembass@mbox.vol.cz

Denmark
Suite 301
Clarion Hotel Neptune
Sankt Annae Plads 18–20
DK-1250 Copenhagen K
Tel: +45 33 962 031
Fax: +45 33 962 031

Egypt
1st Floor
23A Ismail Mohamed Street
Zamalek
Cairo
Tel: +202 73 61 288
Fax: +202 73 65 299

Finland
Bulevardi 57 23
Helsinki 00120
Tel: +3589 69 62 820
Fax: +3589 69 62 830
e-mail: cyemb.hel@kolumbus.fi

France
23 Rue Galilee
75116 Paris
Tel: +331 47 208 628
Fax: +331 40 701 344
e-mail: embrecyp@worldnet.fr

Germany
27 Waltstrasse
10179 Berlin
Tel: +4930 30 86 830
Fax: +4930 27 591 454
e-mail: cyprusembassy@t-online.de

and

Consulate General
3 Rothenbaumchaussee
20148 Hamburg
Tel: +4940 41 07 497
Fax: +4940 41 07 246
e-mail: cyconsulate-hamburg@k-online.de

Greece
16 Herodotou Street
10675 Athens
Tel: +301 72 32 727
Fax: +301 72 31 927
e-mail: cyempkl@hol.gr

and

Consulate General
37 Leoforos Nikis
1st Floor
54622 Thessaloniki
Tel: +3031 260 611
Fax: +3031 274 984
e-mail: cycom@idealcom.net

Hungary
V. Dorottya u.3
III Floor
1051 Budapest
Tel: +361 26 66 045
Fax: +361 26 60 538

India
106 Jor Bagh
New Delhi 110003
Tel: +9111 46 97 503
Fax: +9111 46 28 828
e-mail: cyprus@del3.vsnl.net.in

Iran
328 Shahid Karimi Street
Dezashib
Tehran
Tel: +9821 22 19 842
Fax: +9821 22 19 843
e-mail: cypembth@www.dci.com.ir

Ireland
71 Lower Leeson Street
Dublin 2
Tel: +3531 67 63 060
Fax: +3531 67 63 099
e-mail: embassyofcyprusdub@eircom.net

Israel
50, Dizengoff Street
64332 Tel Aviv
Tel: +9723 52 50 212
Fax: +9723 62 90 535
e-mail: cyprus@netvision.net.il

Italy
15 Via Francesco Denza
00197 Rome
Tel: +3906 80 88 365
Fax: +3906 80 88 338
e-mail: emb.rome@flashnet.it

Kenya
Eagle House
5th Floor
Kimathi Street
PO Box 30739
Nairobi
Tel: +2542 220 881
Fax: +2542 331 232
e-mail: cyphc@net2000ke.com

Libya
Shara Al Tel
Ben Ashour
PO Box 3284, Central Post Office
Tripoli
Tel: +21821 36 01 274
Fax: +21821 36 13 516

Netherlands
15 Surinamestraat
2855 GG The Hague
Tel: +3170 34 66 499
Fax: +3170 39 24 024
e-mail: cyprus@xs4all.nl

Portugal
1 Avenue De Liberdade 229
1250–142 Lisbon
Tel: +351 21 31 94 180
Fax: +351 21 31 94 189
e-mail: chipre@clix.pt

Russia

U1. B. Nikitskaya 51, (Gertsena)
Moscow 121069
Tel: +7095 29 02 154
Fax: +7095 20 01 254
e-mail: cyprusemb@col.ru

South Africa

Corner of Church and Hill Street
Arcadia 0083
Pretoria

and

PO Box 14554
Hatfield 0028
Tel: + 2712 34 25 258
Fax: +2712 34 25 596
e-mail: cyprusib@mweb.co.za

Spain

C/Serrano 23 (2D)
28001 Madrid
Tel: +3491 57 83 114
Fax: +3491 57 82 189
e-mail: cyembassy@mx4.redestb.es

Sweden

37 Birger Jarlsgatan
4th Floor
PO Box 7649
103 94 Stockholm
Tel: +468 245 008
Fax: +468 244 518
e-mail: cy.emb@ebox.tninet.se

Syria

Akram Al-Ojjeh Street
Bld. No. 106
Eastern Mezzeh-Fursan

and

PO Box 9269
Damascus
Tel: +96311 61 30 812/3
Fax: +96311 61 30 814
e-mail: cyemb@scs-net.org

United Kingdom
93 Park Street
London W1K 4ET
Tel: +44 207 49 98 272/4
Fax: +44 207 49 10 691
e-mail: cyphclondon@dial.pipex.com

United States
2211 R. St, North-West
Washington DC 20008
Tel: +1202 46 25 772
Fax: +1202 48 36 710
e-mail: cypembwash@earthlink.net

and

Consulate General
13, East 40th Street
5th Floor
New York, NY 10016
Tel: +1212 68 66 016/7
Fax: +1212 44 71 988

Yugoslavia
9 Diplomatska Kolonija
11040 Belgrade
Tel: +38111 36 72 725
Fax: +38111 36 71 348
e-mail: cyprus@EUnet.yu

Cyprus trade centres overseas

Austria
Parkring 20
A-1010 Vienna
Tel: +431 51 30 634
Fax: +431 51 30 635
e-mail: cyprus-trade@vienna.at

Czech Republic
36 Budecska Street
120 00 Prague 2
Tel: +4202 2225 4152
Fax: +4202 2225 4081
e-mail: cytrade@id.cz

Egypt
23A Ismael Mohamed Street
1st Floor
Zamalek
Cairo
Tel: +202 73 61 288
Fax: +202 73 65 299

France
42 Rue de la Bienfaisance
75008 Paris
Tel: +331 4289 6086
Fax: +331 4289 6077
e-mail: chypre@wanadoo.fr

Germany
42–44 Friedrichstrasse
D-50676 Cologne
Tel: +49221 272 358
Fax: +49221237 013
e-mail: info@zypern-wirtshaft.de

Greece
36 Voukourestiou Street
10673 Athens
Tel: +301 36 46 320
Fax: +301 36 46 420
e-mail: ctcath@otenet.gr

Israel
14th Floor, Top Tower
Dizengoff Centre
50 Dizengoff Street
64332 Tel Aviv
Tel: +972 3525 8970
Fax: +972 3620 0078
e-mail: ctc@urbis.net.il

Russia
UI Dimitria Ullanova
16 Korp.2 Kv.127
Moscow 107292
Tel: +7095 12 42 659
Fax: +7095 12 42 427
e-mail: cytrade@cityline.ru

Sweden
37 Birger Jarlsgartan
4th Floor
PO Box 7649
10394 Stockholm
Tel: +468 240 941
Fax: +468 207 533
e-mail: cyprustradecentre.sweden@chello.se

United Arab Emirates
AlGhurair Centre, Office Tower
6th Floor, Office No. 635
PO Box 11294
Dubai
Tel: +9714 22 82 411
Fax: +9714 22 75 700
e-mail: cycentre@emirates.net.ae

United Kingdom
29 Princes Street
3rd Floor
London W1R 7RG
Tel: +44 207 62 96 288
Fax: +44 207 62 95 244
e-mail: cytradecentreuk@btinternet.com

United States
13 East 40th Street
New York, NY 10016
Tel: +1212 21 39 100
Fax: +1212 21 32 918
e-mail: ctcny@cyprustradeny.org

Employers & Industrialists Federation (OEB)

Employers & Industrialists Federation (OEB)
30 Grivas Dhigenis Avenue
PO Box 21657
1511 Nicosia
Cyprus
Tel: +357 22 665 102
Fax: +357 22 669 459
Web site: www.oeb-eif.org

Exhibition and conference services

Cyprus State Fairs Authority
Georgiou Seferi Street
Engomi
PO Box 23551
1684 Nicosia
Tel: +357 22 352 918
Fax: +357 22 352 316
Web site: www.csfa.org.cy

Options Cassoulides
114 A. Loukaide Street
Oasis Complex
Block E, 4th Floor
PO Box 54723
3727 Limassol
Cyprus
Tel: +357 25 843 600
Fax: +357 25 340 830
Web site: www.options.com.cy

Suricom Consultants Ltd
John Kennedy Avenue
Iris House
2nd Floor, Suite 2
PO Box 53184
3301 Limassol
Cyprus
Tel: +357 25 589 418
Fax: +357 25 589 296
Web site: www.suricom.com.cy

Foreign diplomatic representation in Cyprus

Australia
4 Annis Komninis Street
1060 Nicosia
Tel: +357 22 753 001
Fax: +357 22 766 486
e-mail: auscomm@logos.cy.net

Bulgaria
13 Constantinou Paleologou Street
Engomi,
2406 Nicosia
Tel: +357 22 672 486
Fax: +357 22 676 598
e-mail: Bulgaria@cytanet.com.cy

China
28 Archimidou Street
PO Box 24531
2411 Engomi
1300 Nicosia
Tel: +357 22 352 182
Fax: +357 22 353 530

Cuba
7 Yiannis Taliotis Street
Strovolos
2014 Nicosia
Tel: +357 22 512 332
Fax: +357 22 512 331
e-mail: embacuba@spidernet.com.cy

Czech Republic
48 Arsinois Street
Acropolis
PO Box 25202
Nicosia
Tel: +357 22 421 118
Fax: +357 22 421 059

Egypt
3 Egypt Avenue
PO Box 21752
1097 Nicosia
Tel: +357 22 680 651
Fax: +357 22 664 265

France
12 Ploutarchou Street
PO Box 21671
Engomi
2406 Nicosia
Tel: +357 22 779 910
Fax: +357 22 781 052

Germany
10 Nikitaras Street
1080 Nicosia
Tel: +357 22 451 145
Fax: +357 22 665 694
e-mail: germanembassy@cytanet.com.cy

Greece
8 Byron Avenue
PO Box 21799
1513 Nicosia
Tel: +357 22 680 645
Fax: +357 22 680 649

India
3 Indira Gandhi Street
Montparnasse Hill
Engomi
PO Box 25544
1515 Nicosia
Tel: +357 22 351 741
Fax: +357 22 350 402
e-mail: India@spidernet.com.cy

Iran
42 Armenias Street
Acropolis
PO Box 28908
Nicosia
Tel: +357 22 314 459
Fax: +357 22 315 446

Israel
4 Grypari Street
PO Box 25159
1307 Nicosia
Tel: +357 22 664 195/6
Fax: +357 22 663 486

Italy
11 25th March Street
Engomi
2408 Nicosia
Tel: +357 22 357 635
Fax: +357 22 357 616

Lebanon
1 Vassilissis Olgas Street
1101 Nicosia

and

PO Box 21924
Engomi,
1515 Nicosia
Tel: +357 22 774 216
Fax: +357 22 776 662

Libya
14 Estias Street
PO Box 23669
1041 Nicosia
Tel: +357 22 317 366
Fax: +357 22 316 152

Poland
12–14 Kennedy Avenue
Flat 302
1087 Nicosia
Tel: +357 22 753 517
Fax: +357 22 753 784

Romania
83 Kennedy Avenue
PO Box 2210
1077 Nicosia
Tel: +357 22 379 303
Fax: +357 22 379 121
e-mail: romemb@cylink.com.cy

Russia
Corner Agiou Prokopiou Street
and Archbishop Makarios III Avenue
2406 Engomi
1514 Nicosia
Tel: +357 22 774 622
Fax: +357 22 774 854
e-mail: transl@cytanet.com.cy

Slovak Republic
4 Kalamatas Street
2002 Strovolos
PO Box 21165

1514 Nicosia
Tel: +357 22 311 681
Fax: +357 22 311 715

Switzerland
46 Themistocles Dervis Street
MEDCON Building
6th Floor
PO Box 20729
1663 Nicosia
Tel: +357 22 766 261
Fax: +357 22 766 008

Syria
24 Nikodimou Myonla Street
Ayios Antonios
1071 Nicosia

and

PO Box 21891
1514 Nicosia
Tel: +357 22 764 481/2
Fax: +357 22 756 963

United Kingdom
Alexander Pallis Street
PO Box 21978
1587 Nicosia
Tel: +357 22 861 100
Fax: +357 22 861 125
Web site: www.Britain.org.cy

United States
Corner Metochiou and Ploutarchou Streets
2406 Engomi
Nicosia
Tel: +357 22 776 400
Fax: +357 22 780 944
e-mail: amembsys@spidernet.com.cy

Yugoslavia
2 Vassilissis Olgas Street
Engomi
1101 Nicosia
Tel: +357 22 777 511
Fax: +357 22 775 910

Hotels (5 Star)

Aeneas Hotel, Ayia Napa
(Meridien Hotel)
Tel: +357 23 724 000
Fax: +357 23 723 677
Web site: www.aeneas.com.cy

Alion Beach Hotel, Ayia Napa
Tel: +357 23 722 900
Fax: +357 23 722 901
Web site: www.nissi-beach.com

Amathus Beach Hotel, Limassol
Tel: +357 25 832 000
Fax: +357 25 327 494
Web site: www.amathus-hotel.com

Coral Beach Hotel and Resort, Paphos
Tel: +357 26 621 601
Fax: +357 26 621 742
Web site: www.coralbeach.com.cy

Four Seasons Hotel, Limassol
Tel: +357 25 310 222
Fax: +357 25 310 887
Web site: www.fourseasons.com.cy

Hawaii Grand Hotel & Resort, Limassol
Tel: +357 25 634 333
Fax: +357 25 634 588
Web site: www.hawaiihotel.com

Hilton Cyprus, Nicosia
Tel: +357 23 724 000
Fax: +357 23 723 677
Web site: www.aeneas.com.cy

Le Meridien Limassol Spa & Resort, Limassol
Tel: +357 25 862 000
Fax: +357 25 634 222
Web site: www.lemeridien-cyprus.com

Louis Apollonia Beach Hotel, Limassol
Tel: +357 25 323 351
Fax: +357 25 321 683
Web site: www.louishotels.com

Paphos Amathus Beach Hotel, Paphos
Tel: +357 26 964 300
Fax: +357 26 964 222
Web site: www.pamathus.com

St Raphael Resort, Limassol
Tel: +357 25 636 100
Fax: +357 25 636 394

Human resources consultants

Jacovos Christofides
Human Resources Consultant
Lozanis 2a
2023 Strovolos
Nicosia
Cyprus
Tel: +357 22 510 911
Fax: +357 22 318 882
Contact: Jacovos Christofides
e-mail: JChristofides@valicom.com.cy

Lawyers and legal consultants

Andreas Coucounis & Co
9 Archbishop Makarios III Avenue
Lazaros Centre, Suites 101–02
PO Box 40519
6305 Larnaca
Cyprus
Tel: +357 24 654 697
Fax: +357 24 626 106
Web site: www.coucounis.com

Chrysses Demetriades & Co. Law Office
Fortuna Court
284 Makarios III Avenue
3105 Limassol
Cyprus

and

PO Box 50132
3601 Limassol
Cyprus
Tel: +357 25 582 424
Fax: +357 25 587 191, +357 25 588 055
Web site: www.demetriades.com

Costas Indianos & Co
4 Diagorou Street
Kermia House, Office 601
PO Box 21574
1510 Nicosia
Cyprus
Tel: +357 22 675 231
Fax: +357 22 669 678
Web site: www.indianos.com.cy

CP Erotocritou & Co
23 Olymbion Street
Libra Tower, 4th Floor
PO Box 50437
3605 Limassol
Cyprus
Tel: +357 25 363 665
Fax: +357 25 341 500
Web site: www.c.p.erotocritou.com

Tassos Papadopoulos & Co
2 Sofouli Street
Chanteclair Building, 2nd Floor
1096 Nicosia
Cyprus
Tel: +357 22 677 999
Fax: +357 22 669 090
Web site: www.papadopoulos.com

Management consultancy

Deloitte & Touche
Corner Themistocles Dervis and Florinis Streets
PO Box 21675
1512 Nicosia
Cyprus
Tel: +357 22 360 300
Fax: +357 22 360 400
Web site: www.deloitte.com.cy

Totalserve Management Ltd
Totalserve House
17 Gr. Xenopoulou Street
3106 Limassol
Cyprus

and

PO Box 54425
3724 Limassol
Cyprus
Tel: +357 25 866 000
Fax: +357 25 866 001
Web site: www.totalservecy.com

Market research

ACNielsen AMER
5 Limassol Avenue
PO Box 23962
1687 Nicosia
Cyprus
Tel: +357 22 337 660
Fax: +357 22 337 655
Web site: www.acnielsen.com

Ministries and government agencies relevant to business

Cyprus Securities and Exchange Commission
32 Stasikratous
4th Floor
PO Box 24996
1306 Nicosia
Cyprus
Tel: +357 22 875 475
Fax: +357 22 754 671
Web site: www.cysec.gov.cy

Cyprus Tourism Organisation
19 Limassol Avenue
2112 Nicosia
Cyprus

and

PO Box 24535
1390 Nicosia
Cyprus
Tel: +357 22 337 715, +357 22 691 144
Fax: +357 22 331 644
Web site: www.cto.org.cy
e-mail: informationcentre@cto.org.cy

Ministry of Commerce, Industry and Tourism
6A Araouzos Street
(off Limassol Avenue)
1421 Nicosia
Cyprus
Tel: +357 22 867 100, +357 22 867 112
Fax: +357 22 304 924, +357 22 375 120
Web site: www.cyprustrade.gov.cy
e-mail: mintrade@spidernet.com.cy

Newspaper – financial

Financial Mirror
89–91 Prodromou Street
Strovolos
2063 Nicosia
Cyprus

and

PO Box 16077
2085 Nicosia
Cyprus
Tel: +357 22 678 666
Fax: +357 22 678 664
Web site: www.financialmirror.com

Public relations consultants

Christian Alexander Public Relations & Event Planning
53 Kennedy Avenue
Office 101
PO Box 28929
2084 Nicosia
Cyprus
Tel: +357 22 318 431
Fax: +357 22 510 489

Cypronetwork Consultancy Group
Corner 2, Zinonos Rossidi & Agias Fylaxeos Street
PO Box 3318
Limassol
Cyprus
Tel: +357 25 730 540
Fax: +357 25 730 441
Web site: www.cypronetwork.com

Real estate consultants

Antonis Loizou & Associates
68A Kennedy Avenue
1076 Nicosia

and

PO Box 6634
1640 Nicosia
Cyprus
Tel: +357 22 424 853
Fax: +357 22 428 681

Shipping and ship management consultants

Deloitte & Touche
Tax Services
Eftapaton Court
256 Makarios III Avenue
3105 Limassol
Cyprus

and

PO Box 53180
3301 Limassol
Cyprus
Tel: +357 25 857 700
Fax: +357 25 356 010
Web site: www.deloitte.com.cy

Totalserve Management Ltd
Totalserve House
17 Gr. Xenopoulou Street
3106 Limassol
Cyprus

and

PO Box 54425
3724 Limassol
Cyprus
Tel: +357 25 866 000
Fax: +357 25 866 001
Web site: www.totalservecy.com

Strategy consultants

Civilitas Research
13 Queen Olga Street
PO Box 16183
2086 Nicosia
Cyprus
Tel: +357 22 492 555
Fax: +357 22 495 040
Web site: www.Civilitasresearch.com
Contact: Dr James Ker-Lindsay, Managing Director
e-mail: james.lindsay@civilitasresearch.com

Tax consultants

Deloitte & Touche
Tax Services
Eftapaton Court
256 Makarios III Avenue
3105 Limassol
Cyprus

and

PO Box 53180
3301 Limassol
Cyprus
Tel: +357 25 857 700
Fax: +357 25 356 010
Web site: www.deloitte.com.cy

Totalserve Management Ltd
Totalserve House
17 Gr. Xenopoulou Street
3106 Limassol
Cyprus

and

PO Box 54425
3724 Limassol
Cyprus
Tel: +357 25 866 000
Fax: +357 25 866 001
Web site: www.totalservecy.com

Appendix 3

Contributors' Contact Details

ACNielsen AMER
5 Limassol Avenue
PO Box 23962
1687 Nicosia
Cyprus
Tel: +357 22 337 660
Fax: +357 22 337 655
Web: www.acnielsen.com
Contact: Soulla Kellas, Director, Customised Research
e-mail: Kellas.soulla@Cyprus.ACNielsen.com
Contact: Anna Rita Hadjigavriel, Director, Client Sales & Service
e-mail: Hadjigavriel.Annarita@Cyprus.ACNielsen.com

Antonis Loizou & Associates
68A Kennedy Avenue
1076 Nicosia

and

PO Box 6634
1640 Nicosia
Cyprus
Tel: +357 22 424 853
Fax: +357 22 428 681
Contact: Antonis Loizou, Senior Partner
e-mail: aloizou@logos.cy.net

Central Bank of Cyprus
80 Kennedy Avenue
1076 Nicosia
Cyprus

and

PO Box 25529
1395 Nicosia
Cyprus
Tel: +357 22 714 100
Fax: +357 22 378 153
Web site: www.centralbank.gov.cy

Christian Alexander Public Relations & Event Planning
53 Kennedy Avenue
Office 101
PO Box 28929
2084 Nicosia
Cyprus
Tel: +357 22 318 431
Fax: +357 22 510 489
e-mail: Alexander@cytanet.com.cy
Contact: Christina Pissi Patsalides, Director

Chrysses Demetriades & Co. Law Office
Fortuna Court
284 Makarios III Avenue
3105 Limassol
Cyprus

and

PO Box 50132
3601 Limassol
Cyprus
Tel: +357 25 582 424
Fax: +357 25 587 191, +357 25 588 055
Web site: www.demetriades.com
Contact: Christos Mavrellis
e-mail: christos@demetriades.com
Contact: Demosthenes Mavrellis
e-mail: demosthenes@demetriades.com

Civilitas Research
13 Queen Olga Street
PO Box 16183
2086 Nicosia
Cyprus
Tel: +357 22 492 555
Fax: +357 22 495 040
Web site: www.Civilitasresearch.com
Contact: Dr James Ker-Lindsay, Managing Director
e-mail: james.lindsay@civilitasresearch.com

Cyprus Securities and Exchange Commission
32 Stasikratous
4th Floor
PO Box 24996
1306 Nicosia
Cyprus
Tel: +357 22 875 475
Fax: +357 22 754 671
Web site: www.cysec.gov.cy
Contact: Dr Marios Clerides, Chairman
e-mail: chairman@cysec.gov.cy

Cyprus Stock Exchange
Kampou Street
Strovolos
PO Box 25427
1309 Nicosia
Cyprus
Tel: +357 22 712 300
Fax: +357 22 570 308
Contact: Nondas Metaxas, Director General/CEO
e-mail: info@cyse.com.cy

Cyprus Telecommunications Authority
Telecommunications Street
PO Box 24929
1396 Nicosia
Cyprus
Tel: +357 22 701 690
Fax: +357 22 701 766
Web site: www.cyta.com.cy
Contact: Andreas Theodorou, Officer, Regulatory Affairs, Business
Management Support
e-mail: andreas.theodorou@cyta.com.cy

Cyprus Tourism Organization
19 Limassol Avenue
2112 Nicosia
Cyprus

and

PO Box 24535
1390 Nicosia
Cyprus

Tel: +357 22 337 715, +357 22 691 144
Fax: +357 22 331 644
Web site: www.cto.org.cy
Contact: Information Centre
e-mail: informationcentre@cto.org.cy

Deloitte & Touche
Corner Themistocles Dervis and Florinis Streets
PO Box 21675
1512 Nicosia
Cyprus
Tel: +357 22 360 300
Fax: +357 22 360 400
Web site: www.deloitte.com.cy
Contact: Pieris Markou, Partner
e-mail: pmarkou@deloitte.com

Tax Services
Eftapaton Court
256 Makarios III Avenue
PO Box 53180
3301 Limassol
Cyprus
Tel: +357 25 857 700
Fax: +357 25 356 010
Web site: www.deloitte.com.cy
Contact: Antonis Taliotis, Partner
e-mail: ataliotis@deloitte.com
Contact: Costas Georghadjis, Partner
e-mail: cgeorghadis@deloitte.com

Employers & Industrialists Federation (OEB)
30, Grivas Dhigenis Avenue
PO Box 21657
1511 Nicosia
Cyprus
Tel: +357 22 665 102
Fax: +357 22 669 459
Web site: www.oeb-eif.org
Contact: Kostas Christophidis, Assistant Director General
e-mail: cchristophides@oeb-eif.org
Contact: Michael Antoniou, Head, Industrial Relations & Labour
Legislation Department
e-mail: mantoniou@oeb-eif.org

Ernst & Young
Nicosia Tower entre
36, Byron Avenue
PO Box 21656
1511 Nicosia
Cyprus
Tel: +357 22 674 000
Fax: +357 22 677 005, +357 22 677 004
Web site: www.cy.eyi.com
Contact: George Kourris, Country Managing Partner
e-mail: george.kourris@cy.eyi.com
Contact: Yiannakis Theoklitou, Partner in charge of AABS (Assurance and Advisory Business Services) in Cyprus and South East Europe
e-mail: Yiannakis.theoklitou@cy.ey.com

Financial Mirror
89–91 Prodromou Street
Strovolos
2063 Nicosia
Cyprus

and

PO Box 16077
2085 Nicosia
Cyprus
Tel: +357 22 678 666
Fax: +357 22 678 664
Web site: www.financialmirror.com
Contact: Fiona Mullen, Assistant Editor
e-mail: mullen@financialmirror.com

Jacovos Christofides
Human Resources Consultant
Lozanis 2a
2023 Strovolos
Nicosia
Cyprus
Tel: +357 22 510 911
Fax: +357 22 318 882
Contact: Jacovos Christofides
e-mail: JChristofides@valicom.com.cy

Laiki Group
154 Limassol Avenue
2025 Nicosia
Cyprus

and

PO Box 22032
1598 Nicosia
Cyprus
Tel: +357 22 811 330
Fax: +357 22 811 492
Web site: www.laiki.com
Contact: Sofronis Eteocleous, Manager, Economic Research and
Planning
e-mail: seteocleous@laiki.com
Contact: Marios Charalambides, Officer, Economic Research &
Planning
e-mail: mcharalambides@laiki.com

Ministry of Commerce, Industry and Tourism
6A Araouzos Street
(off Limassol Avenue)
1421 Nicosia
Cyprus
Tel: +357 22 867 100, +357 22 867 112
Fax: +357 22 304 924, +357 22 375 120
Web site: www.cyprustrade.gov.cy
e-mail: mintrade@spidernet.com.cy

PG Economides & Co.
Chartered Certified Accountants
Totalserve House
17 Gr. Xenopoulou Street
PO Box 53117
3300 Limassol
Cyprus
Tel: +357 25 866 300
Fax: +357 25 866 301
Web site: www.pgeconomides.com
Contact: Peter G Economides, Senior Partner
e-mail: economides@pgeconomides.com

Pyramis DDB Advertising Ltd
49 Elia Papakyriakou Street
2415 Engomi
Makedonitissa
Nicosia

and

PO Box 22438
1521 Nicosia
Cyprus
Tel: +357 22 592 232
Fax: +357 22 591 399
Web site: www.ddbcy.com
Contact: Vasilis A P Metaxas, Managing Director
e-mail: vmetaxas@ddbcy.com

The Cyprus Development Bank Ltd
50 Archbishop Makarios II Avenue
PO Box 21415
1508 Nicosia
Cyprus
Tel: +357 22 846 500
Fax: +357 22 846 604
Web site: www.cyprusdevelopmentbank.com
Contact: Maria Georgiadou, Business Development Manager
e-mail: mariag@cdb.com.cy

The Philip Dew Consultancy Limited
(Registered office)
Julia House
3 Themistocles Dervis Street
PO Box 21612
1591 Nicosia
Cyprus

and

(Main operational office)
PO Box 11836
Bahrain
Tel: +973 1170 0886
Fax: +973 1170 0729
e-mail: pdew@batelco.com.bh

Totalserve Management Ltd
Totalserve House
17 Gr. Xenopoulou Street
3106 Limassol
Cyprus

and

PO Box 54425
3724 Limassol
Cyprus
Tel: +357 25 866 000
Fax: +357 25 866 001
Web site: www.totalservecy.com
Contact: Peter G Economides, Chairman
e-mail: economides@totalserve.com
Contact: Emily Yiolitis, Director/Legal Consultant
e-mail: yiolitis@totalservecy.com

Index

accountants   243–45
accounting   22
  principles   55–56
  record-keeping requirements
    53–54
  reporting requirements   54–55
advertising   183–90
  agencies   186–87
  costs   189–90
  Internet   189
  newspapers   188
  outside   189
  radio   188
  TV   187–88
agriculture   10, 146
airlines   235, 245–46
airports   235
AKEL   15–16
Aliens and Immigration Law
    228
anti-money-laundering measures
    160–63
arbitration proceedings   95–97
  international   97
auditing requirements   56
auditors   243–45

balance of payments   45–46
banking   22, 34–35, 153–59

capital adequacy   157
  regulation and supervision
    98–104
banks   153–59, 246–47
  commercial   154–55
  co-operative credit institutions
    158
  International Banking
    Institutions   158–59
  specialized credit institutions
    155
business
  dress   238
  establishing a   109–29
  etiquette   239
  family   224
  international   22
business consultancy services
    22, 247–48
business incubators   49

Central Bank of Cyprus   xv, 35,
    46, 98–104, 119–20, 153, 160,
    228, 270
Central Bank of Cyprus Law
    98–103, 153
  banks' shareholdings   100
  credit facilities   100
  Directives   101–03

immovable property   100
large shareholdings in banks
    100–01
Chamber of Commerce and
    Industry   248
chartered surveyors   246
Chrysostomides, Kypros   16
Clerides, Glafkos   16, 19
climate   238
clothing   238
Companies Law   92, 118
companies
    foreign participation in Cyprus
        117–20
    formation and operation of
        118–19
    legal requirements   56–57,
        59–60
    offshore   147
computing   23
constitution   91–92
Council of Ministers   18, 91, 136,
    222
Courts, the   91–92, 95–96
currency   239
Cyprus
    archaeology   145
    climate   4
    cultural heritage   28
    geography   3
    geology   4
    history   5–6
    living in   145–49
    map of   xxv
    reasons for popularity
        135–36
    regional role   200–01
Cyprus Company   111, 112–14
Cyprus Constitution   91–92
Cyprus Development Bank
    169–75, 276

Cyprus Employers and
    Industrialists Federation
    (OEB)   xviii, 48, 211, 221,
    254, 273
Cyprus Institute   23
Cyprus International Branch
    114
Cyprus International Partnership
    114
Cyprus International Trust   111,
    115
Cyprus issue/problem   17–20
    impact on the property market
        139–40
Cyprus Securities and Exchange
    Commission   xvi–xvii, 35,
    176–78, 179, 266, 272
    duties, responsibilities and
        powers   176
    organizational structure
        177
Cyprus Telecommunications
    Authority (CYTA)   xvii, 37,
    38, 39, 272
Cyprus Tourism Organization
    (CTO)   xvii, 27–29, 266,
    272–73
    Strategic Plan for Tourism
        (2010)   27–29
Cyprus Workers Confederation
    219, 230

Democratic Party (DIKO)   16
Democatic Rally (DISY)   16
Denktash, Rauf R   17, 18, 19
Deposit Protection Scheme
    103–04
    see also banking
design companies   23
diplomatic representation
    overseas   248–54

double taxation treaties   10,
    78–84, 111, 117
  anti-avoidance provisions
    79
  benefits   80
  tax sparing credits   80–83
  tie breaker clause   83–84
  withholding taxes   85–87

economy   7–14
  challenges   12–14
  key indicators   7
  living standards   8
  performance of   12
  structure of   7–8
education system   23, 148
educational attainment   198–99,
    225
electricity   239
employee statutory rights
    207–11
  collective agreements
    211–15
  during employment   207–09
  termination of employment
    209–11
engineering   23–24
EU (European Union)   35, 41
  accession to   10–11, 12–13, 15,
    19–20, 35, 94, 96, 118,
    136–37, 159, 176, 223
  acquis communautaire   94, 96,
    159, 207
European Investment Bank (EIB)
    172
exchange control   239
exports   25, 41–43, 44, 47, 49–50
external debt   46

financial and business services
    9–10, 34–35

foreign diplomatic representation
    in Cyprus   257–61
foreign investment   8, 47, 118
  real estate market   133–44
foreign trade   41–45
foreign workers   215, 228

government   15–20
Greece   43–44
Greek Orthodox Church   242
gross domestic product (GDP)   7,
    12, 46–48
  by sector   11

health care   148–49, 235
hotels (5 star)   262–63
House of Representatives   16, 18,
    91, 222
human resources   205–32
  consultants   263
  developing   230–31
  employee rights   207–18
  industrial relations   219–23
  management   224–32
Human Resources Development
    Authority (HDRA)   228, 230,
    231

Iacovou, George   16
imports   43–44, 45
independence   5, 6, 15, 183
industrial relations   219–23
  collective bargaining   220–21
  employers' associations   220
  Industrial Relations Code (IRC)
    221
  trade unions   219, 230
inflation   12
insurance sector   34–35, 164–68
  life   166
  non–life insurance   166–67

international business   111–16
International Business
     Companies (IBCs)   113, 117
international clubs   242
International Labour
     Organization (ILO)   207, 222
instruments   216–18
International Trusts   105–07
Internet, the   189, 203

Labour Advisory Body   220
labour law   207, 215–16, 228–30
   see also employee statutory
     rights
language   237–38
Larnaca   3
lawyers   263–64
legal consultants   263–64
legal dispute proceedings   95–97
legal framework   92–94
legal services   24
Limassol   3

Makarios, Archbishop   18
management consultancy   265
manufacturing industry   44,
     47–50
   government support for   49
   'New Industrial Policy'   48
marine and shipping   24
market research industry
     200–04, 265
   industry developments   204
   size and structure   201–02
marketing   181–204
   advertising   183–90
   current position   197–98
   market research   200–04
   public relations   191–95
media, the   183–84
minerals   4

mining   10
Ministry of Commerce, Industry
     and Tourism   266, 275

newspapers   188, 241
   financial   266–67
Nicosia   3
   map of   xxvi

Office of the Superintendent of
     Insurance   35

Pancyprian Federation of Labour
     219, 230
Papadopoulos, Tassos   16
Paphos   3
passports   235
petrol   240
pharmaceuticals   43
political parties   15–17
PR Professionals   194, 195
private healthcare   24
privitization   10
property ownership   131–49
   acquisition of immovable
     property by aliens   142–44
   living in Cyprus   145–49
   real estate market   133–41
public holidays   237
public relations (PR)   191–95
   consultants   267
   independent agencies   193
   internal   193–94
   large corporations   192
   semi-governmental
     organizations   192
   sponsorships   194
public sector   11

radio   184, 190, 241
   advertising   188

real estate market   133–41
  commercial/retail   139
  consultants   267
  foreign demand   134
  indicative property prices   141
  industrial   139
  limitations on foreign
      acquisitions   136
  locations to buy   137
  office   139
  potential investors   138
  reasons for Cyprus' popularity
      135–36
  residential   138–39
Register of Ships   123–25
religion   17, 149, 242
returns   133–34
risk management   24
road system   146

salary levels   227–28, 229–30
sales and marketing   24
shipping and ship management
    121–29
  consultants   268
  fees payable by Cyprus ships
      126–29
  formation of a shipping entity
      122–23
  legislation   122
  ownership of Cyprus ships
      122
  Register of Ships   123–25
shipping companies   113
Social Insurance Fund   212,
    214
Socialist Party (EDEK)   16
Stock Exchange   xvii, 8, 34, 35,
    45, 56, 120, 179–80, 272
strategy consultants   268
Supreme Court   94, 93

tax calendar   58–59, 66
taxation   10, 57–59, 61–72,
    128–29
  capital gains tax   73–74, 141
  company income   113–14
  corporate tax   62
  exempt income   62, 67–68
  immovable property tax   74
  property   140–41
  rates of   67
  residence rules   62, 66–67
  Social Coherence Fund   75
  Social Insurance Fund   75
  Special Contribution for
      Defence Law   70–72
  special modes of   69–70
  Stamp Duty   76–77
  Value Added Tax (VAT)
      75–76
  see also double taxation treaties
tax consultants   269
telecommunications   37–40, 146,
    240
  international network   38
  mobile telephony   38–39
  national network   38
television (TV)   183, 184–85, 190,
    241
  advertising   188
tourism   8–9, 12, 25, 26–33,
    146–47
  arrivals   29–31
  foreign investment   120
  holiday accommodation   31–32
  receipts from   29–31
  vulnerability of   8–9, 13
  see also Cyprus Tourism
      Organization (CTO)
trade centres overseas   254–56
trade unions   219, 221, 230
transport   240–41

Trusts   115–16
Turkey   15, 20, 170
Turkish Cypriot political system
    17
'Turkish Republic of Northern
    Cyprus'   3, 6, 15, 18
    see also Cyprus issue/problem

unemployment   14
United Kingdom   30
University of Cyprus   14, 23

visas   235

water   239
work permits   215
workforce
    academic qualifications   225
    see also human resources
working hours   236

Index of Advertisers

Antonis Laizou   vi
Cyprus International Institute of Management   ii
CYTA   36
The Ministry of Commerce, Industry and Tourism   v
Moore Stephens   63
Pafilia Property Developers   2

Other titles in this series from Kogan Page

Doing Business with Azerbaijan
Doing Business with Bahrain
Doing Business with China
Doing Business with Croatia
Doing Business with the Czech Republic
Doing Business with Egypt
Doing Business with Estonia
Doing Business with Georgia
Doing Business with Germany
Doing Business with Hungary
Doing Business with India
Doing Business with Kazakhstan
Doing Business with Libya
Doing Business with Lithuania
Doing Business with Malta
Doing Business with Oman
Doing Business with Poland
Doing Business with Qatar
Doing Business with the Russian Region of Krasnodar Krai
Doing Business with Saudi Arabia
Doing Business with Slovenia
Doing Business with Slovakia
Doing Business with Spain
Doing Business with South Africa
Doing Business with Turkey
Doing Business with Ukraine
Doing Business with the United Arab Emirates